J. KEIR HARDIE

J KEIR HARDIE, 1914

J. KEIR HARDIE

A Biography

By

WILLIAM STEWART

With an Introduction by

J. RAMSAY MACDONALD

CASSELL & COMPANY, LTD.
LONDON, NEW YORK, TORONTO, AND MELBOURNE

Printed at the London Works of
THE NATIONAL LABOUR PRESS, LIMITED
8 9 10 Johnson's Court Fleet Street E C 4

AUTHOR'S PREFACE

THE one man of all Keir Hardie's associate most fitted to write an account of his life an work was the late J. Bruce Glasier His know ledge of the Labour and Socialist movement in all it phases and aspects, his long and close intimacy wit Hardie both in public and private life, his sympatheti perception of the motives and environment and heredit which went to the formation of Hardie's character, an influenced his actions, and his own fine gift of literar expression, qualified him above all others to be Kei Hardie's biographer.

The Fates ruled otherwise. Before Mr Glasier ha begun to collect and assort the material for the work, h was himself stricken with the illness, which, heroicall borne through two years of pain, ended in his death. I was at Mr Glasier's request while on his bed of sicknes that I, not very confidently, undertook the work Th Memorial Committee adopted Mr. Glasier's suggestio that I should be appointed to take his place. The wor therefore came to me both as a request and as a com mand I have performed it to the best of my ability whether well or ill, must be left to the judgment of other.

To those friends who were most familiar with Kei Hardie's habits of life it will be unnecessary to explai that the task has not been quite easy. Though he had th intention of some day writing a book of reminiscence. the daily call of the Labour and Socialist movement le, him without any leisure to sit down to it systematicall)

and when he died he had not even made that provisic
for posthumous fame which seems customary with pe
sons who have figured in public life   He kept no diar
and he preserved few letters, though he must han
received many from important people   If it be tru
as has been said, that letters are the raw material (
biography, this particular biography has been produce
at a disadvantage   That is not entirely true, howeve
Much of the material for a life of Hardie is to be foun
not in his private but in his public writings which we,
voluminous, and, to a considerable extent, self-revealin,
But the very wealth and abundance of this kind (
material have rendered the work difficult if interestin,

I found it necessary to go through with some selectiv
care the two volumes of "The Miner," twenty-on
volumes of the "Labour Leader," several volumes (
the "Merthyr Pioneer," and also to refer to othu
Socialist papers, to the columns of the contemporai
daily press, and to the pages of "Hansard."

There will be differences of opinion as to whethu
this material has always been used in the best way, an
also as to whether certain events and episodes have bec
over or under emphasised   These differences cannot l
helped. I had to use my own judgment and have doit
so, and the result must stand.

For information concerning the early period of Ke
Hardie's life I am indebted to several members of th
family, especially to his brothers, George, David an
William. Mrs Keir Hardie also was most helpful t
supplying those domestic details which seemed necessai
while for some of the early Ayrshire experiences I hat
to thank Councillor James Neil of Cumnock, an

AUTHOR'S PREFACE

everal quite obscure but sterling men of the pits who
ere associated with Hardie in his scantily recorded
pioneering days

For an account of the historic Mid-Lanark election
here was a fair amount of information available, though
it had to be dug out. Not so, however, with regard to
the West Ham election, and I have specially to thank
Councillor Ben Gardner for his valuable help in this
connection. There is a probability that he, and also the
many Merthyr friends, notably Llewellyn Francis, John
Ban, Councillor Stonelake and Emrys Hughes, may
think I have not made the fullest use of the very valuable
information which they placed at my disposal. They
will, however, I have no doubt, realise that I had to be
governed by a sense of proportion, and had to consider
each phase of Hardie's life in its relation to his whole
career

I do sincerely believe, however, that the book as it
stands contains nearly all that is essential to a true
understanding of the character of Keir Hardie and of
his life work, and thereby makes it possible for readers
to form a just estimate of the great service which he
rendered to the working people, not of his own country
only, but of the world, and therefore to Humanity.

WILLIAM STEWART.

September 9th, 1921

LIST OF ILLUSTRATIONS

INTRODUCTION

THE purposes of biography are manifold, but they have this common end : to interpret the subject and show forth what manner of man he was of whom the writer writes. That done faithfully, the biographer can launch his work upon the waters and trust to the winds and the currents for a prosperous voyage.

But what is "faithfully"? A patient and accurate accumulation of facts and events strung upon time as boys used to hang rows of birds' eggs upon strings? A cold, impartial scrutiny of a life made from a judgment seat placed above the baffling conflicts of doubting conscience, groping reason and weak desire? Biographies may be so written. But the life of him who has stood in the market place with a mission to his fellows, who has sought to bring visions of greater dignity and power into the minds of the sleeping and vegetating crowds, who has tried to gather scattered and indifferent men into a mighty movement and to elevate discontented kickings against the pricks into a crusade for the conquest of some Holy Land, cannot be dealt with in that way. He must submit to the rigid scrutiny; the dross that is in him, the mistakes and miscalculations which he made, must be exposed with his virtues, wisdoms and good qualities. But to portray such a man, the biographer has not only to scrutinise him objectively; he must also tell how he appeared to, and was *felt* by, the people who were influenced by him, and preserve for the future the hero or the saint who received the homage of leadership and the worship of affection. The glamour of the myth gathers round all great popular leaders and becomes an atmosphere as real to their personality as the colour of cloud and sun is real to a landscape. Were we to separate what is inseparable, we might say that such a man has two beings, that which the critic alone can see, dissecting him as though he lay a lifeless thing upon a table, and that which the artist sees regarding him as one of the living formative forces of his time.

In the latter way the biography of Keir Hardie must be treated if it is to be a full interpretation of the man. Mr. Stewart, who has done this book, writes of his hero, frankly and unashamedly, as a worshipper. He is a disciple who for many years has enjoyed the intimacy of his master, and he sees with the eye and writes with the pen which reveal the inspiring leader to us. He has gathered from a great mass of details the outstanding incidents in Hardie's life, and through the deeds has shown the man. He has also preserved for all who may read his book, and especially for those in whose memories those precious days of pioneering have no place, the inspiration that made the work possible and brought forth from chaos the Labour Movement.

Everyone who came in contact with Hardie felt his personality right away at the outset. His power never lay in his being at the head of a political organisation which he commanded, for the organisation of the Independent Labour Party was always weak compared with its influence, and he had ceased to be an official of the miners before their combination became really formidable; nor did it lie in his ability to sway the crowd by divine gifts of speech and appeal, for his diction though beautifully simple was rarely tempestuous, and his voice had few of the qualities that steal into the hearts of men and stir them in their heights and depths; more certainly still he never secured a follower by flattery nor won the

INTRODUCTION

ear of a crowd by playing down to it. He set a hard task
before his people and gave them great ends to pursue.
He left no man in peace in the valley gutter, but winded
them on the mountain tracks. What then was the
secret of the man? I who have seen him in all relationships, at the height of triumph and the depths of
humiliation, on the platform and at the fireside, dignified
amongst strangers and merry amongst friends,
generally fighting by his side but sometimes in conflict
with him, regard that secret as first of all his personality
and then his proud esteem for the common folk and his
utter blindness to all the decorations of humanity. He
was a simple man, a strong man, a gritty man.

Hardie was of the "old folk." Born in a corner of
Scotland where there still lingered a belief in the
uncanny and the superhuman, where Pan's pipes were
still heard in the woods, the kelpie still seen at the fords
and the fairy still met with on the hills, and born in the
time of transition when the heart and imagination paid
homage whilst the reason was venturing to laugh, he went
out into the world with a listening awe in his soul;
brought up in surroundings eloquent with the memory
of sturdy men who trusted to the mists to shield them
from the murderous eyes of the Claverhouses and their
dragoons, and dotted with the graves and the monuments
of martyrs to a faith—dreary moors "where about the
graves of the martyrs the whaups are crying," and grey
farmhouses where in the "killing times" women
lamented over their husbands and sons murdered at
their doors for loyalty to God and the Covenant—
surroundings, moreover, which in later times had seen
Burns at the plough dejected, and had heard him singing
his songs of love, of pity, of gaiety, he went out a strong
man in heart and in backbone, with the spirit of great
tradition in him; nurtured by a mother who faced the

B   xvii

J. KEIR HARDIE

hard world like a woman of unconquerable soul, whose tears were followed by defiance and whose sighs ended with challenge, he went out like a knight armed with a sword which had the magic of conquest tempering its steel. That was his birthright, and that birthright made him a gentleman, whether running errands for a baker in Glasgow, or facing the "overfed beasts" on the benches of the House of Commons. Such men never fear the face of men and never respect their baubles.

From the same sources came his comfort in the common folk. All great human discovery is the discovery of the wisdom that comes from babes and sucklings, as all great artistic achievement depends on the joy that dwells in the simple. It has been said that there is the false ring of peevishness in Burns' "A man's a man for a' that," and it may be that resentment gives a falsetto note to some of the lines. But when the great labour leader comes, whether he be born from the people or not will be of little concern, the decisive thing will be whether he values in his heart, as Burns did, the scenes and the people from which spring not only "Scotia's grandeur," but the power which is to purify society and expose the falseness and the vulgarity of materialist possession and class distinctions. The mind of the labour leader must be too rich to do homage to "tinsel show," too proud of its own lineage to make obeisance to false honour, and too cultured to be misled by vulgar display.

> A title, Dempster merits it;
> A garter gie to Willie Pitt;
> Gie wealth to some be-ledger'd cit,
>   In cent. per cent.
> But give me real sterling wit,
>   And I'm content.

A working class living in moral and social parasitism on its "betters" will only increase the barrenness and the futility of life. In the end, it is perhaps a matter of good taste and self-respect, and these are birthrights and are not taught in the schools. They belong to the influences which life assimilates as plants assimilate a rich or an impoverished air and sap. Perhaps the Scotsman is peculiarly fortunate in this respect. No country has had a meaner aristocracy or a sturdier common people. Partly its education, partly its history, partly its church government and system of worship, partly the frugality which nature imposed upon it for so many generations, laid up a store of independence in the characters of many of its people, and Burns awoke this into activity. I doubt if any man who received the historical birthright of Scotsmen at his birth, ever accepted a tinsel honour without feeling that he was doing wrong and somehow abandoning his country.

Be these things as they may, Hardie had those native qualities which never became incompetent to value the honour and the worth of a kitchen fireside, of a woman who, like his mother, toiled in the fields, of a man who earned his living by the sweat of his brow, subduing Heaven the while. He said a life-long Amen to the words which Scott puts in the mouth of Rob Roy on Glasgow bridge: "He that is without name, without friends, without coin, without country, is still at least a man; and he that has all these is no more"—Hardie's democratic spirit might have added "and is often something less." When he became famous, his world widened and he mixed with people in different circumstances. But he met them as the self-respecting workman, all unconscious of difference and with neither an attempt nor a desire to imitate them. The drawing-rooms of the rich never allured him into a sycophantic servitude, a chair at a workman's fireside hard to sit upon never robbed that fireside of its cheery warmth. The true gentleman is he who acts like a gentleman unconsciously. Therefore, this quality eludes him who would write of it, for an explanation of it suggests consciousness of it. Only when the ruling class habits sought to impose themselves on him by authority did he resent them and become conscious of his own nature—as when he went to the House of Commons in a cloth cap, or when, in an outburst of moral loathing, he replied to the jeers of a band who had returned to the House radiant in the garb and the demeanour of those who had risen from a well replenished table, by the epithet "well-fed beasts,"—and then his native good taste speedily asserted itself and he became natural.

Experience in the world strengthened this part of his nature. Whether as a baker's messenger forced to pass moral judgment on the man of substantial respectability, or as a Trade Union official studying the results of the work of directors, managers and such like, or as a politician in touch with the political intelligence and general capacity of "the ruling classes," he saw no inferiority in his fellow workmen. He found them careless, disorganised, indifferent; but their lives remained real and their common interests were the true interests. They were the robust stem upon which every desirable thing had to be engrafted.

Thus it was that the sober people, the people prepared for idealistic effort, the people whose ears detected the ring of a genuine coin and had become tired of the spurious or ill-minted thing, the people who were laying the foundations of their new cities on the rock of human worth, were drawn to him, honoured him, believed in him and loved him. It is very difficult for a man made of that material to do justice to "the classes" in these times—to their qualities, their lives, their interests, and even their worship—but Hardie was catholic, and rarely have his friends heard from his lips an unjust condemnation of those people. Charity lay even in his most emphatic condemnations.

Of Hardie's work it is easy to judge even at this early day, so distinctive was it. He will stand out for ever as the Moses who led the children of labour in this country out of bondage—out of bondage, not into Canaan, for that is to be a longer job. Others had described that bondage, had explained it, had told what ought to come after it. Hardie found the labour movement on its industrial side narrowed to a conflict with employers, and totally unaware that that conflict, if successful, could only issue in a new economic order; on its political side, he found it thinking only of returning to Parliament men who came from the pits and workshops to do pretty much the same work that the politicians belonging to the old political parties had done, and totally unaware that Labour in politics must have a new outlook, a new driving force of ideas and a new standard of political effort. When he raised the flag of revolt in Mid-Lanark, he was a rebel proclaiming civil war; when he fought the old Trade Union leaders from the floor of Congress, he was a sectary; when the Independent Labour Party was formed in Bradford, it was almost a forlorn hope attacked by a section of Socialists on the one hand and by the labour leaders in power on the other. What days of fighting, of murmuring, of dreary desert trudging were to follow, only those who went through them know. Through them, a mere handful of men and women sustained the drudgery and the buffetings. Hardie's dogged—even dour—persistence made faint-heartedness impossible. One has to think of some of those miraculous endurances of the men who defied hardship in the blank wilderness, the entangled forest, the endless snowfield, to get an understanding of the exhaustion of soul and mind and body which had to be undergone between 1890 and 1900, in order to create a Labour Movement.

For this endurance Hardie had an inexhaustible inner resource. He knew

> The hills where his life rose,
> And the sea where it goes.

He was one of the sternest champions which his class has ever produced, and yet his was no class mind. His driving and resisting power was not hate nor any of the feelings that belong to that category of impulse. When I used the expression "communal consciousness," for the first time in a book I had written, as the antithesis to "class consciousness," which some Socialists regarded as the shibboleth test of rectitude, he wrote me saying that that was exactly what he felt. But even that was not comprehensive enough. His life of sense was but the manifestations of the spirit, and to him "the spirit" was something like what it was to the men whose bones lay on the Ayrshire moors under martyrs' monuments. It was the grand crowned authority of life, but an authority that spoke from behind a veil, that revealed itself in mysterious things both to man's heart and eyes. He used to tell us tales and confess to beliefs, in words that seemed to fall from the lips of a child. Had he not found his portion where blows had to be given and to be fended, and where the mind had to be actively wary every moment of the day in advancing and retreating, he would have been one of an old time to whom a belief in mystic signs and warnings would have been reverence and not superstition, and by whom such signs would have been given. Those who knew him have often met him looking as though a part of him were absent in some excursion in lands now barred to most of

mankind. This, I believe, explains the hospitality he
always gave to every new attempt to express the truth,
explains his devotion to the cause of women as it was in
his lifetime and, above all, explains the mysterious
affinity there was between himself and children. His
whole being lay under the shadow of the hand of the
crowned Authority which told him of its presence now
by a lightning flash, now by a whisper, and now by a
mere tremor in his soul like what the old folk believed
went through the earth when night died and the day was
born. The world was life, not things, to him.

Thus, his Socialism was not an economic doctrine, not
a formula proved and expressed in algebraic signs of x
and y. He got more Socialism from Burns than from
Marx; "The Twa Dogs," and "A Man's a Man for a'
that," were more prolific text books for his politics than
"Das Kapital." This being the spirit of his handiwork,
the Independent Labour Party, is one reason why it
became the greatest political influence of our time and
threw into an almost negligible background, both in its
enthusiastic propaganda and practical capacity, all other
Socialist bodies in this country.

The inconsistencies which are essential attributes of
human greatness are the cause of much trouble to the
ordinary man, but these inconsistencies do not belong
to the same order of things as the unreliabilities of the
charlatan or the changefulness of the time-server.
Hardie's apparent waywardness often gave his colleagues concern. He was responsive to every movement and hospitable to the most childlike thoughts—
—so much so that in a battle he not infrequently seemed
to be almost in the opposing ranks, as at that Derby
Conference, described by Mr. Stewart, when he sorely
tried the loyalty of our own women by going out of his
way to greet those who had done everything in their

power to harass and insult them. A great man has so many sides to which the various voices of the day make appeal. He is not only one man but several—not only man, but woman too. But greatness is inconsistent only in the things that do not matter very much, and in the grand conflict of great issues he stood up as reliable as a mighty boulder in a torrent. The strength of hills was his for exactly the same reason as he had the trustful mind of a child. What appeared to be inconsistency was indeed manysidedness. No man was more generously international in his outlook and spirit, and yet to the very core of his being he was a Scotsman of Scotsmen, and it is not at all inappropriate that I came across him first of all at a meeting to demand Home Rule for Scotland. A man who held in no special esteem the "book lear" of universities, he, nevertheless, warmed in interest to all kinds of lore, and he read choicely and was ever ready to sit at the feet of whomsoever had knowledge to impart. Always willing to listen, he was never ready to yield; loyal like a man, he was, nevertheless, persistent in his own way sometimes to a fault; humble in the councils of friends, he was proud in the world. Looking back at him now, the memory of his waywardness only adds to affection and admiration. One sees how necessary it was for his work.

There is one other inconsistency of greatness which he showed only to friends. He could stand alone, and yet he could not. "No one can ever know," he once said to me, "what suffering a man has to endure by mis-representation." He required a corner in the hearts of his people where he could rest and be soothed by regard. He therefore felt keenly every attack that was crudely cruel. For instance he was sorely struck by the brutally vile cartoon which "Punch" published of him when he was in India. (I knew of the letters which Lord Minto was sending home expressing pleasure at his conduct in India, and I cheered him by telling him of them.)

But sorest of all was the wound which the war made upon him. Like every intelligent man who kept his head, he saw that the most worthless elements in the country would ride the whirlwind, that the people would be worked up into a state of mind that would not only defy every appeal to reason, but would prolong the agony and settle it, as all wars have hitherto been settled, by crushing debts, ruined ideals and a peace which would only be a truce to give time for the sowing of new seeds of war. He knew that when the clash came it could not be ended until the conditions of a settlement arose, and he joined heartily with the small group in the country who took the view that those conditions were political and not military, and that, therefore, whilst the soldier was holding the trenches, the politician should be as busy as the munition worker creating the political weapons which were to bring peace. He also knew that, when the war comes, the safety of every country is endangered by its enemy and that adequate steps must be taken to protect it. But he saw that problem in its fulness and not with military blinkers limiting his vision to recruitment, guns and poison gas. He was quite well aware that the sky would speedily be darkened by black clouds of lies and misrepresentations, innocent and deliberate. That was in the day's work, and he knew that in time the attitude of his colleagues and himself would first of all be understood and that, later on, people would wonder why it took them so long to see the same things. He saw the Treaty of Versailles before 1915 was very far spent, and he was content to endure and wait. That is not how he was wounded. The deadly blow was given by the attitude of old colleagues. When he returned from his first meeting in his constituency on the outbreak of war, described by Mr. Stewart, he was a crushed man, and, sitting in the sun on the terrace of the House of Commons where I came across him, he seemed to be looking out on blank desolation. From that he never recovered. Then followed the complete mergence of the Labour Party in the war-lusty crowd. The Independent Labour Party kept as trusty as ever, but he felt that his work was over, that all he could do in his lifetime was to amount to no more than picking up some of the broken spars of the wreckage. As Bunyan puts it, "a post had come from the celestial city for him." And so he died.

The outlook has already changed. The floods are subsiding and his work stands. We are still too near to that work to see it in its detailed historical relations; the day and its events are too pressingly close and urgent to enable us to view the results of it in a lasting setting. Of this we are assured, however : in its great purposes and general achievements it is permanent. It is well with him and his memory.

"I shall be satisfied when I awake."

J. Ramsay MacDonald.

J. KEIR HARDIE

J. KEIR HARDIE

CHAPTER ONE

THE MAKING OF AN AGITATOR

JAMES KEIR HARDIE was born on August 15th, 1856, in a one-roomed house at Legbrannock, near Holytown in Lanarkshire, amongst the miners, of whom he was to become one, and with whose interests he was to be closely identified all through life.

His father, David Hardie, was not, however, a miner, nor of miner stock. He was a ship carpenter by trade, drawn into this district by the attractions of Mary Keir, a domestic servant, who became his wife and the mother of the future labour agitator. Both parents were endowed with strong individuality of character, of a kind not calculated to make life smooth for themselves or their offspring; but it was undoubtedly from the mother that the boy inherited that resourcefulness and power of endurance which enabled him, through a full half-century of unceasing strife, to develop and, in some measure, realise those ideals of working-class independence and organisation with which his name is associated.

Not much is known of Keir Hardie's years of infancy, but that they were not overflowing with joy may be surmised from the fact that in his eighth year we find the

family—increased in numbers—living in the shipbuilding district of Glasgow in very straightened
circumstances even for working folk.

Latterly, the father had been following his trade at
sea, but was now trying to settle down to work in the
shipyards, not an easy thing to do at a time when trade
was dull and employment scarce. This may account for
the fact that the home was, now on the Govan side, now
on the Partick side, and never got itself really established
as a steady going working-class household. A brief
period of regular employment was broken by an accident
which incapacitated the breadwinner for many weeks,
during which there were no wages nor income of any
kind, and as a consequence there was an accruing
burden of debt. Those were not the days of Compensation Acts and Workmen's Insurance.

At this period we get our first real glimpse of the boy
Keir Hardie and of the conditions under which his
character developed. Hardly had the father recovered
from his illness and started to work when a strike took
place in the shipbuilding trade. One of Hardie's
earliest recollections was of attending a trade union
meeting with his father who advised against the strike on
the ground of lack of funds and slackness of trade.
During this dispute the family were compelled to sell
most of their household goods, and what was worse, to
enlist the boy of seven as one of the breadwinners. His
first job was as a message boy to the Anchor Line Steam-
ship Company, and as school attendance was now impossible, the father and mother devoted much of their
time in the evenings to his education, and were at least
able to teach him to read, and to love reading, which is
the basis of all education.

After a short time spent as a message boy, he was sent
into a brass-finishing shop, the intention being to

apprentice him to that trade, but when it was learned that the first year must be without wages, brass finishing was abandoned, and his next place was in a lithographer's in the Trongate at half-a-crown a week. That did not last long and we find him serving as a baker's message boy at three shillings a week. From this he went to heating rivets in Thompson's shipyard on a fifty per cent. rise in wages, four shillings and sixpence a week. He would probably have continued at this employment and Clyde-side would have had the nurturing of a great agitator, but a fatal accident to two boys in the shipyard frightened the mother, and once more he became a baker's message boy.

All this experience was crowded within the space of two years and while he was still but a child. Many other working-class children have had similar experiences. Several generations of them in fact, have been denied all knowledge of the natural joys of childhood in order that the present industrial system might be founded and run. Whether that tremendous historical fact finds any reflection in the mentality of the present day British working class need not be discussed here, but it is undoubted that these child-time experiences left an indelible mark on the character of Keir Hardie. It was a period of his life to which in after years he seldom referred, but always with bitterness. The manner of its ending forms the theme of one of the few autobiographical notes which he has left us, and for that reason, if for no other, his own description of it may be given.

There had been a great lock-out of Clyde shipworkers lasting six weary months. The Union funds were soon exhausted. In the Hardie household everything that could be turned into food had been sold. The boy's four shillings and sixpence a week was the only income. One child, next in age to Keir, took fever and died, and another child was about to be born. "The outlook was black," says Hardie, looking back upon it, "but there was worse to come, and the form it took made it not only a turning point in my life, but also in my outlook upon men and things. I had reached an age at which I understood the tragedy of poverty, and had a sense of responsibility to those at home far beyond my years. I knew that, despite the brave way in which my mother was facing the situation, she was feeling the burden almost too great for her to bear, and on more than one occasion I had caught her crying by herself. One winter morning I turned up late at the baker's shop where I was employed and was told I had to, go upstairs to see the master. I was kept waiting outside the door of the dining-room while he said grace—he was noted for religious zeal—and, on being admitted, found the master and his family seated round a large table. He was serving out bacon and eggs while his wife was pouring coffee from a glass infuser which at once—shamefaced and terrified as I was—attracted my attention. I had never before seen such a beautiful room, nor such a table, loaded as it was with food and beautiful things. The master read me a lecture before the assembled family on the sin of slothfulness, and added that though he would forgive me for that once, if I sinned again by being late I should be instantly dismissed, and so sent me to begin work.

"But the injustice of the thing was burning hot within me, all the more that I could not explain why I was late. The fact was that I had not yet tasted food. I had been up most of the night tending my ailing brother, and had risen betimes in the morning but had been made late by assisting my mother in various ways before starting. The work itself was heavy and lasted from seven in the morning till closing time.

"Two mornings afterwards, a Friday, I was again a

4

few minutes late, from the same source, and was informed
on arriving at the shop that I was discharged and my fortnight's wages forfeited by way of punishment. The
news stupefied me, and finally I burst out crying and
begged the shopwoman to intercede with the master for
me. The morning was wet and I had been drenched in
getting to the shop and must have presented a pitiable
sight as I stood at the counter in my wet patched clothes.
She spoke with the master through a speaking tube,
presumably to the breakfast room I remembered so well,
but he was obdurate, and finally she, out of the goodness
of her heart, gave me a piece of bread and advised me to
look for another place. For a time I wandered about
the streets in the rain, ashamed to go home where there
was neither food nor fire, and actually discussing whether
the best thing was not to go and throw myself in the
Clyde and be done with a life that had so little
attractions. In the end I went to the shop and saw the
master and explained why I had been late. But it was
all in vain. The wages were never paid. But the
master continued to be a pillar of the Church and a
leading light in the religious life of the city !''

A poignant reminiscence for any human being to carry
through life, and explanatory of the ready sympathy for
desolate children characteristic of the man in after years;
and also of his contempt for that kind of hypocrisy which
covers up injustice under the cloak of religion.

The upshot of it all was that the father in sheer despair
went off again to sea, and the mother with her children,
removed to Newarthill, where her own mother still lived,
and quite close to the place where Keir was born.

Thus there had arrived, as he himself has said, a
turning point in his life, deciding that his lot should be
cast with that of the mining community and determining
some other things which, taken altogether, constituted a

somewhat complex environment and impulse for a receptive minded lad growing from boyhood to adolescence.

Both parents had what is called in Scotland a strictly religious upbringing, and had encouraged the boy to attend regularly at Sunday School. The Glasgow experience had changed all that. They were persons of strong individuality. The mother especially had a downright way of looking at life, and had no use for the forms of a religion which sanctioned the kind of treatment which she and those she loved had passed through. Henceforward the Hardie household was a free-thinking household, uninfluenced by "kirk-gaun" conventionalities or mere traditional beliefs. Priest and Presbyter were not kept outside the door, but there was free entrance also for books critical of orthodoxy or secular in interest, and on the same shelf with the Bible and the Pilgrim's Progress might be found Paine's "Age of Reason" and works by Ingersoll, together with Wilson's "Tales of the Borders" and the poems of Burns. All the members of the family grew up with the healthy habit of thinking for themselves and not along lines prescribed by custom.

Almost immediately on coming to Newarthill the boy, now ten years of age, went down the pit as trapper to a kindly old miner, who before leaving him for the first time at his lonely post, wrapped his jacket round him to keep him warm. The work of a trapper was to open and close a door which kept the air supply for the men in a given direction. It was an eerie job, all alone for ten long hours, with the underground silence only disturbed by the sighing and whistling of the air as it sought to escape through the joints of the door. A child's mind is full of vision under ordinary surroundings, but with the dancing flame of the lamps giving life to the shadows, only a vivid imagination can conceive what the vision must have been to this lad.

At this time he began to attend Fraser's night school at Holytown. The teacher was genuinely interested in his pupils and did all he could for them with his limitations of time and equipment. There was no light provided in the school and the pupils had to bring their own candles. Learning had now a kind of fascination for the boy. He was very fond of reading, and a book, "The Races of the World," presented to him by his parents, doubtless awakened in his mind an interest in things far beyond the coal mines of Lanarkshire. His mother gave him every encouragement. She had a wonderful memory. "Chevy Chase" and all the well-known ballads and folk-lore tales were recited and rehearsed round the winter fire. In this manner and under these diverse influences did the future Labour leader pass his boyhood, absorbing ideas and impressions which remained with him ever afterwards.

The father returned from sea and found work on the railway then being made between Edinburgh and Glasgow. When this was finished, the family removed to the village of Quarter in the Hamilton district, where Keir started as pit pony driver, passing from that through other grades to coal hewing, and by the time he was twenty had become a skilled practical miner, and had also gained two years' experience above ground working in the quarries.

He was in the way however of becoming something more than a miner. At the instigation of his mother he had studied and become proficient in shorthand writing, and through the same guidance had joined the Good Templar movement which was then establishing itself in most of the Scottish villages. He became an enthusiastic propagandist in the Temperance cause, and it was in this sphere that he really began to take a part in public work. His habit of independent thinking too, had led him, not to reject religion but only its forms and shams and doctrinal accretions, and he was associating himself with what seemed to him the simplest organised expression of Christianity, namely the Evangelical Union. He was, in fact, like many another earnest soul at his time of life seeking outlets for his spiritual vitality. Because of the part he was now playing in local public affairs his brother miners pushed him into the chair at meetings for the ventilating of their grievances, and appointed him on deputations to the colliery managers, posts which he accepted, not without warning from some of his friends in the Temperance movement as to the dangers of taking part in the agitations going on in the district—warnings which, to a youth of his temperament, were more likely to stimulate forward than to hold back. Without knowing it, almost involuntarily, he had become a labour agitator, a man obnoxious to authority, and regarded as dangerous by colliery managers and gaffers.

The crisis came for him one morning when descending No. 4 Quarter pit. Half-way down the shaft, the cage stopped and then ascended. On reaching the surface he was met by the stormy-faced manager who told him to get off the Company's grounds and that his tools would be sent home. "We'll hae nae damned Hardies in this pit," he said, and he was as good as his word, for the two younger brothers were also excommunicated. The Hardie family was having its first taste of the boycott. Keir now realised that he was evidently a person of some importance in the struggle between masters and men, and a comprehension of that fact was perhaps the one thing needed to give settled direction to his propagandist energies, hitherto spent somewhat diffusely in movements which afforded no opportunity of getting at close quarters with an enemy. By depriving him of his means of livelihood, the enemy itself had come to close quarters with him. He had been labelled an agitator and he accepted the label.

The mining industry was at this time in a deplorable condition from the men's point of view. The few years of prosperity and comparatively high wages during the Franco-Prussian War had been followed by severe depression, which, as usual, pressed more acutely upon wages than upon dividends. The West of Scotland miners, perhaps through lack of the right kind of leadership, had not taken advantage of the prosperous years to perfect their organisation, and when the slump came were completely at the mercy of the employers. In the attempt to resist reductions the Lanarkshire County Union, after some desultory and disastrous strikes, had collapsed. A chaotic state of matters existed throughout Lanarkshire. There was no cohesion or co-ordination, each district fighting for its own hand. During these black years the miners were crushed down to 2s. per day in the Quarter district where Hardie was now boycotted, and to 1s. 8d. and 1s. 9d. in the Airdrie district.

Here then was Hardie in the reawakening of the need amongst the miners to reorganise for self-preservation. A large-scale strike was impossible. Limitation of output was the only alternative, and that meant a still further reduction of the weekly wage already at starvation point. Yet men and women, disorganised as they were, made the sacrifice all over Lanarkshire. The miners, always good fighters, were beginning to lift their heads again. What was wanted was leadership. By driving Hardie from one district to another the employers themselves made him a leader of the men. The family moved to Low Waters, near the Cadzow collieries; and here

J. KEIR HARDIE

Hardie began to show that resourcefulness which in future years was to carry him through many a difficult situation. He opened a tobacconist's and stationer's shop, while his mother set up a small grocery business. His painfully acquired shorthand proficiency now also came into play, and he became correspondent to the "Glasgow Weekly Mail," for the Coatbridge and Airdrie district, thus modestly making his first entrance into the world of journalism, a sphere in which he might easily have made great progress but for the insistent call of the labour movement. The appointment at least gave him greater freedom to carry on his work among the miners.

In the month of May, 1879, the masters had intimated another reduction of wages. This had the effect of quickening the agitation. Huge meetings were held every week in the Old Quarry at Hamilton, and at one of these meetings on July 3rd, 1879, Hardie was appointed Corresponding Secretary. This gave him a new outlet and enabled him to get in touch with representative miners all over Lanarkshire. On July 24th, three weeks after his appointment, he submitted to a mass meeting rules for the guidance of the organisation. These were adopted, and at the same meeting he was chosen as delegate to attend a National Conference of Miners to be held in Glasgow the week following. Speaking at a meeting of miners at Shieldmuir in August of this year, he declared that over-production had been the ruin of the miners, and said that he held in his hand a letter from Alexander Macdonald, M.P., reminding the Lanarkshire miners that they were in the same position as in 1844 when, by united action, wages were raised from 3s. to 5s. per day. The following week, at a mass meeting, he was appointed Miners' Agent, with a majority of 875 over the highest vote cast for other candidates. He was now twenty-three years of age and he had found his vocation. He was to be a labour agitator.

Probably he himself did not realise how uphill and thorny was the path he had entered upon, nor how far it would lead him. Almost immediately a curious and well-nigh unbelievable incident brought home to him some of the difficulties of his task. On September 4th, a huge demonstration was held at Low Waters at which Alexander Macdonald was the chief speaker. Hardie moved the resolution of welcome to the veteran agitator, and in a somewhat rhetorical passage, excusable in an immature platform orator, he spoke of Macdonald as an "unparalleled benefactor of the mining community," and compared his work for the miners to that of "Luther at the rise of Protestantism." He had said just exactly the wrong thing to an audience, two-thirds of whom were Irish Roman Catholics, to whom the name of Luther was anathema, and Protestantism more obnoxious than low wages. There were loud murmurs of disapprobation, and Hardie had actually to be protected from assault. How often has this tale to be told in the struggle of labour for justice and liberty! These sectarian quarrels have now partially died out in Lanarkshire, but for many years they were of the greatest service to the employing class.

At another National Conference held at Dunfermline, on October 16th of the same year, Hardie was made National Secretary, an appointment which denoted, not the existence of a national organisation, but the need for it. The Scottish Miners' Federation was not formed till some years later. Hardie's selection at least indicates how far he had already advanced in the confidence of his fellow workers.

As a result of all this agitation, sporadic strikes took place early in 1880 at several collieries in Lanarkshire, the most memorable of these being at Eddlewood, where there were conflicts with the police and subsequent trials of pickets for alleged intimidation. In connection with this strike Hardie made his first visit into Ayrshire to warn the miners there against coming to Lanarkshire. The hunger of the women and children drove the men back to work, but deepened the discontent, and in August, against the advice of Hardie, another strike, general over the whole of Lanarkshire, took place and lasted for six weeks. How it was carried through without Union funds it is difficult to imagine. Public subscriptions were raised. The colliery village bands went far afield throughout Scotland and even across the border, appealing for help. No strike money was paid out but only food was given. Hardie with the other agents got local merchants to supply goods, themselves becoming responsible for payment. At his home a soup kitchen was kept running, and all had a share of what was going until further credit became impossible. In the end there was a sum unpaid, but the merchants, some of themselves originally from the miner class, did not press their claims too hard and freed the agents from their bond. The strike was lost, but the Union, though shaken, remained, and Hardie, having fought his first big labour battle, emerged from what seemed defeat and disaster, stronger and more determined than ever to stand by his class. He accepted a call from Ayrshire to organise the miners there, and, as will be shown, made good use of the experience gained in Lanarkshire.

At this time, he also added to his responsibilities in another direction. He became a married man. His agitation activities had not prevented him from taking part in the social life of the countryside, nor from forming the associations which come naturally to all healthy human beings in the springtime of life. He was not then, nor at any time, the austere Puritanical person he has sometimes been represented to be. A Puritan he was in all matters of absolute right or wrong, and could not be made to budge from what seemed to him to be the straight path. But with that limitation he was one of the most companionable of men. He could sing a good song, and dance and be merry with great abandon. He had his youthful friendships and love affairs, more than one, culminating as usual, in a supreme affection for one lass above all the others; and so it came about that, just before migrating into Ayrshire, he was married to Miss Lillie Wilson, whose acquaintance he had made during his work in the Temperance movement. The two young folk settled down in Cumnock to make a home for themselves, neither of them probably having any idea that in days to come the male partner would have to spend so much of his life outside of that home, returning to it periodically—as a sailor from his voyaging or a warrior from his campaigning—to find rest and quiet and renewal of strength for the storms and battles of a political career.

The labour movement owes much to its fighting men, and to the women also, who have stepped into the furies of the fray, but not less does it owe to the home-keeping women folk whose devotion has made it possible for the others to do this work. Such was the service rendered by Mrs. Keir Hardie in the quietude of Old Cumnock. The home was at first an ordinary room and kitchen house, and later a six roomed cottage and garden known to all members of the I.L.P. as "Lochnorris."

Hardie had come to Cumnock nominally as the Ayrshire Miners' Secretary, but there was really no Ayrshire Miners' Union. To get that into being was his task. The conditions were similar to those in Lanarkshire. At most of the collieries there were a few rebel spirits, keeping the flame of discontent alive and ready to form themselves into Union committees if given the right stimulus and support. It was from these the invitation to Hardie had come, and it was through co-ordinating these that a move could be made for general organisation. The first skirmishes are always won by the few pioneers who have the stout hearts and the burning vision.

It took nearly a year to get the organisation together, and by the beginning of August, 1881, a demand was formulated, on behalf of the whole of the miners of Ayrshire, for a ten per cent. increase of wages. The demand was refused. There was no alternative but to strike or go on working at the masters' terms. In the latter case, the Union would be destroyed before it had begun to exist. The question was, could the men all over the county be got to strike? Would they risk a stoppage, knowing that there could be no strike pay? Mass meetings were summoned in various parts of the county to be addressed by Hardie and other speakers to decide the question: "Strike or no strike"? but the question settled itself almost intuitively.

The present writer has heard old miners, who were young men then, describe what happened. It is interesting as a comparison with present day methods of calling a strike. On the Saturday, at the end of the rows and on the quoiting grounds, the talk was: "Would there be a strike?" Nobody knew. On the Sunday coming home from the kirk the crack was the same: "Would there be a strike?" On Sunday night they laid out their pit clothes as usual, ready for work next morning, but for ten long weeks they had no use for pit clothes. On Monday, long before dawn, there was a stir on the Ayrshire roads.

At two in the morning the Annbank brass band came playing through Trabboch village and every miner, young and old, jumped out of bed and fell in behind.

THE MAKING OF AN AGITATOR

Away up towards Auchinleck they went marching, their numbers increasing with every mile of the road. On through Darnconner, and Cronberry and Lugar and Muirkirk, right on to Glenbuck by Aird's Moss where the Covenanter Martyrs sleep, then down into Cumnock, at least five thousand strong. Never did magic muster such an army of the morning. It was as though the fairies had come down amongst men to summon them to a tryst. Over in the Kilmarnock district similar scenes were being enacted. The bands went marching from colliery to colliery and

> "The rising sun ower Galston Muir,
> Wi' glorious light was glintin"

upon processions of colliers on all the roads round about Galston village and Hurlford and Crookedholm and Riccarton, making, as by one common impulse, towards Craigie Hill which had not witnessed such a mustering of determined men since the days of William Wallace.

Ere nightfall a miracle had been accomplished. For the first time in its history, there was a stoppage nearly complete in the Ayrshire mining industry. At last the Ayrshire miners were united and, win or lose, they would stand or fall together. The fields were ripening to harvest when the men "lifted their graith." Ere they went back to work the Cumnock hills were white with snow, and by that time Keir Hardie was at once the most hated and the best respected man in Ayrshire. It was the Lanarkshire experience over again—an experience of sacrifice and endurance. The bands went out collecting money. The women folk and the children went "tattie howkin'" and harvesting. Thrifty miners' families who had saved a little during the prosperous years of the early 'seventies, threw their all into the common stock. The farmers, many of them, gave meal and potatoes to keep the children from starving. Here and there was an occasional break away, and the pickets were out, and the police and the military, and there were skirmishes and arrests and imprisonments. Hardie toiled night and day directing the relief committees, restraining the wild spirits from violence, advocating the men's claims temperately and persuasively in the local press, addressing mass meetings all over the county and keeping the men in good heart. "God's on our side, men," he declared. "Look at the weather He's giein' us!" And it seemed true. It was the finest fall of the year in Ayrshire within the memory of man, and, but for the pinch of hunger, was like a glimpse of Heaven to men accustomed to sweat ten hours a day in underground darkness. Whoever wants to know why it is so easy to get the miners to take an idle day, let him try a few hours "howkin' coal" and he will understand.

So the fight went on from week to week, till at last the winter came as the ally of the coalowners. Boots and clothes and food were needed for the bairns, and for the sake of the bairns the men went back to work. But they went back as they came out, altogether, maintaining their solidarity even in defeat. Nor were they wholly defeated. Within a month the coalowners discovered that trade had improved, and, without being asked, they advanced wages, a thing unprecedented in the coal trade. That ten weeks' stoppage had put a wholesome fear into the hearts of the coalowners, and they had also learned that a leader of men had come into Ayrshire. Here ended the second lesson for Keir Hardie the agitator. In the impoverished condition of the miners, the formation of the Union was for the present impracticable, and, recognising this, he settled himself down quietly as a citizen of Cumnock, and bided his time.

CHAPTER TWO

IT is not clear what Hardie's sources of income were in those early days in Ayrshire. He had determined to work no more underground for any employer. No colliery manager would have the chance a second time to drive him out. There was no miners' organisation to pay him a wage, though he ceased not from doing organising work. The likelihood is that he had kept up his press connections formed while in Lanarkshire, and that there was some little income from that quarter. He wrote occasional verses, amateurish, but of the kind acceptable in the "Poet's Corner" of provincial papers, and there would be an odd seven and sixpence for these. He was never a spendthrift, and probably both he and his lass had a small "nest egg" laid by before they joined partnership, and with this were prepared to go on for a month or two until the man could make good. He had great faith in himself, and she had great faith in him, and what more could any newly-married couple want for starting out in life?

Before long the financial question was solved. The pastor of the Evangelical Union church which Hardie joined had eked out a somewhat scanty stipend by writing notes for the local "Cumnock News." The pastor, in bad health, went off for a holiday, and asked Hardie to write his notes while he was away. He never returned, and Hardie found himself writing the notes practically as a member of the staff, and as he, with his knowledge of the miners' conditions and a decidedly literary turn of the pen, was just the kind of man wanted for such a paper, he was, by and by to all intents and purposes, acting as editor.

The "Cumnock News," it should be said, was an off-shoot of the "Ardrossan and Saltcoats Herald," which then was, and still is, one of the most ably conducted of Scottish provincial papers. Its editor and proprietor, Mr. Arthur Guthrie, was a man with literary and artistic tastes, and in politics a staunch Liberal, a fact which, however we may regard Liberalism now, was of some democratic value in those days, in a shire largely dominated by the county families. It required some fortitude to stand up against the Bute, the Eglinton and the Dundonald interests, not to speak of the coal-owning magnates of whom the Baird family was the most powerful.

It will thus be seen that Hardie's first editorial experience was on the side of the Liberal Party. There is no evidence that he took much interest in politics before he came into Ayrshire, but he could not help doing so now, nor could any active-minded working man. The political question of the hour was the extension of household franchise to the counties, and as it was to the Liberal Party that the workers looked for that boon, it was natural that the earnest and thoughtful sections of them should be Liberals. Hardie became a member of the Liberal Association, and, naturally, being the kind of man he was, was an active and prominent member. He was, however, a very complex personality, this new-comer into the social and political life of Ayrshire, and neither the Liberal Association nor the " Cumnock News " could absorb more than a small part of his energies. He was still active in temperance work, and, as a matter of course, became Grand Worthy Chief of the local Good Templars' Lodge. He took his share of the church work and filled the pulpit on occasions when the absence of the appointed minister made that necessary, and frequently his voice was to be heard at the street corners in Cumnock and in some of the neighbouring villages, preaching the Gospel of Christ as he understood it. He formed an evening class two nights a week for the teaching of shorthand writing, himself acting as teacher without fee or reward, and he gathered round him a group of students, who, we may be sure, learnt more things than shorthand.

At this time his reading of books became more comprehensive if not more systematic. That latter could hardly be with his mode of life. He then read Carlyle's " Sartor Resartus " for the first time and became acquainted with some of the writings of Ruskin and of Emerson. Fiction does not seem to have attracted him much, except in the form of ballads and folk-lore, though, strange to say, he himself wrote one or two stories when later he had control of a paper of his own. With Robert Burns he had of course been familiar since childhood. " I owe more to Robert Burns than to any man, alive or dead," he once wrote. As a boy it was the tender humanitarianism of the Scottish peasant poet to which his nature responded, and he has told how the "Lines on Seeing a wounded Hare" thrilled him with pity and anger. He was gaining in mental power and self reliance during these years, though with no settled purpose as to the use he would make of the knowledge and strength he was acquiring, except that all the time he had one fixed immediate object in view : the formation of an Ayrshire Miners' Union.

This event took place in August, 1886. The exact date is not known nor the place of nativity, early records having apparently been lost. James Neil, of Cumnock, who took an active part in the early work of the Union, has recollections of a delegate meeting in Mauchline, at which Andrew Fisher, of Crosshouse, (afterwards Prime Minister of Australia) was present, and he thinks this may have been the initial meeting, which is not unlikely, Fisher, like Neil himself, being one of the original delegates. Whether that was so or not, one thing is certain. The Union was formed in 1886, and Hardie was appointed its Organising Secretary. Henceforth, the coal magnates of Ayrshire had a new force to reckon with. Hardie's allowance—it could hardly be called a salary—was £75 a year, but as he was earning his living in other ways, he devoted the money to the starting of a monthly paper, and in the beginning of the following year produced "The Miner," of which we shall have something to say in due course.

This same year the Scottish Miners' Federation was formed, and to this also Hardie was appointed Secretary, perhaps on the principle that the willing horse gets the heaviest burden. That he was willing there can be no doubt. Since the days of the Lanarkshire strike, seven years before, he had realised the need for the Scottish miners being united in one organisation, and he was ready to take his share in the work.

There was also being borne in upon him and others a belief that the time had come for organised Labour to consider what use could be made of the new political opportunities which had been presented to it. The passing of the 1884 Franchise Act, which extended household franchise to the counties, brought great hopes to the workers, though it found them, for the moment, unable to take advantage of it. It gave political power to practically all the adult miners in the country, and the leaders of the miners began to take thought as to how it could be utilised.

For the most part they held to the belief that in the Liberal Party organisation lay the medium by which the representatives of Labour could reach Parliament. Liberalism, simply because it was traditionally opposed to Toryism, was accepted as embodying the progressive spirit of the nation. The leader of the Liberal Party was W. E. Gladstone, then in the heyday of his popularity. The workers generally were willing to trust Gladstone, but amongst them were a considerable number who, having begun to imbibe Socialist ideas, had doubts as to the genuineness of the Liberal Party's professions of goodwill to labour. They knew that although it might be true that the Tory Party was dominated by the landed interests, there were not a few territorial magnates in the councils of Liberalism. They also knew that the Liberal Party policy was directed largely on behoof of the manufacturing and commercial interests, and they felt that, as in the very nature of things these interests must collide with those of the workers, to strengthen the Liberal Party might be like making a stick for labour's back. Yet, on the whole, they were willing to give it a trial, induced by the knowledge that there were in the Liberal Party a few honest, sincere and able men, friendly to labour—men such as Cunninghame Graham, the Radical Member for North-West Lanark, Conybeare, Stephen Mason, Dr. G. B. Clark, and a few others, who, with Burt and Fenwick and Abraham already representing the miners, were expected to force the pace inside the Liberal Party. In Cunninghame Graham especially, great hopes were centred. He had won North-West Lanarkshire as a Gladstonian Liberal in the 1886 election. In his election campaign Graham had thoroughly familiarised himself with the needs and aspirations of the miners, had wholeheartedly adopted their programme of reforms, and had

D 21

advocated the passing of an Eight Hours' Bill, the establishment of a wage court, and the nationalisation of minerals; he had, moreover, made it quite clear that he supported such measures only as necessary transitional steps towards Socialism. Two years later he was to prove his sincerity by introducing the Miners' Eight Hours' Day Bill into Parliament, and by going to prison in defence of free speech. He had already, by his originality of utterance, caught the attention of the House of Commons, and the fact that he came of aristocratic lineage added piquancy to his sometimes savage sarcasms against the ruling classes. Altogether, he was a picturesque and dashing Parliamentary figure; and that this man, holding views that were little short of revolutionary, should still be a recognised member of the Liberal Party, helped to sustain working-class faith in Liberalism and probably helped to delay, until the psychological moment was past, the formation of a clearcut, working-class party. The right moment was at the passing of the Franchise Act.

Keir Hardie, though himself a member of the Liberal Party, was amongst the doubters, and he, for one, resolved to put the matter to the test at the earliest opportunity, and in his capacity as Secretary of the Ayrshire Miners' Union, made preparations accordingly. In May, 1887, at demonstrations of the Ayrshire miners held on Irvine Moor and on Cragie Hill, the following resolution was adopted: "That in the opinion of this meeting, the time has come for the formation of a Labour Party in the House of Commons, and we hereby agree to assist in returning one or more members to represent the miners of Scotland at the first available opportunity."

Shortly afterwards Hardie was adopted as the miners' candidate for North Ayrshire, and immediately there developed a situation which has been repeated hundreds of times since all over the country, and which can best be shown by quotations from a speech delivered by Hardie at Irvine in October of that same year. It is his first recorded political utterance, and defines very clearly his attitude at that stage of his development. It shows that he was not yet prepared to fight on a full Socialist programme, and also that he was not unwilling to work through the Liberal Party, provided its methods were honestly democratic. He was, in fact, putting Liberalism to the test of allegiance to its own avowed principles. He said, "The Liberals and Conservatives have, through their organisations, selected candidates. They are both, as far as I know, good men. The point I wish to emphasise, however, is this : that these men have been selected without the mass of the people being consulted. Your betters have chosen the men, and they now send them down to you to have them returned. What would you think if the Miners' Executive Council were to meet in Kilmarnock and appoint a secretary to the miners of Ayrshire in that way? Your candidate ought to be selected by the voice and vote of the mass of the people. We are told that Sir William Wedderburn is a good Radical and that he is sound on the Liberal programme. It may be all true, but we do not know whether it is or not. Will he, for example, support an Eight Hour Bill? Nobody has asked him, and nobody cares except ourselves. Will he support the abolition of private property in royalties? Well, he is a landlord and not likely to be too extreme in that respect. Is he prepared to establish a wage court that would secure to the workman a just reward for his labour? Nobody knows whether he is or not. Is he prepared to support the extension of the Employers' Liability Act, which presently limits the compensation for loss of life, however culpable the employers may be, to three years'

wages? Nobody knows. I am not surprised at the
action of the Liberal Association in opposing me. This
is what has been done in nearly every case where a
Labour candidate has been brought forward. I have
been asked what course I intend to take, and my reply is,
the same as formerly. I will endeavour to have a Labour
Electoral Association formed in every town and village
in the constituency. When the time comes for an election I will judge how far circumstances justify me in
going forward. If the working men are true to themselves, I will insist on a plebiscite being taken between
myself and the Liberal candidate, and then let the man
who gets most support go to the poll. If the Liberal
Association refuses to take this course, working men
will then see how much their professions of friendship
are worth. I am not specially anxious to go to Parliament, but I am anxious and determined that the wants
and wishes of the working classes shall be made known
and attended to there. Meantime, I recommend my
friends not to pledge themselves to either of the candidates now before them till they see what the future
may bring forth."

There was nothing revolutionary in all this; Socialism was not even hinted at; Liberalism was not condemned; it was to be put upon its trial, and the test
of its sincerity was to be its willingness within its own
organisation to provide a fair field for labour. The one
thing that does emerge from this utterance and others
during this period is Hardie's class feeling, inherent in
his very nature, derived from and intensified by his own
life experience, and avowed at a time when he had probably made no acquaintance with Marxian philosophy.

"I am anxious and determined that the wants and
wishes of the working classes shall be made known and
attended to in Parliament." From that fundamental

political creed he never deviated during the whole of his life. It was his basic article of faith, the impregnable rock upon which he stood immovable and incorruptible : Loyalty to the working class. The party politicians never could understand this, and therefore they never understood Keir Hardie. The simple straightforward-ness and steadfastness of the man were baffling to them, and afterwards, in the House of Commons, when he kept at arm's length all Parliamentary intriguers and even held aloof from some who may have desired from quite friendly motives to be on terms of social fellowship with him, it was ascribed to boorishness on his part. It was nothing of the sort, as those who were on terms of intimacy with him well knew. It was the expression at once of his own individuality and of his class loyalty. He was a man who could not be patronised, and he was jealous for the independence of the working people, of whom he believed himself to be representative. When, many years afterwards, George Bernard Shaw charac-terised him as "the damndest natural aristocrat in the House of Commons," there was more truth in the description than Shaw himself realised. If to be an aristocrat is to have pride of caste, Keir Hardie was an aristocrat. He possessed pride of class in the superla-tive degree, in a much greater degree than the average working man himself has ever possessed it. Hardie was willing at all times to associate with members of the other classes for the furtherance of the objects he had in view—with Fabian middle class people, with clergy-men, and artists, and litterateurs, but always on terms of equality. At the first hint of patronage, either on the ground of class or cultural superiority, he drew back and went his own way, alone if need be.

Unforeseen events decided that his first parliamentary contest should be elsewhere than in North Ayrshire, but

J. KEIR HARDIE

it was here, in the year 1887, that he first threw down his challenge to Liberalism to prove its sincerity, and called upon his fellow workers to prepare to make use of their political opportunities self-reliantly and with a sense of the dignity of their class. "So long as men are content to believe that Providence has sent into the world one class of men saddled and bridled, and another class booted and spurred to ride them, so long will they be ridden; but the moment the masses come to feel and act as if they were men, that moment the inequality ceases." Thus he wrote in "The Miner" at this time. He himself had reached that stage very early in life and in his own personality he typified his conception of what the working class ought to be.

The year 1887 was a very busy one for Keir Hardie. He had already acquired that capacity for work which in future years frequently astonished his colleagues of the Independent Labour Party. As already recorded, the Scottish Miners' Federation had been formed in the autumn of 1886 and he had accepted the position of Secretary. A personal paragraph in the first Annual Report gives only a partial indication of his activities. "Conscious," he says, "of many defects in the performance of my duties, I have yet tried to do my best. It has been hard sometimes to bear the blame of unreasonable men, though this has been more than compensated for by the tolerance of the great mass. There is scarcely a district in Scotland where my voice has not been heard, with what effect it is for others to say. I find, leaving out the deputations to London and the big conferences, that I have attended on behalf of the Federation 77 meetings, 37 of which have been public, and 40 Executive and conference meetings, involving 6,000 miles of railway travelling. I have sent out over 1,500 letters and circulars, and over 60,000 printed leaflets. This has involved a very considerable amount of work, but I am persuaded it has not been labour in vain." A reference to the balance sheet shows under the heading of "Salaries" : "J. K. Hardie, £3 15s."—a remuneration certainly not commensurate to the work done, but probably bearing some proportion to the earnings of the miners themselves, for in this same report it is recorded that "wages still continue very low, ranging from 2s. 6d. to 4s. per day, the average being about 3s. 3d. Work is, however, very unsteady, and thus the earnings of the men cannot be more than 12s. per week." Those were hard times for underground workers, and not unduly prosperous ones for their leaders. Another interesting item in the financial statement runs : "Donation from meeting in Edinburgh (Socialist), £11 8s. 6d."—probably some public gathering under the auspices of the newly-formed Socialist League, willing thus early to help forward the work of industrial organisation. The concluding exordium is in the genuine Keir Hardie vein familiar to all who ever had the good fortune to work along with him. "May the experience of the past not be lost on us in the future. There are a number of young and ardent spirits in our ranks who, if they can be laid hold of, will ensure the success of our movement in years to come. Ours is no old-fashioned sixpence-a-day agitation. We aim at the complete emancipation of the worker from the thraldom of wagedom. Co-operative production, under State management, should be our goal, as, never till this has been obtained, can we hope for better times for working people." Thus spake the optimist.

He was himself prevented from being present at this first annual meeting of the Federation. The death of his second-born child, Sarah, two years of age, had naturally affected him very keenly, and made it impossible for him at the time to be interested in anything else

J. KEIR HARDIE

than this first domestic affliction which came upon him.
Two other children were left, James, born in 1881, and
Agnes, born in 1885, but as usually happens, the one that
was taken had no peer in the minds of the bereaved
parents. Another boy, Duncan, born this same year,
1887, helped to fill the gap thus made in the little family
circle.

The visits to London mentioned in the report were
to interview the Home Secretary in favour of improvements in the Government's Mines Bill, and of
Donald Crawford's Bill to abolish the truck system,
introduced and passed during the Parliamentary session
of that year. The miners sought to have an eight-hours
clause for boys, together with one making it penal for
an employer to keep men in the pit when they desired to
get out. Hardie's deputation colleagues were R. Chisholm Robertson of Stirlingshire, John Weir of Fife-
shire, and Robert Brown of the Lothians, all at that
time active in promoting organisation in their various
districts. They also, on this occasion, did some lobby-
ing of Members to support their proposals, and in the
course of this Keir Hardie doubtless got ample confirmation of the need for direct Labour representation, and
was strengthened in his growing belief that such representation should be independent of existing political
parties. We can also see the effect which the subsequent result, when the Eight Hours Amendment was
defeated actually owing to the action of the Liberal-
Labour members from mining districts, Burt, Fenwick
and Abraham, had upon his attitude to certain of the
older Trade Union leaders and both their industrial and
political policy.

One notable amendment of the Bill, secured very
largely through pressure by Hardie and other outside
agitators, was the prohibition of the employment of boys

under twelve. "What a difference," he commented in
"The Miner," "from the time when children were taken
into the pit almost as soon as they were out of the cradle."
What a difference, he might have said, from the time
when he himself went down the pit at ten years of age !
What a difference, we might say, from the present time,
when fourteen is the minimum school-leaving age.
Verily, the agitators have not laboured in vain.

Reference is made above to "The Miner," a monthly
journal of which he was the founder and editor, and to
which, as a matter of fact, he contributed about one-third
of the letterpress. Its first number appeared in January,
1887, and it was published for two years, being discon-
tinued at the end of 1888, partly because of the usual
lack of support from which all purely Labour journals
have suffered, but chiefly because by that time Hardie
himself was becoming too deeply involved in political
propagandist agitation to be able to give the necessary
time to the work of supervision. It was a very remarkable
paper, and to those who are fortunate enough to possess
the two volumes, it mirrors in a very realistic way the
social conditions of the collier folk of that time, and also
throws considerable light on the many phases and
aspects of the general Labour movement in the days
when it was gropingly feeling its way through many
experiments and experiences towards political self-
reliance and self-knowledge.

The journal is peculiarly valuable to us in that it
reveals Hardie himself as a man growing and developing, and becoming more and more self-assertive. It
began as "The Miner: a Journal for Underground
Workers." When it had reached the second year it had
become "The Miner: an Advanced Political Journal.
Edited by J. K. Hardie," thus definitely proclaiming
the aim of its controller—if not yet of the workers whose

interests it advocated. It was at once the germ and the precursor of the "Labour Leader," which was to be for many years almost the personal organ of Keir Hardie, and is now the firmly established and influential exponent of the Independent Labour Party, of which he was the founder. In its pages you can discern him, tentatively, but ever more boldly, finding expression for his Socialist convictions, and from being a miners' leader, steadily aspiring towards becoming a people's leader. He was quite sure of himself, and of his purpose, but not quite sure of the approval of his readers. "The miners of Britain," he said in his first leading article, "stand sorely in need of an organ to ventilate their grievances, *and teach them the duty they owe to themselves.* The paper, while dealing primarily with purely mining affairs, will advocate reform in *every direction* which promises to bring relief to the toiling millions," and throughout the career of the paper he is found giving a platform to the pioneers and protagonists of schemes of working-class betterment, no matter what their label might be. Land Nationalisers, Socialists, Anarchists, Trade Unionists, are all given room to state and argue their case, and ever and anon he lets it be known where he himself stands and where he is going.

"The capitalist has done good service in the past by developing trade and commerce. His day is now nearly past. He has played his part in the economy of the industrial system, and must now give way for a more perfect order of things wherein the labourer shall be rewarded in proportion to his work." That is not exactly Socialism, but the idea of evolution in industry towards Socialism has seldom been more tersely stated; nor, indeed, has the general purpose of Socialism been more accurately defined. And again, "The world to-day is sick and weary at heart. Even our clergy are for the most part dumb dogs who dare not bark. So it was in the days of Christ. They who proclaimed a God-given gospel to the world were the poor and the comparatively unlettered. We need to-day a return to the principles of that Gospel which, by proclaiming all men sons of God and brethren one with another, makes it impossible for one, Shylock-like, to insist on his rights at the expense of another.''

There was no lack of idealism in the journalistic fare served up to the working miners who turned to their trade journal for news of the daily conflicts with employers and managers, and found that in plenty, along with the idealism. We have here the manifestations of what I might call the spiritual consistency which formed the fibre of Hardie's character, and was in large measure the secret of his power to win the allegiance even of those whose belief in Socialism had a more materialistic foundation.

His energy at this time seems to have been inexhaustible. Besides this editorial and journalistic work, he was a member of Auchinleck School Board, and, in addition to his secretarial duties for the Scottish Miners' Federation, he was still acting as secretary of the Ayrshire Miners' Union, and in that capacity displaying an amount of vigour surprising to his associates and disconcerting to colliery managers and officials with whom he was perforce in continual conflict. Conducting what are known as "partial" strikes, bringing the men out, now in one corner of Ayrshire, now in another, on questions of wages, on questions of illegal deductions of weight, on questions of victimisation; holding mass meetings, and calling idle days here, there, and everywhere, with a view to enforcing the policy of restriction of output which at this time was the only alternative policy to a general strike in resistance to wage reductions; and in one way and another keeping the whole Ayrshire area in that condition of unrest which was the only possible means of giving active expression to the discontent seething throughout the entire mining community of Scotland. There was indeed very ample justification for this agitation. "With coal selling in Glasgow at 1s. per cwt., and public works stopped for want of fuel; with mounted policemen riding down inoffensive children nearly to death, and felling quiet old men with a blow from a baton; with the wives and children of thirty thousand men not on the verge but in the very throes of starvation; with all this, and much more that might be named, a condition of things is being fostered which can only end in riot, as unhappily has been in Lanarkshire." This is his picture of the condition of the miners at that time, a picture the truth of which can easily be verified from the columns of the contemporary newspapers. He was in favour of a general strike throughout England, Scotland and Wales, but the unity of organisation which could bring that to pass was yet far away, and guerilla fighting was the only possible tactics. "If the miners were Highland crofters," he said, "or African slaves, or Bulgarians, people would be found on every hand getting up indignation meetings to protest against the wrongs inflicted upon them by the capitalists, but because they are *only* miners nobody heeds them."

The miners have now found means of making *everybody* heed them, and Hardie and his colleagues had already begun the forging of the weapons for that achievement. It was on a motion from Scotland that, at a Conference in Manchester in April, 1887, it was agreed that "The Federations be admitted to the Miners' National Union on payment of one farthing per member quarterly, this money to be spent in furthering legislative work and in holding conferences for the consideration of the state of trade and wages, such conferences to have power to issue such recommendations as may seem necessary for the improvement of the same." Thus was laid the basis of the now powerful Miners' Federation of Great Britain.

Any account of this period of Hardie's life would be incomplete without a reference to the colliery disaster at Udston, in Lanarkshire, which took place on the 28th May, 1887, and by which eighty-five lives were lost. He, immediately on getting the news, hurried through from Ayrshire and joined with the other agents in the relief work and in comforting the bereaved relatives. Many of the men who had been killed were his own personal friends, lads he had worked with underground or companioned in play and sport and sociality when he and they were growing into manhood. He was able to visualise the conditions under which they had met their death in the fiery mine with never a chance to escape, and he believed that it was only the parsimony of the mineowners that prevented the methods being used which would make such accidents impossible.

This belief deepened his conviction that there would never be proper protection for the miners except through compulsory legislation in the framing of which the miners themselves should have a voice. Yet in after years one of his chief difficulties was to convince the miners themselves of that fact, and that they should trust only in themselves for the passing of protective laws. On this occasion, in "The Miner," he impeached both the colliery management and the Government inspectors for gross neglect of their duties. But of course "The Miner" was read only by miners, and only by a small number of them.

The end of 1887 brought his severance—voluntarily on his part—from the two Ayrshire papers, the "Ardrossan Herald" and "Cumnock News," with which he had been connected since 1882.

During that time in addition to supplying the news of the district, he had contributed under the *nom de plume* of "The Trapper," a weekly article, headed "Black Diamonds, or Mining Notes Worth Minding." His farewell words to the readers were indicative alike of the character of his work on these local papers and of his aspirations for the future in the wider field upon which he was now entering :—

"I have tried to practice what I preached by showing, so far as I knew how, that manhood was preferable to money. Nor have I the least intention of changing. Circumstances have for the time being directed my course a certain way; for how long I cannot tell, but these make it all but impossible for me to continue writing "Black Diamonds.' . . . I feel like giving up an old friend in thus taking leave, but that the great tide of human progress may keep flowing steadily shoreward till it washes away all the wrong and the sin and the shame and the misery which now exist, is now, and for ever will be, the sincere prayer of your friend 'The Trapper.' Good Bye."

CHAPTER THREE

MID-LANARK—THE SCOTTISH LABOUR PARTY

IN the spring of 1888 came the opportunity for which he had been waiting and preparing, but it arose, not, as he had hoped, in Ayrshire, but in Lanarkshire. The resignation of Mr. Stephen Mason from the representation of Mid-Lanark made a by-election necessary.

The constituency was pre-eminently mining and there was a natural expectation that the Liberal Party would give preference to a miner as candidate. Almost as a matter of course Hardie's name was suggested and a requisition numerously signed by electors in the Division was presented to him, requesting him to stand as Labour candidate. In "The Miner" he made known his attitude. "For the first time, so far as Scotland is concerned, a serious attempt is to be made to run a genuine Labour candidate for the constituency, and my own name has been put forward in that connection. I desire to define my position clearly. I earnestly desire to see Labour represented in Parliament by working men. Should the choice of the electors fall on me, I am prepared to fight their battle. Should another be selected by them, I will give that other as hearty and ungrudging support as one man can give another. The constituency is essentially one for returning a Labour candidate. Much depends on the position taken up by the Liberal Association. It may or may not select a Labour candidate. In either case my advice would be that the Labour candidate should be put forward. Better split the party now, if there is to be a split, than at a general election, and if the Labour Party only make their power felt now, terms will not be wanting when the general election comes.''

The prospect of the contest aroused widespread interest. It was recognised that, not only the Liberal professions in favour of Labour representation, but the workers themselves, were to be tested, and that, in the result, it would be shown whether in a typical working-class constituency the workers were yet ready to use their newly-acquired political power in the interest of their own class and irrespective of old party traditions. The press immediately got busy. The Scottish Liberal papers, ''The Glasgow Daily Mail'' and the ''Scottish Leader,'' began to confuse the issues, to put forward the names of various middle-class candidates, to besmirch and misrepresent Hardie, and to talk about ''Tory gold.'' On the other hand the London ''Star'' wrote as follows :—''Mr. Hardie is certainly the best man for the constituency. One or two of his stamp are greatly needed to look after Scottish Labour interests in Parliament, especially as those interests are about to lose the advocacy of Mr. Stephen Mason.''

The Tory ''Ayrshire Post'' said : ''Among the candidates brought forward for the expected vacancy in Mid-Lanark, through the retirement of Mr. Stephen Mason, is Mr. J. Keir Hardie, Cumnock. A correspondent interested in the election asks us whether there is any truth in the rumour that Mr. Hardie was a Unionist in 1886. The rumour is an absurd one. Mr. Hardie has been a consistent and pronounced Home Ruler since the beginning of the controversy. Whatever faults he may have, sitting on the hedge is not one

of them.   Right or wrong, you know what he means.''
So began the campaign of lies and innuendo of which
he was to have a plentiful experience in future years,
and the very fact that the Tory press was inclined to
speak of him respectfully was adduced as proof that he
was in league with the Tories.

Hardie pursued his way steadily, unmoved by any
calumny.   On the 15th March he offered himself as a
candidate for selection by the Mid-Lanark Liberal
Association.   On the 21st of the same month he withdrew his name from the official list for the following
reasons.   ''The Executive of the Association, without
giving the electors a chance of deciding on the merits
of the respective candidates, have already, at the
instance of outsiders, and without regard to fitness,
decided who the candidate is to be.''   The Liberal
candidate finally adopted was Mr. J. W. Phillips, a
young Welsh lawyer, who ultimately made his way to
the House of Lords as Lord St. Davids.   The Tory
candidate was Mr. W. R. Bousfield.   Hardie stood
therefore as an Independent Labour candidate,
the first of the kind in British politics; and for
that reason, if for no other, this Mid-Lanark election
is historical.   As a Labour candidate but, be it noted,
not yet as a Socialist, did he stand.   In his letter to the
Liberal Association, he claimed that he had all his life
been a Radical of a somewhat advanced type, and from
the first had supported Mr. Gladstone's Home Rule
proposals.   In his election address he said, ''I adopt in
its entirety the Liberal programme agreed to at
Nottingham, which includes Adult Suffrage; Reform of
Registration Laws; Allotments for Labourers; County
Government; London Municipal Government; Free
Education; Disestablishment.   On questions of general
politics I would vote with the Liberal Party, to which I

have all my life belonged." His proposals for Labour and Land legislation, though going far beyond the Liberal programme, were not at all comprehensively Socialistic. An Eight Hours' Day for Miners, an Insurance and Superannuation Fund supported from Royalties, Arbitration Courts, and the creation of a Ministry of Mines were his mining proposals; the reimposition of the four shillings in the pound Land Rent, payable by the landlord to the State, the establishment of a Land Court, compulsory cultivation of waste lands, taxation of land values and nationalisation of royalties were his land programme. On the question of Home Rule he said, "I will support the Irish Party in winning justice for Ireland, and in the event of a difference between them and the Liberal Party, would vote with the Irish"; and to this he added, "I am also strongly in favour of Home Rule for Scotland, being convinced that until we have a Parliament of our own, we cannot obtain the many and great reforms on which I believe the people of Scotland have set their hearts."

His chief appeal however for differentiation as between himself and the other candidates was on the ground of class representation. He submitted an analysis of all the interests represented in Parliament, showing that out of the 72 members sent from Scotland, not one represented the working people. "Why is it," he asked, "that in the richest nation in the world those who produce the wealth should alone be poor? What help can you expect from those who believe they can only be kept rich in proportion as you are kept poor?

'Few save the poor feel for the poor, the rich know not how hard,
It is to be of needful food and needful rest debarred.'

"I ask you therefore to return to Parliament a man of yourselves, who being poor, can feel for the poor, and whose whole interest lies in the direction of securing for you a better and a happier lot?"

Encouragement came from many quarters.

The recently formed Labour Electoral Association, which during this election assumed the title of National Labour Party, sent through its treasurer, Edward Harford, £400 with the assurance : "You can have more if needed.

-This body subsequently proved itself unable to stand the strain of divided allegiance to Liberalism and Labour. The secretary, T. R. Threlfall, wrote declaring the election to be ''particularly a test question as to how far the professed love of the Liberal Party for Labour representation is a reality.''

The Scottish Home Rule Association, both through its Edinburgh and its London Committees, adopted him as its candidate, the Metropolitan section passing the following resolution, "That this meeting hails with gratitude the appearance of Mr. J. K. Hardie, the tried and trusted champion of the rights of the Scottish Miners, as a Labour candidate for Mid-Lanark, and trusts that the working men in that constituency will rally round him and do themselves the honour of returning the first genuine Labour representative for Scotland." In transmitting the resolution, the Secretary, J. Ramsay MacDonald, sent the following letter, the terms of which he himself has probably long ago forgotten. As this was the first correspondence between two men who were later to be in close comradeship, it is set down here for preservation. It shows, amongst other things, that Mac-Donald, like Hardie, had not yet lost hope in the Liberal Party.

J. KEIR HARDIE

"Scottish Home Rule Association.
"23 Kelly Street, Kentish Town, London.

"Mr. J. Keir Hardie,

"Dear Mr. Hardie,—I cannot refrain from wishing you God-speed in your election contest. Had I been able to have gone to Mid-Lanark to help you—to do so both by 'word and deed'—would have given very great pleasure indeed. The powers of darkness—Scottish newspapers with English editors (as the 'Leader'), partisan wire-pullers, and the other etceteras of political squabbles—are leagued against us.

"But let the consequences be what they may, do not withdraw. The cause of Labour and of Scottish Nationality will suffer much thereby. Your defeat will awaken Scotland, and your victory will re-construct Scottish Liberalism. All success be yours, and the National cause you champion. There is no miner— and no other one for that matter—who is a Scotsman and not ashamed of it, who will vote against you in favour of an obscure English barrister, absolutely ignorant of Scotland and of Scottish affairs, and who only wants to get to Parliament in order that he may have the tail of M.P. to his name in the law courts.

I am, Dear Sir,
Yours very truly,
"J. RAMSAY MACDONALD,
"Hon. Secretary, S.H.R.A."

The Parliamentary Committee of the Highland Land League, through its Chairman, J. Galloway Weir, also endorsed the candidature. The Glasgow Trades Council did likewise, and the Executive Council of the British Steel Smelters' Association. Lady Florence Dixie wrote: "If the miners put you in they will know

40

that, at least, they have a representative who will be the slave of no Party, but who will speak fearlessly for Scotland and her people's interests." Cunninghame Graham sent a characteristic epistle in which he expressed the hope that all Scotsmen would see the importance of not returning an Englishman, and concluded, "a good coat is useful enough against the weather, but why poor men should bow down and worship one, knowing that it will not warm *their* backs passes my comprehension."

Hardie resisted all inducements to retire, including an offer from the Liberal Party, the nature of which had best be disclosed in his own words many years afterwards.

"In 1888 I came out as the Labour candidate for the Mid-Division of Lanarkshire. The whole story of that campaign will be told some day—Bob Smillie could tell it—but for the moment I confine myself to one little incident. Mr. T. R. Threlfall, Secretary to the Labour Electoral Association, came North to take part in the contest. One evening Threlfall did not turn up at the meeting for which he was advertised, and shortly after I got back from my round he turned up at the hotel bubbling over with excitement. 'I've settled it,' he cried excitedly. 'I've been in conference with them all the evening, and it's all fixed up.' 'In conference with whom, and settled what?' I asked. 'In conference with the Liberals,' he replied, 'at the George Hotel, and you've to retire.' I don't quite know what happened then, but I remember rising to my feet and Threlfall ceased speaking. Next morning he returned home to Southport. On the day of his departure Mr. Schnadhorst, the then chief Caucusmonger of the Liberals, invited me to meet him at the George Hotel. I replied that I was quite prepared to receive in writing anything he had to say. The following day, Mr.

J. KEIR HARDIE

C. A. V. Conybeare, then M.P. for the Camborne Division of Cornwall, induced me to pay a visit to Sir George Trevelyan, also at the George Hotel. Sir George was very polite, and explained the unwisdom of Liberals and Labour fighing each other. They wanted more working men in Parliament, and if only I would stand down in Mid-Lanark he would give me an assurance that at the General Election I would be adopted somewhere, the party paying my expenses, and guaranteeing me a yearly salary—three hundred pounds was the sum·hinted at—as they were doing for others (he gave me names). I explained as well as I could why his proposal was offensive, and though he was obviously surprised, he was too much of a gentleman to be anything but courteous. And so the fight went on."

The contest was fought with great bitterness, especially on the part of the Liberals, who did not scruple to introduce sectarian and religious animosities, and who were able to make great play with the Irish Home Rule question in a constituency where the Irish electorate bulked largely. The United Irish League seems to have believed implicitly at that time in the willingness and ability of Mr. Gladstone to carry the Liberal Party with him in establishing Home Rule, and although Hardie had the support of Mr. John Ferguson, the leading champion of the Irish cause in the West of Scotland, and himself on the Council of the Liberal Party, the official mandate went against Hardie. He had thus to fight both the Liberal machine and the Nationalist machine, and had only an impromptu organisation wherewith to counter them. When the end came, he got 617 votes, and the Liberal went to the House of Commons—and in due course higher up. Looking back over the years and the events which separate us from this historical contest, how tragic is "the might-have-been."

But the election had cleared the air, and had settled one thing for ever, the impossibility of a Labour Party *within* the Liberal Party. That gives it its permanent place in the history of the Labour movement. From that day onward, the coming of the Independent Labour Party was a certainty, and that it should be a Socialist Party was equally certain from the very nature of the political developments arising out of the competitive commercialist system and the growing demands of the workers for a higher standard of life, which it was quite evident could not be realised merely through the industrial organisations then existing.

The capitalist and the landowning classes both relied upon political force for the maintenance of their privileges. To combat these, Labour political force was necessary. Only a minority of the working class leaders were able to diagnose the disease and apply the remedy. Amongst that minority was the defeated Labour candidate for Mid-Lanark. Henceforth there was to be no temporising so far as he was concerned—no accommodating other interests. The issues and the policy were to be alike clear. A new chapter in Labour politics was opened.

The next step was quickly taken. On May 19th, twenty-seven men met in Glasgow. Mr. John Murdoch, a man well known in connection with the Highland Crofters' agitation, sturdy in frame as in opinions, presided, and Hardie explained the object for which the meeting had been called, viz., the formation of a *bona fide* Labour Party for Scotland. A Committee was formed to arrange for a conference to be held without delay to form such a Party. The members of the Committee were Duncan Macpherson, Keir Hardie,

Charles Kennedy, George Mitchell and Robert Hutchison. Two of these at least, Mitchell and Hutchison, were avowed Socialists, the latter an exceedingly able open-air speaker, who, with Bruce Glasier, carried the Socialist message into many far distant corners of Scotland. These two were, in fact, the voices in the wilderness heralding the coming of the great army of propagandists that was to follow. Three months later, on August 25th, the Conference was held in the Waterloo Rooms, Glasgow, and the Scottish Parliamentary Labour Party was duly formed and office-bearers elected. The Hon. President was R. B. Cunninghame Graham; Hon. Vice-Presidents, Dr. Clark, M.P., and John Ferguson. The Chairman of Executive was J. Shaw Maxwell, who afterwards became first secretary of the national Independent Labour Party. Keir Hardie was Secretary, and George Mitchell, Treasurer. Thus one more office of responsibility was added to Hardie's already numerous duties. He was now Secretary of the Ayrshire Miners' Union, of the Scottish Miners' Federation, of the Scottish Parliamentary Labour Party, and editor of "The Miner." In the creation of all these enterprises on behalf of labour his was the active mind, and it cannot be said that he shirked in any way his share of the toil which their promotion involved.

Amongst those who took part in this memorable meeting was a delegate from Larkhall named Robert Smillie, who has been heard of in the world since then. Hardie and he were already fairly close friends and fellow workers in the common cause, and remained so till death broke the bond of comradeship. Smillie, though still working in the pits, was, at the period of this meeting, already busy organising the Lanarkshire miners and serving them in a representative capacity on the Larkhall School

Board. In such probationary ways and through such manifold experiences do working class leaders evolve. This is the kind of service for which the qualifying degrees do not emanate from any university, though the university might be helpful if it were available.

The newly formed party discussed and adopted a lengthy and detailed programme which need not be reproduced here. The most far-reaching of the proposals, such as the "State acquisition of railways, and all other means of transit," "A National Banking System and the Issue of State Money only," remain yet unfulfilled, though now well within the range of practical politics. The formulation of these demands thirty years ago indicates how far these men were in advance of their time, and in what manner they were feeling their way towards a statement of Socialist aims which, by its very practicality, would be acceptable to their fellow workmen. They were not dreamers by any means. They were out for realities. They related the hard road at their feet with the justice they saw on the horizon.

Following close upon this memorable meeting at Glasgow, came the annual Trades Union Congress held that year at Bradford. Hardie was a delegate and much in evidence in the debates, being practically leading spokesman for the advanced section, who made use of the Congress as a propaganda platform in favour of Parliamentary Labour Representation and the Legal Eight Hours' Day. He also presided at an outside fraternising meeting of French and British delegates for the purpose of mutual enlightenment on the progress of the working-class movement in both countries. Already he was beginning to be recognised by European working-class leaders as representative of the most progressive and the most fearless elements in the British

Labour movement, and for his part, he was eager to
know and understand the conditions under which they
had to carry on the struggle against the forces of capitalism; he was also, perhaps, desirous of, to some extent,
taking the measure of the personalities who were in the
forefront of that battle.   He had an opportunity of
extending his knowledge at an International Conference which took place in London the following November.   This was Hardie's first International, and for that
reason it is of importance for this memoir, but also for
other reasons.   It was not a fully representative Conference, the German Social Democrats having decided not
to take part through some misunderstanding, which need
not be discussed now after all these years, but which
called for an explanatory circular from the "Socialist
members of the German Reichstag" addressed to "Our
Socialist comrades, and the workers of all countries,"
and including amongst its signatures the names of two
men who take rank amongst the great ones of the
wide-world Socialist movement, William Liebknecht
and August Bebel.   The Conference was called by the
Parliamentary Committee of the Trades Union Congress, and was really a Trade Union, rather than a
Socialist, International.   Naturally, the British delegates were largely in the majority, being seventy-nine
in number as compared with eighteen from France which
sent the next largest number.   Holland sent thirteen,
Belgium ten, Denmark two, Italy one.
  There does not appear to have been any representation from Austria, or Hungary, or Switzerland, or any of
the Balkan countries.   Hardie's observations, comparing the British with the foreigners may be quoted, if
for no other purpose than to illustrate his opinions concerning the British Trade Union movement of that
time. Describing the reception in Westminster Palace

Hotel, he says : "How different we are after all from
our neighbours.   They are gay, light, volatile, ever
ready to flare up into a passion at a moment's notice;
we, stolid (stupid, someone called it), heavy, dullish,
slow to anger (the chairman excepted), and not at all
like men in earnest.   Certainly these foreigners know
what they are about.   They have made up their minds
as to what they want, and mean to have it.   They are
Socialists to a man, and have the fiery zeal which always
characterises earnest men who are fighting for a principle.   Probably some of the earlier trade unionists of
this country exhibited the same characteristics, but now
that the leader of a Trade Union is the holder of a fat,
snug office, concerned only in maintaining the respectability of the cause, all is changed.   Theirs (the
foreigners) may be a madness without method, ours is
a method without life.   A fusion of the two would be
beneficial all round."

Then he goes on to characterise the notables present
at the Congress, his reference to some of the home-made
ones being rather more caustic than was necessary, but
interesting, nevertheless, in view of their subsequent
careers.

"The Chairman, Mr. George Shipton, of the London
Trades Council, has much to do to keep things in order;
next him Mr. Broadhurst, Secretary.   On the floor, Mr.
Burt, philosophic and gentle-looking as ever, taking no
part in the proceedings, but, like the sailor's parrot,
thinking a lot; Mr. Fenwick, too, growing visibly larger,
much to his regret; Mr. Abraham, 5ft. by 4ft., correct
measurement, so that he is not so broad as he is long,
though I should say he soon will be; his voice is scarcely
so clear as it once was, but he himself is bright, cheerful
and full of *bonhomie* as ever.   There too, was Miss
Edith Simcox, with her strong, sympathetic face.

J. KEIR HARDIE

('Done more for the unskilled workers than all the Parliamentary Committee put together,' is the remark of one
who knows.) Mrs. Besant attends as frequently as she
can. She is not tall, and has a slight stoop, probably
the result of a too close application at her desk; wears
her hair short, and has on a red Tam-o'-Shanter; silver
streaks are not wanting among her tresses. Miss Chap-
man sits wearily through several sittings, wondering
what it is all about. She is president of the Match Girls'
Union, and is a tall, good-looking lassie, with dark and
clear-cut features, despite Bryant & May and their
twenty-two per cent. John Burns keeps running about
and appears to know everybody. He is an Ayrshire
Scotchman of the third generation. A thick-set, black
tyke he is, with a voice of slightly modulated thunder and
a nature as buoyant as a schoolboy's. Among the
foreigners is Anseele of Belgium, probably their best
man. He has 'done' his six months in jail for siding with
the workers, but that has not daunted him any. His power
of speech is amazing, and, as he closes his lips with a snap
at the end of each sentence, he seems to say, 'There! I
have spoken and I mean it.' He is young, vigorous,
and talented, and destined to make his mark. Next in
importance is Hoppenheimer of Paris. Tall and good-
looking, with a head of hair like a divot. He has seen
much life and is greatly trusted by his fellows. Christi-
son is a typical Dane with a bullet head and more given
to action than talking. Mr. Adolph Smith made a
capital interpreter. Lazzari the Italian is easily known.
He wears leather leggings, a black cloak thrown over
his shoulders and a slouch hat. He has only recently
come out of prison, and is quite prepared to be sent back
on his return home. His face is long and sallow; his
eyes dark and bright, and as he stalks about with a
swinging gait, or lounges against a pillar smoking a

cigarette, I call to mind the stories of long ago in which just such a picture figured in my mind's eye as the cruel brigand. Many others might be mentioned, but space is limited.''

The foregoing appeared in "The Miner," and it justifies the belief that if Hardie had not been so absorbed in the cause of Labour, he might have been a prince of journalists.

Hardie was very much to the front at this Conference, which for a whole day discussed "the best means for removing the obstacles to free combination amongst the workers in continental countries," and the following morning on Hardie's recommendation carried the following resolution : ''The Labour parties in the different countries are requested to put on their programme, and work for, by agitation, the abolition of all laws prohibiting or hampering the free right of association and combination, national and international, of the workers.''

On the question of methods he put forward the following proposals, a perusal of which by our modern industrial unionists may indicate to them that the idea underlying their policy is not so very novel after all.

"First. That all unions of one trade in one country combine in electing an Executive Central body for that trade in that country.

"Second. That the Central bodies of the various trades in the different countries elect a General Council for *all* trades.

"Third. That the Central bodies of the various trades in the different countries shall meet in Conference annually and an International Conference shall be held at intervals of not less than three years.''

J. KEIR HARDIE

There was here the conception of an international industrial power capable of being called into action at any given moment of great crisis, which, if it could have materialised in the form, say, of a general strike, might long ago have completely shattered militarism and made impossible the 1914 European calamity, while it would also have undermined the very foundations of capitalism. That it did not materialise is no fault of Keir Hardie. That he was capable of formulating it is proof of his greatness of vision, even if it implied a faith in organised mass intelligence for which working-class environment and tradition gave little justification. To have dreamed the dream was worth while, even if the realisation thereof may be for other generations.

Hardie's resolutions were not carried, but in their stead a long resolution from the foreigners, to which Hardie had no objections and which, according to his summary of it, "provided for the organisation of all workers, the appointment of National Committees, the formation of a distinct political Labour Party, and the holding, if possible, of a yearly International Congress, the next one to meet in Paris the following year." The Conference also decided in favour of a maximum eight hours' day, and, on the motion of Mr. Burt, it resolved : "That arbitration should be substituted for war in the settlement of disputes between nations." Hardie's concluding comments are noteworthy. "The Conference is over. We know each other better. Socialism is in the ascendant and everybody knows it. The marching order has been given, and it is 'Forward!' Henceforth there can be no alienation between British and Continental workers. The Broadhurst school have now Hobson's choice facing them—accept the new gospel or go down before those who will."

Thus ended the activities of the year 1888 with a declaration of Socialism. It had been a tremendous year for Hardie. Packed full of striving from beginning to end, and marking the beginnings of new endeavours which were to engross him henceforth all the days of his life. He had fought his first parliamentary contest. He had thrown down the gauntlet to the existing political parties, and to those working-class leaders who adhered to them. He had joined hands with the overseas fighters for freedom. He had become international. He had embraced Socialism. He had raised up against him in his own country hosts of enemies, but he had also secured troops of friends. The battle was drawn and he took joy in it. Let us have a square look at him, as he appeared at this time to one who was fairly closely associated with him in some of these public events. Mr. Cunninghame Graham, shortly after Keir Hardie's death, and for the purpose of this memoir, supplied the following vivid impression :—

"I first met Keir Hardie about the year 1887 or 1888. He was at that time, in conjunction with Chisholm Robertson, one of the chief miners' leaders in the West of Scotland. I first saw him at his home in Cumnock. I spoke to him for the first time in the office of a paper he was connected with, I think 'The Miner' or 'Cumnock News.' He was then about thirty years of age, I should judge, but old for his age. His hair was already becoming thin at the top of the head, and receding from the temples. His eyes were not very strong. At first sight he struck you as a remarkable man. There was an air of great benevolence about him, but his face showed the kind of appearance of one who has worked hard and suffered, possibly from inadequate nourishment in his youth. He was active and alert, though not athletic. Still, he appeared to be full of energy, and

51

as subsequent events proved, he had an enormous power of resistance against long, hard and continual work. I should judge him to have been of a very nervous and high-strung temperament. At that time, and I believe up to the end of his life, he was an almost ceaseless smoker, what is called in the United States 'a chain smoker.' He was a very strict teetotaller and remained so to the end, but he was not a bigot on the subject and was tolerant of faults in the weaker brethren. Nothing in his address or speech showed his want of education in his youth. His accent was of Ayrshire. I think he took pride in it in his ordinary conversation. He could, however, to a great extent throw this accent aside, but not entirely. When roused or excited in public or private speech it was always perceptible. His voice was high-pitched but sonorous and very far-carrying at that time. He never used notes at that time, and I think never prepared a speech, leaving all to the inspiration of the moment. This suited his natural, unforced method of speaking admirably. He had all the charm and some of the defects of his system. Thus, though he rose higher than I think it is possible to rise when a speech is prepared or committed to memory, he was also subject to very flat passages when he was not, so to speak, inspired. His chief merits as a speaker were, in my opinion, his homeliness, directness and sincerity; and his demerits were a tendency to redundancy and length, and a total lack of humour, very rare in an Ayrshire Scot. This was to me curious, as he had a considerable vein of pathos. He always opened his speeches in those days with 'Men,' and finished with 'Now, men.' This habit, which he also followed in his private speech—when two or three were gathered together—used to give great offence to numbers of paternal capitalists, baillies, councillors, and other worthy men who had not much mental culture and failed to detect Hardie's sincerity, and took the familiar 'men' as something too familiar for their conversing. Hardie's dress at this time was almost always a navy blue serge suit with a hard bowler hat. His hair was never worn long and his beard was well-trimmed and curly. Later on, to the regret of the 'judicious,' he affected a different style of dressing entirely foreign to his custom when a little-known man. He was then, and I believe always, an extremely abstemious eater, and in the long peregrinations about the mining villages of Lanarkshire and Ayrshire, when I was a young, unknown M.P. and he an equally unknown miners' leader, in rain and wind, and now and then in snow, an oatcake, a scone, a bit of a kebbuck of cheese always contented him. He would then sit down by the fireside in the cottage in the mining row, and light up his corn-cob pipe and talk of the future of the Labour Party, which in those days seemed to the miners a mere fairy tale. Now and then I have seen him take the baby from the miner's wife, and dandle it on his knee whilst she prepared tea.

"He had the faculty of attracting children to him, and most certainly he 'forbade them not.' They would come round him in the miners' cottages and lean against him for the first few minutes. One felt he was a 'family man' and so, I suppose, did the children."

Allowing for one or two inaccuracies such as that he was an Ayrshire Scot and "totally lacking in humour," the foregoing may be taken as a tolerably faithful pen-portrait of Keir Hardie in his prime, and presents characteristic features recognisable by his later associates, though deepened and strengthened by the stress of conflict in the wider field upon which he was now entering. It is the portrait of a very earnest, sincere man; resolute and strong, yet tender and kindly, and

F   53

making the most of his opportunities and his gifts in the interest of his "ain folk," the working class. It would be helpful if some graphic pen could re-envisage for us the wider environment, beyond Lanarkshire and Ayrshire, which together with these local conditions and these local struggles, was moulding the character and determining the purpose of Hardie and many other ardent spirits at that time.

It is curious to note how unobservant of the potential significance of these Labour movements were the contemporary publicists and historians. Justin McCarthy's "History of Our Own Times," for example, though it comes down to 1897, makes only the most casual five-word reference in recording the death of Cardinal Manning to the London Dock Strike, and makes no mention of the sympathetic strikes all over the country which followed it. It does not record the imprisonment of Cunninghame Graham and John Burns in maintenance of the right of free speech. It says nothing about the "new Unionism" movement which signalised the entrance into organised industrialism, and thereby into the political field, of the great mass of unskilled workers. It does not chronicle the formation of the Social Democratic Federation, or of the Fabian Society, or of the I.L.P. It passes all these events by unnoticed as if they had nothing whatever to do with the history of our own times, and fails to perceive that they were the beginners of the new social and political forces which were bound, in the very nature of things, to challenge the permanency of the existing order, and become the source of whatever has to be told in the history of the times after our own.

It was a time of turmoil and strife, but also of hope for labouring people, whose most thoughtful representatives were testing and experimenting with new mediums for giving expression and effect to the aspirations of their class.   New organisations were born and lived a little while and then died, but always left behind them some foundations and corner stones for future builders. Labour   Electoral   Associations,   National   Labour Parties, Sons of Labour—modelled on the American Knights of Labour—Hardie was willing to try them all, and also ready to associate with the pioneers and pro-pagandists   whom   these   organisations   called   into activity.   Very remarkable personalities some of them indeed were, though not all with horny hands or toil-furrowed faces.   Keen, intellectual, purposeful,   they carried their message alike to the street corners of the great cities and the village greens of remote country districts.   They brought Socialism into   the   market place.   They elbowed their way into Radical Associa-tions and into Tory Clubs, nor disdained the rostrum of the Y.M.C.A. or the Mutual Improvement Society. Their purpose was to break through the old habits of thought, to undermine stereotyped party formulas, to prepare the way for the new times.

Greatly varied in origin, in temperament, in charac-ter, in talents, were these men of the advanced guard of the modern British Socialist movement—H. H. Cham-pion, ex-army officer, in appearance, patrician to   the finger tips, cool as an iceberg, yet emitting red-hot revolution in the placid accents of clubland; Tom Mann, a working engineer, fresh from the "tanner-an-hour" dock strike, with all its honours full upon him, vigorous, eloquent, strong-lunged, rich-toned, speaking as easily in an amphitheatre as Champion could do in a drawing room, the very embodiment, it seemed, of the common people; Bruce Glasier, a designer and architect, somewhat angular in physical outline, pale of face, yet withal picturesquely attractive at a street corner with

J. KEIR HARDIE

the breeze dishevelling his hair and carrying his high-pitched, musical tones to the far end of the street, his artistic fusing of poetry, economics and politics compelling even the Philistines to stand and listen; James Connolly, a labourer from the Edinburgh Cleansing Department a most un-Celtic-like personality, slow and difficult of utterance, yet undeterred by any disability either of physique or training from delivering his message, a very encyclopædia of statistical facts and figures and of Marxian economics, a victimised industrial martyr even then, but with nothing either in his demeanour or in his political views foreshadowing his tragic and heroic end at the head of an Irish rebellion. And with these sometimes, and sometimes alone, there was a burly, thick-set figure of a man, in blue sailor-like garb, yet withal countrified in appearance, a ruddy-complexioned lion-headed man, William Morris, poet, artist, pre-Raphaelite—and because he was all these and humanitarian to boot, a Socialist. There were others too, rough and uncultured, or refined and bookish, men from the mine and from the factory, and the workshops and the dockyard and the smelting furnace, working men with active brains and great hearts, artists, dons, professional men. Harry Quelch, Pete Curran, Bob Hutcheson, Sandy Haddow, Bob Smillie and many others like unto them crowded into this service. These were the men who, with Keir Hardie, were making Socialism in the 'eighties of the last century. He was with them but not yet entirely of them. He was at close grips with that form of capitalism under whose domination his lot had been cast. Fighting the coalowners and stiffening the men, smoking his pipe in the colliery rows and fondling the bairns, yet all the time, assimilating inspiration from the turmoil beyond, and gradually merging himself in that turmoil. Idealist and enthusiast, yet looking ever to the practical side of things and retaining always his own individuality. The friend-less, forlorn errand boy of Glasgow streets has come far in these twenty-two years. He has still much farther to go in the new world of service that is opening out ahead of him.

CHAPTER FOUR

THE year 1889 is notable in Socialist history as the year in which what is known as the Second International was founded. Its predecessor, formed in 1864, under the style of the International Workingmen's Association by Karl Marx in co-operation with George Odger, George Howell, Robert Applegarth, and other leading British trade unionists, together with representatives from the Continental countries, was rent asunder by disputes between Bakuninists and Marxists, and finally ceased to exist in 1876. But the principles and the purpose which inspired it could not, and cannot, be destroyed. International war, the Franco-Prussian, had, for the time being, defeated international working-class solidarity, as it has once again—may we hope for the last time— in these recent terrible years. The idea of co-ordinated international class effort based upon communion of interests is one of those ideas which, once enunciated, are indestructible except through the disappearance of class. The slogan of the Communist Manifesto, "Workers of the world unite," sounded by Marx twenty years before the first International was formed, may be temporarily overwhelmed by militarist and nationalist war cries, but it re-asserts itself, and must do so until it becomes the ascendant, dominant note in humanity's marching tune.

THE SECOND INTERNATIONAL

The call for international working-class unity was making itself heard once more, and this 1889 Conference in Paris was the answer to the call. Naturally, Keir Hardie was there amongst the others. There were, in fact, two Congresses held simultaneously, one of purely trade union origin, arising out of the decisions of the Conference held in London the previous year, and the other arising out of the decisions of the German Working-Class Party in 1886. But for misunderstandings, unavoidable perhaps in the early stages of so great a thing as an international movement, there need only have been one Congress, for both passed the same resolutions and manifested the same purpose, though one was labelled Possibilist, and the other Marxist.

What is to be noted is, that Hardie attended the avowedly Marxist Congress, thus early affirming his allegiance to the Socialist conception of internationalism. Hyndman, the exponent and standard bearer in Britain of Marxian philosophy pure and undefiled, attended the Possibilist gathering as delegate from the Social Democratic Federation. With him were representatives from the Fabian Society, the Trades Union Congress and the Trade Union movement generally, amongst his colleagues being John Burns, Herbert Burrows, Mrs. Besant, Thomas Burt, M.P., and Charles Fenwick, M.P. Hardie, who at the other Congress represented the Scottish Labour Party, had for companions Cunninghame Graham from the same Party, and William Morris from the Socialist League. Thus, before any political Labour Party had been formed for Great Britain, a Scottish Labour Party was represented in the international movement, due undoubtedly to the influence of its Secretary, Keir Hardie. At this Congress he found himself in the company of many famous

leaders from other lands, including Wilhelm Liebknecht, Jules Guesde, Bebel, Vollmar, Dr. Adler and
Anseele, and, we may be sure, gained education and
inspiration thereby. Both Congresses passed resolutions in favour of an Eight Hours' Day, a Minimum
Wage, prohibition of child labour and unhealthy
occupations, and the abolition of standing armies;
not by any means a revolutionary programme, but one
postulating the demands upon which the organised
workers of all countries might be expected to agree.
The virtue and strength of the International was not in
its programme, but in the mere fact of its existence.
Therein lay incalculable potentialities. The Workers'
International is the adaptation of labour force to meet
the world conditions created by modern capitalism.
It challenges, not any particular form of government
here or there, in this country or in that, but the
capitalist system, which is one and the same in all
countries.

Moreover, the International differentiated itself
from other rebel movements in that it placed no reliance
on underground methods. It came out into the open.
It assumed that labour was now strong enough to stand
upright. It recognised that methods of secrecy made
national working-class co-operation impossible, and that
only by open declaration of ideals and purposes could the
people in the various countries understand and have
confidence in each other. The International was, and
is, an historic phenomenon, vastly more important than
the English Magna Charta, the American Declaration
of Independence, or the Fall of the Bastille. It is the
summation of these and other efforts towards liberty,
seeking not merely to proclaim, but to *establish* the
Rights of Man. Three times it has suffered eclipse.
The Communist League hardly survived its birth-hour

amid the storms and revolutionary turmoil of 1848. The First International—so-called—went down through the blood and fire of the Franco-Prussian War. The Second, of which we are now speaking, was submerged in the frenzies of a world war. Already it emerges once again, the deathless International, and who shall say that it will not this time accomplish its purpose?

They were strong, courageous spirits who conceived the Workers' International and gave it form and stimulus, and lifted it ever and anon out of the very jaws of death. Amongst these Keir Hardie has a foremost place.

The consciousness of having assisted in an event of unparalleled importance to the working class could not but have an expanding effect upon a mind already deeply impressed with a sense of the greatness of the Labour movement, and it is unfortunate that we have no personal record of his impressions at this time. He was not much in the habit of revealing his thoughts in his private correspondence, and his paper, "The Miner," having ceased to exist, we have no printed account of the Paris Congress such as that which he gave of the London one the previous year. It would have been deeply interesting for us to know, not only his thoughts about the personalities whom he met, but also how the great city of Paris looked to the miner from Ayrshire. That this experience constituted another stage in the development of his character cannot be doubted, and the equanimity with which in future years he was able to meet the rebuffs, vexations and scurrilities which assailed him in the course of his work for Socialism, derived itself in large measure from his sense of the magnitude of the cause to which his life was now consecrated.

At home, the chief task of Hardie and other advanced workers was to combat the conservative elements in the

Labour movement itself, as exemplified in the reluctance of the big Trade Unions to adapt themselves to the changing economic and political conditions of the time. After a long heroic struggle the old repressive combination laws had broken down. Trade Unionism had been legalised, an achievement in itself marking a big step in the advance towards liberty, but still only a step. The right to combine, implying the right to strike, was still for large sections of the workers only a right theoretically, as was shown by the failure of Joseph Arch to organise the agricultural labourers, and by the difficuty of incorporating in the general Trade Union movement the immense mass of unskilled labour, male and female, whose low standard of wages continually imperilled the higher standard of the organised sections. This very year another big strike of London Dock labourers had taken place, and there was seen amongst this class of workers much the same sequence of events which Hardie had witnessed amongst the miners of Lanarkshire and Ayrshire, namely, that the strike was a necessary prelude to the Trade Union. First organise and then strike, seems logical, but in the early stages of revolt against economic subjection, necessity, not logic, is the determining factor, and the process is first strike then organise. The strike, resorted to in many cases in sheer desperation by unorganised workers who have been driven to the conclusion that it is better to go idle and starve than to work and starve, emphasises (whether it be partially successful or a complete failure) the need for organisation, and later there comes the conviction that if only the organisation can be made effective enough there will be no need for strikes. "The strike epidemic," as the pressmen called it, of those years, amongst dockers, gasworkers, general labourers, seamen, match girls and other seemingly helpless sections of the community, laid the foundations for the powerful unions of the unskilled —so called—which now play an equally effective part with the craftsmen's associations in determining conditions of employment. But in its immediate economic effects the strike movement of those times did something more than that. It demonstrated the inter-dependence of all sections of labour, and consequently the mutuality of the interests of all. A stoppage of labour in the dockyards, or on the railways, or in the coal mines throughout the country, affected the productive capacity of engineers and textile workers and the distributive capacity of shopkeepers and warehousemen. It played havoc with the idea of an aristocracy of labour. It tended to break down class divisions within the working class. It gave birth to the idea that the Labour cause is one and indivisible.

Synchronising with all this industrial unrest was the fact that the workers now possessed a large measure of political power, and the growing feeling that some means must be found of giving effect to it. In all their disputes, the workers found the Government, whether Tory or Liberal, throwing its weight on the side of the employers. They found that in these disputes they had to fight both Tory and Liberal employers, that directors and shareholders of industrial companies knew no party politics; they even found, as in the case of the strike of the shamefully underpaid women at the Manningham Mills in Yorkshire, a Liberal Cabinet Minister amongst the sweaters. They found further, that Parliament, though elected by the votes of the workers, made not the slightest attempt to deal with the problem of unemployment, but left the employers free to use that problem with its surplusage of labour as a weapon against the workers; and thus there began to evolve, almost without propaganda, a belief in

the need for a political Labour Party—an Independent
Labour Party.

Towards the formation of such a party Hardie now
devoted all his activities. Not only on the propaganda
platform and in the Miners' Trade Union Councils, but
year by year at the annual Trades Union Congress he
had come to be regarded as the chief spokesman of the
new idea of political independence, and was the mark
for all the antagonism which that idea evoked, not only
from the capitalists and landlords, but from the working
classes themselves, and especially from those working-
class leaders who, while believing in political action,
had all their lives and with perfect sincerity been looking
towards Liberalism as the way out. These men
naturally resented any action which tended to weaken
the Liberal Party as being either treason or stupidity.
Passions were aroused and some life-long friendships
broken during this protracted struggle between the
right and left wings of the Labour movement. But
the work went on, and when the General Election of
1892 came along, sufficient progress had been made to
justify the Independents in at least a partial and tentative trial of strength at the polls, as the outcome of
which Keir Hardie found himself in Parliament.

That fact gives some measure alike of the growth of
the labour sentiment towards political independence,
and of the extent to which Hardie was now recognised
as representative not merely of a trade or section or
district, but of the Labour movement nationally.

In 1888, he had claimed the suffrages of the Lanarkshire electors on the grounds that as a miner he was
specially qualified to deal with the interests of the miners,
and that as a Scotsman he was specially qualified to deal
with Scottish affairs. Now, four years later, he was
returned to Parliament by a constituency in which there

was not a single miner and very few Scots. That the miner from Scotland should have been able to appeal successfully to a London community is indicative also of a certain intellectual adaptability on his part, a capacity for identifying himself with the mental and social outlook of people whose environment and habits of thought were very much different from those in which he himself had been reared.

The success of John Burns at Battersea is not so difficult to understand. He was on his native streets, amongst his own people, and spoke in their idioms— a Londoner of the Londoners. Hardie was an incomer, a foreigner almost; and his quick success in this new field of adventure cannot be wholly accounted for, either by the strength of the local Labour organisation, which was only in its incipient stage, or by the intervention of certain accidental circumstances which will be referred to later. Hardie's personality had much to do with his success at West Ham, and especially his power of merging himself without losing himself in the actual life of the people whom he wished to serve.

His presence in West Ham was largely the outcome of the Mid-Lanark contest, which had attracted the attention of advanced politicians all over the country, and amongst them certain democrats in this industrial district of London who were dissatisfied with the Liberal Party policy and were up in arms against the local party caucus. The I.L.P. had not yet been founded, but there was a very influential branch of the Land Restoration League as the result of Henry George's visit to this country some years previously, with groups of Socialists and Radicals anxious to try conclusions with the orthodox parties. From a committee formed of these, Hardie received the invitation to contest the constituency.

J. KEIR HARDIE

The rejection of financial help from Mr. Andrew Carnegie, and the manner of the rejection, emphasised the fact that he was, above all things, a Labour candidate who was not to touch pitch, however offered. Mr. Carnegie, who was by way of being an uncompromising Republican, was also, as the whole world knew, a big employer of labour in America, and as his employees at Pittsburg were at that very time on strike and were up against Mr. Carnegie's "live wires" and hired gunmen, the West Ham share of the donations went to help the strikers.

The election of Hardie and Burns was the first practical indication to the orthodox politicians that there were new elements in society with which they would have to reckon. Even yet they hardly realised the significance of what had taken place. They were being kept too busy with other matters to be able to take serious note of the new movement. Not without reason, they were concerned with the malcontents of Ireland more than with the malcontents of Labour. Their last Franchise Act had created a formidable British-Irish electorate, able to decide the fate of governments—or at least so it seemed for a time—and the rival competitors for parliamentary power were busy on the one hand placating the Irishmen, and on the other stirring up and rallying all the possible reserves of British prejudice against the Irish. They were, in fact, endeavouring to keep the British voters divided, no longer merely as Liberals and Conservatives, but as Home Rulers and Unionists. In this they were only too successful, but were too engrossed in the congenial political manoeuvring in which British statecraft seems to live and move and have its being, to realise the significance of the entry into Parliament of a man like Hardie. They were to have it fully brought home to them within the next three years.

That Hardie was on this occasion favoured by a certain element of luck must be admitted. The local Liberal Party were taken at a disadvantage through the sudden death of their selected candidate, and, with little time to look for another and the knowledge that Hardie had already secured a strong following, they made a virtue of necessity, and, though never officially recognising him, joined forces with the forward section. They even persuaded themselves that Hardie could be regarded as a Liberal Member and be subject to official party discipline.

They had no grounds for such a belief in any utterances of the Labour candidate. On the contrary, he had made explicit declarations of his independence of party control. "I desire," he said in his election address, "to be perfectly frank with the body of electors, as I have been with my more immediate friends and supporters in the constituency. I have all my life given an independent support to the Liberal Party, but my first concern is the moral and material welfare of the working classes, and if returned, I will in every case place the claims of labour above those of party. Generally speaking, I am in agreement with the present programme of the Liberal Party so far as it goes, but I reserve to myself the absolute and unconditional right to take such action, irrespective of the exigencies of party welfare, as may to me seem needful in the interests of the workers." At a Conference of Trade Unions, Temperance Societies, Associations and Clubs, asked if he would follow Gladstone, he answered : "So long as he was engaged in good democratic work, but if he opposed Labour questions he would oppose him or anybody else." "Would he join the Liberal and Radical Party?" In reply, he said *"he expected to form an Independent Labour Party."*

On these conditions he entered the House of Commons

untrammelled and unpledged—except to his own conscience—perhaps the only free man in that assembly.

He had hardly taken his seat, and the new Government had not even been formed, when he began to be
troublesome to the House of Commons' authorities. On
August 18th, we find him interrogating the Speaker as
to procedure, and as this was his first Parliamentary
utterance and foreshadows fairly well his subsequent
policy, the question may be given in full. "Mr.
Speaker," he said, "I rise to put a question of which I
have given you private notice. Perhaps you will allow
me to offer one word of explanation as to why I put the
question. On Thursday, last week, I gave notice of an
amendment to the Address, but when the amendment
then before the House was disposed of there was so much
noise and confusion that I did not hear the main question
put, and I anticipated that to-day there would be an
opportunity of discussing the point embodied in my
amendment. I find that under the ordinary rules of the
House there will be no such opportunity. The question
which I desire to put now, Sir, is whether, in view of the
interest which has been awakened on the question of holding an autumn session for the consideration of measures
designed to improve the condition of the people, there is
any way by which the sense of the House can now be
taken for the guidance of the ministry now in process of
formation?" The Speaker, as was to be expected, ruled
that the question could not be raised until a Government
had been formed. And as no autumn session was held,
it was February of next year before Hardie could begin
his Parliamentary work on behalf of the unemployed.

An incident which occurred at this time illustrates
in a very vivid way his determination to keep himself
clear of all entanglements which might in any way interfere with his personal and political independence. It

had best be described by himself, especially as his manner of telling the story brings out some of those characteristics which governed his actions all through life.

"I was elected in July, and on getting home was told that two quaintly dressed old ladies had spent a week in the village making very exhaustive inquiries about my life and character. Later in the year, we were spending a few days with my wife's mother, in Hamilton, and learned they had been there also and had visited my wife's mother. They told her frankly their errand. They knew that, as a working man, I would be none too flush of money, and they were anxious to help in this respect, provided they were satisfied that I was dependable. Their inquiries into my public character were assuring, but—was I a good husband? A mother-in-law was the best authority on that.

"The upshot was that I received, through an intermediary, an invitation to call upon them in Edinburgh, which I did. They explained that from the time of the Parnell split they had been helping to finance the Parnellite section of the Irish Party, but that they also wanted to help Socialism, and believed that Nationalism and Socialism would one day be working together. They therefore proposed to give me a written agreement to pay me £300 a year so long as I remained in Parliament, and to make provision for it being continued after they had gone. To a man without a shilling, and the prospect of having to earn his living somehow, the offer had its practical advantages, and I promised to think it over. A few days later I wrote declining the proposal, but suggesting as an alternative that they should give the money to the Scottish Labour Party, the I.L.P. not yet having been formed.

"But this gave mighty offence. They had all their lives been accustomed to having things done in their own way, and, as I learned subsequently, their attachment was to persons rather than causes. For my part, I was probably a bit quixotic and had made up my mind to 'gang my ain gait' without shackle or trammel of any sort or kind. Besides, I knew that they had made a charge against a leading member of the Land Restoration League of having appropriated to his own use money intended for other purposes, and I was taking no risks."

And thus it came about that for the second time Keir Hardie had refused an income of £300 a year. The two elderly ladies were the Misses Kippen of Edinburgh, and, as will appear, they did not allow this rebuff to destroy their interest in Hardie's career, nor in the cause with which he was identified.

The following year, during the Parliamentary session, an experience of another kind provided him with an amusing indication of the insidious methods which might be used to influence his Parliamentary conduct. He was invited to a seance in an artist's studio, the special inducement being the prospect of a talk with Robert Burns. He took with him a number of friends, Bruce Wallace, Frank Smith, S. G. Hobson and others well known in the Labour movement of that time. The medium delivered messages from Parnell, Bradlaugh, Bright and other distinguished persons resident in the spirit world, including Robert Burns, and they all with one accord advised Hardie to vote against the Irish Home Rule Bill! As Hardie supported Home Rule on every possible occasion, we must suppose that these eminent shades were duly disgusted. Hardie never learned who were responsible for the seance, but they must have taken him to be a very simple-minded person—either that, or they were so themselves.

In the interval between his election and the opening of his Parliamentary career, an event of even greater

I.L.P.

importance than his election to Parliament had taken place. The Independent Labour Party had been formed, and when he returned to Westminster it was with the knowledge that there was an organised body of support outside. Even in these first few weeks, however, he had, partly by accident and partly by design, managed to become a conspicuous Parliamentary figure, and to inaugurate a sartorial revolution in that highly conventional assembly. The intrusion of the cloth cap and tweed jacket amongst the silk hats and dress suits was most disturbing and seemed to herald the near approach of the time when the House of Commons would cease to be the gentlemen of England's most exclusive club-room. It conveyed an ominous sense of impending change, not at all modified by the fact that the cloth cap had arrived in a two-horse brake with a trumpeter on the box. Hardie's participation in these shocks to the House of Commons' sense of decency was quite involuntary. He wore the clothes which were to him most comfortable.

The charabanc was the outcome of the enthusiasm of a few of his working-class constituents who desired to convey their Member to St. Stephen's in style, and being a natural gentleman always, he accepted their company and their equipage in the spirit in which it was proferred. In the result, the vulgar sarcasms of the press made him the most widely advertised Member of the new Parliament and even for a time overshadowed the discussion as to whether Rosebery or Harcourt would succeed Gladstone in the premiership.

Meantime, while the press humorists were making merry, the Independent Labour Party was getting itself formed.

Following upon the formation of the Scottish Parliamentary Labour Party, in 1888, similar organisations had sprung up in various districts of England, notably in Yorkshire and Lancashire and on the North-East coast. All these bodies had the same object, namely, the return to Parliament of Labour Members who would be independent of the Liberal and Tory parties.

A most notable factor in bringing those organisations into being was "The Workman's Times," founded in 1890, under the vigorous editorship (and latterly proprietorship) of Mr. Joseph Burgess, who in due course became a prominent personality in the Independent Labour Party, in the formation of which he took an active part. Though published in London, the paper, through its localised editions, had a considerable circulation throughout Lancashire and Yorkshire, especially amongst the textile workers.

It consistently and ably advocated independent Labour representation, with Socialism as the objective. It ceased to exist in 1894, but by that time it had done its pioneering work and helped to make an Independent Labour Party not only possible, but inevitable.

There was also the Social Democratic Federation operating chiefly in London, but with branches scattered here and there throughout the country, and having the same political objective as the others. Between all these bodies, however, there was no organised cohesion, except to some extent in Scotland, where the Scottish Labour Party had brought into existence some thirty branches, all affiliated to a Central Executive, of which Hardie was Secretary. The time had now arrived for unifying all these bodies into one National Party. With two independent Labour Members now in Parliament (for it was fully believed that Burns, whose Socialist declarations had been even more militant than Hardie's, would be sturdily independent) it was felt that a strong organisation was needed in the country to sustain and reinforce these Parliamentary representatives and to formulate a policy which would define clearly the Socialist aspirations of the new movement. In September, the annual meeting of the Trades Union Congress was held at Glasgow. By a greatly increased majority, the resolution in favour of independent Labour representation, which had been passed at three previous meetings of the Congress, was reaffirmed, but unlike what had happened on previous occasions it was not allowed to fall into complete neglect. That same day, an informal meeting of delegates favourable to the formation of a Party in conformity with the resolution was held, and it was decided that a conference of advanced bodies willing to assist in promoting that object should be called.

On January 13th and 14th, 1893, the conference was held in the Labour Institute, Bradford. Delegates to the number of one hundred and twenty-one mustered from all parts of England and Scotland. All manner of Labour and Socialist societies were represented, the chief however being Labour clubs, branches of the Social Democratic Federation and the Fabian Society, the Scottish Labour Party, and several trade organisations. Keir Hardie was elected Chairman, and despite many forebodings of dissension and failure, the gathering set itself to the task of formulating a constitution in a thoroughly earnest and harmonious spirit. The name "Independent Labour Party," which had already become a common appellation of the new movement and had been assumed by many of the local clubs, was adopted almost unanimously in preference to that of the "Socialist Labour Party."

Without hesitation, however, the Conference declared the primary object of the Party to be the "collective ownership and control of the means of production, distribution, and exchange." Thus, though rejecting the word Socialist from its title, the Party became an avowedly Socialist or Social Democratic organisation. Among the delegates present at this historic Conference were Bernard Shaw, Robert Blatchford, Pete Curran, Robert Smillie, Katherine St. John Conway (afterwards Mrs. Bruce Glasier), F. W. Jowett, Joseph Burgess, James Sexton, Ben Tillett, Russell Smart, and many other notable workers for Socialism.

Mr. Shaw Maxwell, well known in Glasgow Labour circles, but at that time resident in London, was appointed Secretary, and Mr. John Lister, of Halifax, Treasurer. The National Administrative Council consisted of delegates representing the London District, the Midland Counties, the Northern Counties, and Scotland, their names being : Katherine St. John Conway, Dr. Aveling, son-in-law of Karl Marx, Pete Curran, Joseph Burgess, Alfred Settle, William Johnson, W. H. Drew, J. C. Kennedy, George S. Christie, A. Field, A. W. Buttery, William Small, George Carson and R. Chisholm Robertson.

Not all of those who took part in these memorable proceedings were able to continue their allegiance through the years of storm and trouble which followed. Robert Blatchford, failing to get the constitution made as watertight against compromise as he desired, in due course seceded. Others fell away for exactly the opposite reason, because the constitution, from their point of view, lacked elasticity. On the whole, however, the defectionists were comparatively few, and even they could not undo the work they had helped to accomplish in those two eventful days in Bradford. They had founded one of the most remarkable organisations that has ever existed in this or any other country—a political party and something more—a great social fellowship,

I.L.P.

joining together in bonds of friendship all its adherents in every part of the land and forming a communion comparable to that of some religious fraternity whose members have taken vows of devotion to a common cause.

This fraternal spirit was the outcome of the nature and method of the propaganda carried on by the new Party and of the character of the propagandists, who were mostly of the rank and file; and also of the character of the Party newspaper, which made its appearance almost simultaneously with the Party itself. The "Labour Leader," promoted by the Scottish Labour Party on the initiative of Hardie, and edited by him, came out as a monthly periodical devoted to the interests of the I.L.P.

On entering Parliament, he had quickly realised that if he were to be able to stand there alone, ostracised as he was sure to be by all the other parties, and subject to the misrepresentations of the entire political press, he would require at least one newspaper which would keep him right with his own people. Its most valuable feature for promoting a sense of unity and fellowship amongst the readers consisted in the brief reports of the doings of the branches in the various districts, whereby they were brought together, so to speak, all the year round. Men and women who had never met face to face, nevertheless got to feel an intimate comradeship the one with the other.

During the first year, the "Labour Leader" was produced monthly, and afterwards weekly. It had, as we shall see, amongst its contributors writers and artists of great ability, some of them perhaps with a greater literary gift than Hardie himself, but throughout it continued to be mainly the expression of Hardie's personality. It came to be spoken of by friends and enemies alike as "Keir Hardie's paper."

75

J. KEIR HARDIE

At this period he had good reason to be satisfied with the way things were going. He had gained a footing in Parliament, and had sufficient confidence in himself to believe that from that position he could command the attention of the nation to the questions in which he was interested. The political party for which he had laboured incessantly during five strenuous years, had now come into existence and promised to become a power in the land. And he had control of a newspaper which, though limited in size and circulation, yet enabled him to reach that section of the community whose support he most valued. All this meant more and ever more work, but he was not afraid of work. It was the kind of work he loved, for the people he loved. It was the work for which he believed himself fitted and destined. And in this frame of mind he prepared to resume his Parliamentary duties.

Hardie had no illusions as to the kind of environment into which he was now entering and certainly had no expectations that the new Government would willingly provide him with opportunities for realising his avowed purpose of forming a new party in the House. The Tory opposition was simply the usual Tory opposition with only one immediate object in view, to defeat the Government and step into its place. On both sides all the vested interests of capital and land were strongly represented. There were fifteen avowed Labour Members in the House, but of these only three had been returned independent of party—John Burns, J. Havelock Wilson and Hardie himself. The others had long ago proved themselves to be very plastic political material. It was hoped that the three Independents would hold together, but that had yet to be proved—or disproved. Hardie was not disposed to wait too long for developments. The unemployed were demonstrating daily on the Embankment and he had pledged himself to raise the question of unemployment. Whatever the others might do, he was going to keep his word. The Government, playing for time to produce its Home Rule measure, had in the Queen's Speech outlined a colourless legislative programme which, while referring vaguely to agricultural depression, quite ignored the industrial distress. Upon this omission Hardie based his initial appeal to the House of Commons.

On February 7th, 1893, he made his first speech in the House of Commons in moving the following amendment to the Address : "To add, 'And further, we humbly desire to express our regret that Your Majesty has not been advised when dealing with agricultural depression to refer also to the industrial depression now prevailing and the widespread misery due to large numbers of the working class being unable to find employment, and direct Parliament to legislate promptly and effectively in the interests of the unemployed.' " There was a large attendance of members curious to see how this reputed firebrand would comport himself in the legislative chamber. If there were any there who expected, and perhaps hoped, to hear a noisy, declamatory utterance in consonance with their conception of working-class agitational oratory, they were disappointed. He spoke quietly and argumentatively, but with an earnestness which held the attention of the House.

"It is a remarkable fact," he began, "that the speech of Her Majesty should refer to one section of industrial distress and leave the other altogether unnoticed, and there are some of us who think that, if the interests of the landlords were not bound up so closely with the agricultural depression, the reference even to the agricultural labourers would not have appeared in the Queen's speech." He went on to justify his action in moving the amendment by referring to his election pledges to raise the question of unemployment in Parliament. He spoke of the extent of the evil and quoted the trade union returns to show that 1,300,000 workers were in receipt of out-of-work pay, and he based upon these and Poor Law statistics, the statement that not less than 4,000,000 people were without visible means of support. His amendment had been objected to, he said, because it contained no specific proposal for dealing with the evil. Had it done so it would have been objected to still more, because every one who wanted to find an excuse for not voting for the amendment would have discovered it in whatever proposals he might have made. The House would agree that he had high authority in this House for "not disclosing the details of our proposals until we are in a position to give effect to them"—which was not quite in his power yet. Meantime, the Government, being a large employer of labour, might do something for the immediate relief of the distress then prevailing. It could abolish overtime, about which he had heard complaints. It could increase the minimum wage of labourers in the dockyards and arsenals to sixpence per hour, and it could enact a forty-eight hour week for all Government employees. It had been estimated that, were the hours of railway servants reduced to eight per day, employment would be found for 150,000 extra workingmen. The Government might also establish what is known as home colonies on the idle lands about which they heard so much discussion in that House. One of the most harrowing features connected with the problem of the unemployed was not the poverty or the hardship they had to endure, but the fearful moral degradation that followed in the train of enforced idleness. In every season of the year and in every condition of trade, men were unemployed. The pressure under which industry was carried on to-day necessitated that the young and the strong and the able should have preference in obtaining employment, and if the young, the strong and the able were to have the preference, then the middle-aged and the aged must, of necessity, be thrown on the street. They were now discussing an address of thanks to Her Majesty for her speech. He wanted to ask the Government, what have the unemployed to thank Her Majesty for in the speech which had been submitted to the House? Their case was overlooked and ignored. They were left out as if they did not exist.

This amendment was seconded by Colonel Howard Vincent, a Tory Member, and in the division he had the support of many Tories who were, doubtless, more anxious to weaken the Government than to help the unemployed, Sir John Gorst being probably the only member of that Party who was sincere in his approval of Hardie's action. John Burns did not take part in the debate, while Cremer, a Liberal-Labour Member and actually one of the founders of the International, spoke against the amendment and explained that he had already put himself "right with his constituents"; so that, literally, Hardie stood alone as an Independent Labour representative voicing the claims of the unemployed worker in his first challenge to capitalism upon the floor of the House of Commons. One hundred and nine Members voted with Hardie, 276 against him. The division was mainly on party lines. He had proved that honesty is the best tactics and had successfully exploited the party system for his own purpose. The spectacle of the Liberals voting against the unemployed, and the Ayrshire miner leading the Tory rank and file into the revolutionary lobby was not calculated to enhance the credit of either of these official parties. The Liberals never forgave him for having compelled them to make exposure of their own inherent reactionism.

The approval or disapproval of either of the official parties did not affect Hardie in the slightest degree, and he continued to seize every opportunity which the Rules of the House allowed to give publicity to the grievances of all classes of workers. A mere list of the questions which he asked during his first Parliamentary session almost forms an index to the social conditions of the country at that time. On the same day on which he moved his unemployment amendment, we find him asking the Postmaster-General to state why certain Post Office officials had been refused leave to attend a meeting of the Fawcett Association. On March 7th, he was inquiring as to the dismissal, without reason assigned, of certain prison warders. On the 9th, he was back again at the unemployment question, demanding from the Local Government Board information as to the number of unemployed in the various industries, and what steps local authorities were taking to deal with the matter. On the 10th, he wanted to know why men on strike had been prosecuted for playing musical instruments and collecting money, while organ-grinders and others were not interfered with for doing the same thing. On the 13th, he inquired whether it was intended to submit a measure that Session to enable local authorities to deal effectively with the severe distress prevailing all over the country, and followed this up with another question indicating how this could be done. This question is still so relevant to present-day problems that it may be given in full : ''I beg to ask the Chancellor of the Exchequer whether he contemplates, in connection with the Budget proposals for next year, such a rearrangement of the system of taxation as is known as a graduated Income

Tax, by means of which the contribution to the revenue, local and imperial, would bear a relative proportion to income; also whether he will make such provision in the Budget estimates for next year as would enable the Local Government Board to make grants to any Board of Guardians, Town and County Councils, or committees of responsible citizens willing to acquire land or other property and to undertake the responsibility of organising the unemployed in home colonies and affording them the opportunity of providing the accessories of life for themselves and those dependent on them." The same day he was inquisitive as to the pay of House of Commons' policemen. On April 13th, he raised the question of the inadequacy of the staff of Factory Inspectors, and wanted to know whether it was proposed to appoint sub-inspectors from the ranks of duly qualified men and women who had themselves worked in the factories and workshops.

On this day also, he put the first of a series of questions which continued daily, like the chapters in a serial story, for the following five weeks, and gave conspicuous illustration of the alliance of the Government with the employing classes against the workers. What is known in the history of industrial revolt as the Hull Dock Strike had broken out, and the Government had, with great alacrity, sent soldiers and gunboats to the scene of the dispute. Day after day Hardie attacked the Government in the only way available, with questions, some of which were ruled out of order, but many of which had to be answered, either evasively or with a direct negative, but, either way, revealing the Government bias. "Had the shipowners refused all efforts at a compromise or towards conciliation?" "In these circumstances, would the Government order the withdrawal of the military forces?" "By whose authority were the

military and naval forces of the State sent to Hull to aid
the shipowners in breaking up a Trade Union registered
under an Act of Parliament?'' The answers not being
satisfactory, he moved the adjournment of the House in
order to get the whole question of military interference
discussed, but less than forty Members rose, and, says
"Hansard," "business proceeded." Nothing daunted,
he returned to the attack, and asked the Secretary of
State for War whether he was aware that soldiers were
being used at Hull in loading and unloading ships. He
asked Asquith whether a lady journalist who had taken
part in a meeting of locked-out dockers had been refused
access to the docks by police? He asked particulars
regarding the number of magistrates at Hull; how many
were shipowners or dock directors, and how many were
working men, and elicited the following illuminative
reply :—

"Thirty-nine magistrates, of whom there are four
shipowners, nineteen shareholders in ships. Dock
directors (no information). No working men."

He followed this up with the question : "Was a Bench
composed exclusively of shipowners and dock directors
capable of giving an unbiassed opinion on the question
of the means desirable to be taken for the protection of
their own property? Was it true that additional forces
had been requisitioned, and were they to be sent?" The
answer was : "Yes." "Was the chief obstacle to a settlement of the dispute a Member of this House and a supporter of the Government (the reference being to Wilson,
of the Shipping Federation)?" but this was ruled out of
order by the Speaker as being a matter "not under the
cognisance and control of the Government."

Day after day, and week after week, he persisted with
his damaging catechism. Burns and Havelock Wilson
joined him from time to time, until at last a day was

granted to the latter to move a resolution on the question, he, as secretary of the Trade Union most deeply involved, being recognised as specially representative of the men on strike. A big debate ensued in which Front Bench men took part, and during which Hardie delivered an impassioned speech of considerable length. Burns, Cremer and Hardie all urged Havelock Wilson to divide the House on the question, but that gentleman, for reasons which he doubtless thought satisfactory, withdrew the resolution. Finally, the strike ended, like many others before and since, as a drawn battle in which the workers were the chief sufferers. Never before had any Labour dispute occupied so much of the time of the House of Commons—a fact due to the presence there of one man whose sense of duty to his class was too strong to be overborne by regard for Parliamentary etiquette or party exigencies. He was pursuing, in the interests of labour, the same tactics which the Parnellites had, up to a point, pursued so effectively in the interests of Nationalism, and, had it been possible to have gathered round him at that time a group of a dozen men prepared resolutely to adhere to that policy, the subsequent history of Labour in Parliament would have been much different from what it has been. The dozen men were there, but they were bound by party ties, and lacked both the courage and the vision of Hardie. As it was, he had redeemed his promise to form an Independent Labour Party in the House. He had formed a *Party of one.* And before that Parliament came to an end, both Liberals and Tories had to bear witness to its vitality and effectiveness.

Meantime the I.L.P. outside was growing, thanks not a little to the advertisement it was getting from Westminster. The first Annual Conference at Manchester, in January, 1894, found it with two hundred and eighty

affiliated branches.   At the Conference, Hardie was
elected Chairman; Tom Mann, then an enthusiastic
recruit, undertook the secretaryship.   Ben Tillett—with
a growing reputation as an agitator, and strange though
it may seem, something of a Puritan in social habits—
joined the National Council.   Reports from the districts
showed that the Party would be well represented in the
Municipal elections during the next November, and
would thus have an opportunity of testing in some
degree its electoral support throughout the country.
The I.L.P. was an established factor in the political
life of the nation.

CHAPTER FIVE

HARDIE was as indefatigable outside of Parliament as inside, addressing propaganda meetings all over the country, writing encouraging letters to branch secretaries, and editing the "Labour Leader," which on March 31st, 1894, became a weekly, and for the financing and management of which he made himself wholly responsible. The wages bill of the paper, exclusive of printing, he estimated at £750 a year, which he hoped would be covered by income from sales and advertisements, an optimistic miscalculation which involved him in considerable worry later on, when he found it necessary to dispense with much of the paid service and rely to some extent upon voluntary work by enthusiasts in the cause, who, it should be said here, seldom failed him. The first weekly number contained Robert Smillie's election address as Labour Candidate for Mid-Lanark, where a by-election in which Hardie took an active part was again being fought. In the "Leader," Hardie had an article on the election, a leading article on Lord Rosebery as prospective Premier, and a page of intimate chat with his readers under the heading of "*Entre Nous*," afterwards changed to the plain English of "Between Ourselves," and this quantity of journalistic output he continued for years, while shirking none of the other work that came to him as an agitator and public man. This number contained also an article by Cunninghame

H   85

J. KEIR HARDIE

Graham, the I.L.P. Monthly Report by Tom Mann, "News of the Movement at Home and Abroad," besides literary sketches and verses by various contributors. The paper was edited from London, but printed in Glasgow and distributed from there. There was a working staff at both ends. Of the London experiences, Councillor Ben Gardner of West Ham could doubtless give some interesting reminiscences, while George D. Hardie, Keir's younger brother, could do the same for Glasgow. At the end of the first six months, David Lowe, a young enthusiast from Dundee, with literary tastes and Socialist beliefs, came in as sub-editor and to an appreciable extent relieved Hardie of some of the management worries, besides adding somewhat to the literary flavour of the paper.

With the re-assembling of Parliament, Hardie resumed his efforts to focus attention on the unemployment question, but on bringing forward his resolution, found himself up against a dead wall in the shape of a count-out. By this time, also, his harassing of the Government had raised the ire of West Ham Liberals who had not bargained for quite so much militancy on the part of their representative. From them he received numerous letters of protest with threats of opposition at the next election. To these he made a reply which defined most explicitly at once his own personal attitude and the Parliamentary policy of the I.L.P.

"The I.L.P.," he said, "starts from the assumption that the worker should be as free industrially and economically as he is supposed to be politically, that the land and the instruments of production should be owned by the community and should be used in producing the requisites to maintain a healthy and happy existence. The men who are to achieve these reforms must be under no obligation whatever to either the landlord or the capitalist, or to any party or organisation representing these interests. Suppose, for the sake of argument, that twenty members would be returned to Parliament who were nominally Labour Members but who owed their election to a compromise with the Liberals, what would the effect be upon their action in the House of Commons? When questions affecting the interest of property were at stake, or when they desired to take action to compel social legislation of a drastic character, the threat would be always hanging over them that unless they were obedient to the party Whip and maintained party discipline they would be opposed. In my own case, this threat has been held out so often that it is beginning to lose its effect. I have no desire to hold the seat on sufferance and at the mercy of those who are not in agreement with me, and am quite prepared to be defeated when the election comes round. But I cannot agree to compromise my independence of action in even the slightest degree." This plain speaking was not relished by his Liberal critics, and at one of his meetings in the constituency there was some rowdyism.

In the first month of this particular session, he had the satisfaction of speaking in support of the Miners' Eight Hours' Day Bill, which he himself had helped to draft years before, and of seeing the Second Reading carried by a majority of 81. This result did not, of course, ensure its immediately becoming law, for the obstructive resources of capitalism in Parliament and the opposition of two sections of the miners were strong enough to prevent that for many years to come.

At this time, we also find him addressing meetings in South Wales, as a result of which the I.L.P. got a footing in the Principality which it has held ever since. He had probably no premonition of how close would yet be his own connection with Wales and the Welsh people. But he had made a good beginning towards winning their gratitude, for it was doubtless as the natural sequel to his Welsh visit that in June he blocked the Cardiff Dock Bill and forced thereby the withdrawal of a clause which imposed a tariff of twopence on each passenger landed at Cardiff and a charge for luggage.

And now, certain events happened in the world which produced for Hardie a more trying parliamentary ordeal than he had yet faced, and tested his moral courage to the full. Let us look at these events in the sequence in which they presented themselves to Hardie, and we shall be the better able to understand the feelings and motives which impelled him to act as he did.

On June 23rd a terrible explosion occurred at the Albion Colliery, Cilfynydd, South Wales, by which two hundred and sixty men and boys lost their lives. On the same day a child was born to the Duchess of York. On the following day, June 24th, M. Carnot, the President of the French Republic, was assassinated. On June 26th, 70,000 Scottish miners came out on strike against a reduction of wages.

Now turn to the House of Commons. On June 25th, Sir William Harcourt moved a vote of condolence with the French people. On June 28th, the same Cabinet Minister moved an address of congratulation to the Queen on the birth of the aforesaid royal infant. Never a word of sympathy for the relatives of the miners who had been killed : never a word of reference to the serious state of affairs in the Scottish coalfield. Only one man protested. That man was Keir Hardie.

The House of Commons' situation developed in the following manner. When Harcourt gave notice of his intention to move the vote of condolence with the French people, Hardie inquired whether a vote of sympathy would also be moved to the relatives of the two hundrēd and sixty victims of the Welsh colliery disaster. "Oh, no," said Sir William, "I can dispose of that now by saying that the House does sympathise with these poor people." Hardie put down a notice of an addition to the motion, in which the Queen was to be also asked to express sympathy with the Welsh miners' friends, and the House to be asked to express its detestation of the system which made the periodic sacrifices of miners' lives inevitable. His amendment was ruled out of order, but when the congratulatory motion came on he exercised his right to speak against it, as, he said, "in the interests of the dignity of the House, and in protest against the Leader of the House of Commons declining to take official cognisance of the terrible colliery accident in South Wales." He stood alone, deserted by every other Member, including Labour's representatives, and faced a scene of well-nigh unexampled intolerance. A writer in the "West Ham Herald," describing it, wrote : "I've been in a wild beast show at feeding time. I've been at a football match when a referee gave a wrong decision. I've been at rowdy meetings of the Shoreditch vestry and the West Ham Corporation, but in all my natural life I have never witnessed a scene like this. They howled and yelled and screamed, but he stood his ground." Outside, sections of the press acted in much the same way as the House of Commons' hooligans, and tried to represent his action as a vulgar attack on Royalty. It was, primarily, not an attack on Royalty. He was certainly a Republican, but like most Socialists he regarded the Monarchy as simply an appanage of the political and social system, which would disappear as a matter of course when the system disappeared, and had it not been that the juxtaposition of events threw up in such glaring contrast the sycophancy of society where Royalty was concerned, and its heartlessness where the common people were concerned, he would probably have allowed the vote of congratulation to go through without intervention from him. But he was in fact deeply stirred in a way which these people could not understand. He had brought with him into Parliament a humanism which was greater than ceremony and deeper than formality. He was a miner, and to him the unnecessary death of one miner was of more concern than the birth of any number of royal princes. He regarded these two hundred and sixty deaths as two hundred and sixty murders. He knew that this colliery had long before been reported on as specially dangerous, and that no preventive measures had been taken. He understood, only too well, the grief and desolation of the bereaved women and children. He had been through it all in his early Lanarkshire days, and he was righteously and passionately indignant. The jeers and hootings from Members of Parliament and abuse from the press did not matter to him at all. He took his stand because it was the only thing he could do, and the receipt of nearly a thousand letters of approval from people in all social grades convinced him that besides satisfying his own impulses, he had voiced a deep sentiment in the country.

Hardie was now nearly thirty-eight years of age, and a recognised outstanding figure in British political life. An unusual man, amenable neither to flatteries nor to threatenings—one who could not be ignored. An impression of him, contributed to the "Weekly Times and Echo" by John K. Kenworthy in this same month of June, 1894, is worth reproducing.

"Above all things a spiritual, and yet a simply practical man. Not tall, squarely built, hard-headed, well bodied, and well set up, he is obviously a *bona fide* working man. His head is of the 'high moral' type,

with a finely developed forehead, denoting perception
and reason of the kind called common sense. His brown
hair is worn long and curling somewhat like the 'glory'
round the head of a saint in a painted window, and he
goes unshaved. However, most readers will have seen
him for themselves on some platform or another, though
one needs to be near him to perceive the particularly
deep, straight and steady gaze of the clear hazel eyes,
which is notable. Altogether, one judges him, by
appearances only, to be a close-knit, kindly and resolute
man, all which his performance in life bears out."

A by-election at Attercliffe in July calls for mention
if for no other reason than that it signalises J. Ramsay
MacDonald's entrance into the Independent Labour
Party. The circumstances of the contest confirmed the
I.L.P. belief that the interests behind Liberalism would
not concede willingly a single inch to the claims of
labour for representation. The local Trades Council
had nominated their President, Mr. Charles Hobson,
with the tacit understanding that he would be allowed a
clear field to fight the Tory. Hobson was not what was
called an extremist. He would probably have been
obedient in Parliament to the Liberal Whip, but the
Liberals were taking no risks, and Mr. Batty Langley,
a local employer and ex-mayor, who had, as a matter
of fact, promised to support Hobson, was nominated as
Liberal candidate. After some shilly-shallying Hobson
withdrew, and the I.L.P., with little time for organisation, determined to fight with Mr. Frank Smith as their
candidate. He was defeated, of course, but secured
1,249 votes as against 7,984 for the two reactionary
candidates, a good enough foundation for the victory
which was to come later. The immediate result achieved
was the clear exposure of Liberalism's hostility to
labour.

J. KEIR HARDIE

The following letter from MacDonald is of historical interest to the members of the I.L.P., and is to some extent illustrative of the mental attitude of both the sender and the recipient :—

"20 Duncan Buildings,
"Baldwin Gardens, E.C.

"My dear Hardie,—I am now making personal application for membership of the I.L.P. I have stuck to the Liberals up to now, hoping that they might do something to justify the trust that we had put in them. Attercliffe came as a rude awakening, and I felt during that contest that it was quite impossible for me to maintain my position as a Liberal any longer. Calmer consideration has but strengthened that conviction, and if you now care to accept me amongst you I shall do what I can to support the I.L.P.

"Between you and me there never was any dispute as to objects. What I could not quite accept was your methods. I have changed my opinion. Liberalism, and more particularly local Liberal Associations, have definitely declared against Labour, and so I must accept the facts of the situation and candidly admit that the prophecies of the I.L.P. relating to Liberalism have been amply justified. The time for conciliation has gone by and those of us who are earnest in our professions must definitely declare ourselves. I may say that in the event of elections, I shall place part of my spare time at the disposal of the Party, to do what work may seem good to you.

"Yours very sincerely,
"J. R. MacDonald."

In this manner came into the I.L.P. one whom Hardie afterwards characterised as its "greatest intellectual asset," and whose influence on national and international politics has been very great and still continues.

Meanwhile, the industrial phase of the Labour conflict absorbed Hardie's attention even more than the political. The great strike of Scottish miners continued for sixteen weeks, entailing much suffering throughout the mining community and ending in virtual defeat for the men. Still, though this was foreseen almost from the beginning, it was necessary that the stand should be made for the safeguarding of the sense of unity which had now evolved in Scotland. The strike was in some measure a consummation of Hardie's early efforts on behalf of a national organisation. It was not a sectional strike, but national, embracing the whole of the Scottish mining industry, and in that respect constituted a notable step towards that all-British combination which to-day enables the miners from Scotland to Cornwall to present a united front for the advancement of their common interests. The West of Scotland leadership was now in the capable hands of Robert Smillie, but, naturally, when at home during the Parliamentary recess, Hardie gave all possible assistance and addressed many meetings of the men in Ayrshire and Lanarkshire, besides giving what counsel and support he could through the "Labour Leader."

When it was all over he drove home the Socialist lesson in an article which, by reason of its date, October 20th, 1894, is a complete answer to those who now regard the claim for the nationalisation of the mines as a new revolutionary demand. Revolutionary it may be, but it is not new.

"Now, why," he asked, "were the masters, the Government, the press and the pulpit all arrayed against you?

"There is but one answer. All these are controlled by

the rich and you are the poor. Take the miners. The minerals are owned by the landlords, and they insist on having a royalty of from eightpence to one shilling per ton of coal brought to the surface. The pits are owned by the mineowners, and they and the landlords have the power to say that not one ton of coal shall be dug except on the terms they are willing to grant. Here are the people of Scotland—over four million of them, wanting coal to burn, and willing to pay for it. Here are you, the miners of Scotland, seventy thousand of you, willing to dig the coal in exchange for a living wage. But between you and the public stand the landlords and the mineowners, who say : 'The coal is ours and we won't allow the miners to work nor the public to be supplied unless on our terms.' So long as the landlords and the mineowners own the mines they are within their rights when they act as they have been doing, and the cure lies not in cursing the mineowners nor in striking, *but in making the mines public property.*"

It should be noted that it was only before or after a strike, not while it was taking place, that Hardie asked the men to listen to counsel of this kind. He knew that in the fight for wages, a strike, or the threat of a strike, was the only available weapon, and in the use of it he was with them every time. He knew that they must fight for wages, but he wanted them to have something bigger than wages to fight for, and a different weapon than the strike.

In September the Trades Union Congress was held at Norwich, and Hardie attended practically for the last time as a delegate. He had some time previously relinquished all official positions in the Miners' Association and was therefore disqualified by the new standing order passed this year which declared that a delegate must be either working at his trade or be a paid official of a Trade Union.   And so passed from the Trades Union Congress three men who had taken a prominent part in its deliberations—Keir Hardie, John Burns and Henry Broadhurst.   Hardie especially had left his mark on the Congress.   His connection with the Congress had only existed over a period of eight years, beginning in 1887, when the formation of the Ayrshire Miners' Union gave him a standing as a delegate. In that time the outlook of the Congress towards the principle of Independent Labour Representation, and also towards Socialism, had almost completely changed. That Hardie's personality had much to do with that change is beyond doubt.

As far back as 1869 the Congress had declared in favour of Labour Representation and had reaffirmed the principle on several subsequent occasions.   But no steps had ever been taken to give practical effect to the logical electoral policy implied by such resolutions— unless the return of a few working men to Parliament as adherents of the Liberal Party could be so regarded. Most of the men who had been so returned were members of the Congress.   Mr. Broadhurst, the Secretary of the Parliamentary Committee, had indeed accepted office in the Government as Under-Secretary of the Home Office, and he has himself stated in his auto-biography that the Parliamentary Committee functioned as the Radical wing of the Liberal Party.   He had voted in Parliament against the Miners' Eight Hours' Day Bill, and in all election campaigns he was the Liberal Party's chief platform asset wherever working-class votes required to be influenced.   Naturally, he and his Liberal-Labour colleagues resented vigorously the new policy of absolute political independence, of which Hardie made himself the spokesman. Doubtless they represented quite faithfully the general Trade Union attitude on the question. To change that attitude was the purpose of Hardie and the new men who were pushing their way into the Labour movement.

At first Hardie's position was that of almost complete isolation, as the votes of the Congress testify. At the 1888 Congress, his motion impeaching Broadhurst for having "in the name of the Congress" voted against the Miners' Eight Hours' Day Bill received only 15 votes against 80, while the following year at Dundee, when he made a frontal attack and moved that Broadhurst "was not a fit and proper person to hold the office of Secretary" and accused him of supporting employers of labour and holding shares in sweating companies (a charge which was not denied), he was defeated by 177 to 11.

The Congress and the Trade Union movement were evidently overwhelmingly against him. A weaker man would have accepted defeat of this kind as final. It only made Hardie more stubborn and stimulated him to greater effort. Hardie's Congress record is something of a paradox. He was being defeated all the time, and all the time he was winning. Even in 1891, when he got only eleven supporters to his proposal for a Trade Union Parliamentary Fund for securing Parliamentary representation that was a move forward, being an attempt to give practical effect to the decision which the Congress had just previously arrived at calling for a "strong and vigorous Labour Party" in Parliament. Hardie's amendment was as follows: "and would suggest to the organised trades of this country so to alter their rules as to admit of their subscribing to a Parliamentary Fund to be placed at the disposal of the Congress to secure Labour Representation based upon the decision of this Congress." We have here the germ of present day Labour Party finance. Yet, in 1891, it had only eleven supporters in the Trades Union Congress. Similarly, when, in 1892, on the motion of Ben Tillett, it was decided to recommend the formation of a Parliamentary Fund, and also to give no support to any candidates but those who stood for the "collective ownership of the means of production, distribution and exchange," Hardie was again to the fore with an amendment which placed him once more in the minority. His proposal was for the formation of an Independent Parliamentary group, but it was defeated by 119 votes to 96. Hardie's minorities were always the heralds of future victory.

At that same Congress he had gathered together the elements out of which in the following year was evolved the Independent Labour Party, and now, this year, with the I.L.P. in being, and himself in Parliament as its representative, he could take leave of the Trades Union Congress assured that his eight years of struggle and pioneering had not been in vain.

It was probably on the occasion of this visit to Norwich that an incident occurred revealing to his Trade Union friends another aspect of his nature than that to which they were accustomed in the stress of industrial and political strife. The incident is related by Mr. S. G. Hobson. "Of my various pleasant memories of Norwich," says Mr. Hobson, "perhaps the sweetest was one evening in the Cathedral grounds under an old Norman arch where we stood and watched the sun go down and darkness creep silently upon us. The greensward—smoothed by careful hands for centuries back—seemed to gradually recede from our view. By and by the lights twinkled from many windows, and we knew that worshippers were there to chant the evening service and sing their vesper hymns. Suddenly the voice of

97

old Hardie rose through the stillness, giving vocal expression to the Twenty-third Psalm, and we all joined—Christians and agnostics—blending our voices, not so much in any devotional spirit as out of deference to the influence of the place."

This inherent spiritual emotionalism—if it may be so called—was continually manifesting itself in various ways all through life, whether, as in the early Ayrshire days, in evangelising on the Ayrshire highways and by-ways, or, as in later days, preaching in Methodist pulpits or on Brotherhood platforms, or in association with the votaries of spiritualism and theosophy. He was imbued with an imaginative catholicity of spirit which rendered him responsive to every expression of religious feeling which seemed to him sincere. There is no need to try to explain it. It was involuntary, a part of his nature, and it never hindered, but rather intensified and idealised, his work for Socialism. His spiritual enthusiasm never led him out of touch with reality. In a very literal sense, "the poor he had always with him." He was one of them. And to him their cause was a cause of the devotional spirit.

Just about this time he was penning his letter to the Scottish miners which was afterwards circulated in pamphlet form under the title of "Collier Laddies." We find him also addressing propaganda meetings as far north as Arbroath, and across the channel speaking in Waterford and in the Rotunda at Dublin and reporting upon the Labour movement in Ireland with an optimism which can hardly have been based upon an accurate estimate of the all-absorbent character of the Nationalist movement in that country.

Towards the end of this year, the I.L.P. had an accession of a kind more valuable than it could then know. Philip Snowden, a man quite unknown to public life, joined the I.L.P. He had been living quietly in a remote village amongst the Yorkshire hills, recovering from a very serious illness, and in the period of convalescence had given his mind to a study of social problems, which ended in his becoming a convinced Socialist. The I.L.P. was steadily becoming equipped with capable leadership, and with men of experience in administrative work. Keir Hardie, Ramsay MacDonald, Philip Snowden, Bruce Glasier, Fred Jowett, to name no others, constituted a group which for all-round ability on the platform or in the council chamber could not be surpassed by any of the other political parties.

In the Liberal camp there were evident signs of alarm at the activities of the new party. In July, following close upon the Attercliffe election, Joseph Burgess had polled a substantial vote in a by-election at Leicester, and all over the country the I.L.P. was busy selecting its candidates and choosing the constituencies in which it would fight, many of these being places where the Liberal hold was already somewhat precarious. Lord Rosebery, now Prime Minister, found it expedient to address a meeting in Hardie's constituency at which he demonstrated to his own satisfaction that a united democracy was only possible through the Liberal Party. Hardie, characteristically, replied both by speech and pen, thereby focussing more than ever, national attention on himself as a political personality, and an article which he contributed to the January, 1895, "Nineteenth Century" explaining and vindicating the I.L.P. policy and tactics, attracted much attention.

Nor did his practical work in the House of Commons go entirely without recognition. On January 19th, for example, he was the guest of the Fawcett Association, at that time the one body ventilating the grievances of postal servants, and was presented with an illuminated address, "for the valuable services you have rendered us in the House of Commons on every occasion when you have found it possible to effectually advocate our cause." The address concluded: "We thank you for your resolute adherence to the cause of truth and justice, and esteem you as a man whose promise may be relied on." An extremely comforting assurance to a man who was at that very time being more virulently assailed by the party politicians than any other public man in the country.

Hardie was now preparing for his third Parliamentary session and was determined to go to Westminster this time fortified by an outside agitation which would compel the Government to act on behalf of the unemployed, or to resign, a formidable objective for an apparently solitary and friendless commoner. The distress throughout the country, instead of lessening, was becoming more acute and widespread. Well-intentioned local distress committees and soup kitchens only emphasised, without materially alleviating, the misery, and although the contending politicians might make platform play with Armenian atrocities and with their rival plans for pacifying Ireland, it was not possible to get hungry British electors to concentrate on either of these questions as an election issue. The difficulty was—and is—to get them to concentrate upon anything. That, in fact, is the trouble with which the Labour Party is still faced.

In the first week of January, he appealed through the "Labour Leader" for a small fund with which to begin a national unemployed agitation, and by the time Parliament met in February, with a comparatively trifling expenditure of money, big demonstrations had been held in many of the great industrial centres, Hardie himself taking a leading part in most of them. Many of the

J. KEIR HARDIE, 1893

THE UNEMPLOYED

Liberal Members, with a general election impending, were compelled to make promises to their constituents which it was necessary they should make at least some pretence of redeeming. It was, therefore, with some tremors that the Government faced the House of Commons, notwithstanding Harcourt's jocular attempt to make light of the Opposition forces. "There was no 'true blue' now. They had instead the faded yellow of Birmingham, a little dash of green from Waterford, and a little splotch of red from West Ham." Thus—deliberately or not—reckoning the solitary Keir Hardie as of equal importance with the great Unionist Party. "A splotch of red" said one of the clever rhymers of the "Labour Leader" :—

> "A splotch of red, Sir William V.,
> Only a little splotch of red.
> Your friends sit back and broadly smile
> As you the weary hours beguile
> With little jokes—but time will be
> When you'll not treat so jestingly
> That tiny little splotch of red.
> A hearty, healthy little splotch
> And growing fast; full firmly bent
> On turning out the fools that sport
> With simple men and women's woes,
> Your office is your only thought,
> Your friends but on their seats intent.
> Think you it can be ever so?
> Sir William V., we tell you, no ;
> And all your mocking Parliament."

Hardie's amendment to the address was in exactly the same terms as the one he had moved two years before on first taking his seat, but the circumstances were different. The unemployed agitation had assumed big proportions, the pressure from the constituencies was having considerable effect upon many of the Government supporters who would be compelled to vote with Hardie unless their own leaders could provide them with a plausible alternative; and there was the Tory opposition, willing to use the unemployed question, or any other question, as a means of bringing about a Government defeat.

Mr. T. P. O'Connor, himself an experienced wire puller, described in the "Weekly Sun" the manœuverings which took place. "Some shrewd friends of the Government knew what was in store for them if they were to receive the motion of Mr. Keir Hardie with a blank negative. The Government accordingly considered the situation, with the result that they went carefully through the suggestions that were made to them for meeting with this terrible difficulty which comes periodically athwart the opulence and comfort of this mighty nation and this vast city. The information was conveyed to the friends of the Government that they saw their way to propose a committee which would get a very practical bit of work to do, and which would be obliged to go into the question of the unemployed promptly as well as seriously. Friends of the Government, having considered the terms of what it was proposed to do, were able to announce in turn to the Government that in their opinion this was as much as could be expected, and so all danger of defections from the Liberal ranks disappeared. Whatever happened on other amendments, Ministers were safe on the amendment of Mr. Keir Hardie"— safe, but considerably shaken. Hardie had proved himself a good parliamentary strategist; but he was more than a strategist. He was, in a good cause, perhaps the most stubborn man alive. He persisted with his motion notwithstanding the promised concession, in the value of which he had no faith at all. The scene which ensued was thus described by a Press correspondent:—

"As soon as it was known he was up, Members poured

in from every part, until every bench had its full quota of Members, whilst a crowd stood below the bar and another crowd behind the Speaker's chair. Both front benches were crowded with Ministers and ex-Ministers and the attention of the House was kept unbroken from start to finish.

"The speech was not of the fighting order; the concession just offered by the Government of a special committee having made that impossible, but the interest never flagged for a moment and the chorus of cheers from all parts at the close showed that a responsive chord had been struck. Sir Charles Dilke followed and congratulated Mr. Hardie on having gained the point which for two and a half years he had been constantly fighting for. He quoted Mr. Gladstone's reply to a question put by the Member for West Ham in 1893, in which the Prime Minister refused to agree to the appointment of a committee because it was not the business of the Government to deal with such questions."

Another contemporary impression, contributed to a Northern paper, preserves for us with remarkable vividness the nature of the ordeal through which Hardie had to pass when opposing the Government motion :—

"When the Member for West Ham moved his second amendment, Sir William Harcourt appealed to him to withdraw it, an appeal which was backed by Sir John Gorst, Mr. J. W. Benn, and Sir Albert Rollit, whilst a number of Members tried their influence privately. 'If the Government can find the committee and make an interim report, I will withdraw my amendment'; and the knit brow and the firm mouth showed that the words meant what they said. It was a strange and significant scene as the representatives of rank and titles tried to bend the shaggy pitman to their will. In the end he conquered, and the cheers with which Sir William Harcourt's capitulation was received were really a tribute to Keir Hardie's firmness. It was a little incident, but of great significance."

The "splotch of red" had made an indelible mark. He got the assurance that the committee would get to work immediately and bring in an interim report with all possible speed. He, for his own part, having little faith in a committee appointed reluctantly to save the Government from immediate downfall, refused to associate himself with it.

And now, finally, to complete the picture, take this other contemporary comment from the London "Echo."

"Possibly the new Parliament may see nothing of Keir Hardie, but the chronologist will at least do him the justice of recording how he threw the Government of the day into a blue funk, forced their hand, and then haughtily left the Chamber, disdaining with almost a refinement of cynicism to support their tardy concession, and at the same time deftly eluding the grasp of the clever intriguers who hoped to jockey into a follower the free lance whom their caste pride would not permit to lead them. Verily, the game of party politics is a truculent business, and the fact has never been more poignantly illustrated than in the incidents of a week in which, shocking as it is, the almost houseless poor have been the sport of the strategists in 'high places.' "

In this fashion did Keir Hardie earn the title of "Member for the Unemployed."

CHAPTER SIX

A GENERAL ELECTION—AMERICA—INDUSTRIAL STRIFE

THE Liberal Government, however, though saved for the time being, was, through sheer incapacity to retain the confidence of any substantial section of public opinion, drifting to its doom, and when, at Easter, 1895, the Annual Conference of the I.L.P. met in Newcastle, its deliberations were influenced to some extent by the knowledge that a General Election was near at hand and that the Party might in the course of a few weeks have to make its first trial of strength at the ballot box.

The chief subject of discussion at the Conference was, therefore, on questions of election tactics and policy, but the decisions arrived at involved something more than a question of merely tentative electioneering expediency. They determined the future character and method of the I.L.P. as a political party working for Socialism.

First of all there was the proposal to change the name to that of "National Socialist Party," a proposal which, if it had been adopted when proposed by George Carson at the first Conference, would doubtless have remained permanently. Whether it would have excluded any undesirable moderate elements from the Party can now only be conjectured, but after two years, in which, under the name of I.L.P., the Party had established itself and had become familiar to the British public, without in any way compromising its Socialist aim, it was felt by the great majority that a change was unnecessary. The

Newcastle Conference therefore confirmed the title under which, through good report and evil, British Socialism has sought to utilise the political power of British democracy. Hardie was not strongly partial either way, and would have continued to serve under any Party name which embodied the Socialist objective.

Not so, however, with regard to the other and more vital proposal to introduce into the Constitution a rigid pledge binding all I.L.P. members "to support and vote only for I.L.P. and S.D.F. candidates at any election." This was what was known as the "Fourth Clause," and round it was waged in the press, on the platform and in branch meetings, many a wordy conflict. It was mainly because of the rejection of this clause that Robert Blatchford left the I.L.P. Under this proposal the large majority of I.L.P. adherents would have exercised no vote at all at the oncoming General Election. Some twenty-one candidates had already been chosen, and others were in course of selection, but in upwards of six hundred constituencies, even where their votes might have had a decisive effect as between Liberal and Tory, Socialists under this pledge would be condemned to inaction. Contingent upon this proposal was the other discussion as to whether, in constituencies where there was no Socialist candidate, the vote should be given always against the sitting Member, either Liberal or Tory, the object being to demonstrate the power of the I.L.P. This, of course, was an impossible policy if the abstinence pledge was enforced. Hardie was opposed to the rigidity which such a pledge implied for other reasons. He had an intimate knowledge of the Trade Union and Co-operative movements, and he knew well that even I.L.P. sympathisers within these movements could not be expected, where possible gain to Trade Unionism or Co-operation was obtainable, to exercise such a self-denying political ordinance. To issue a mandate which would not be obeyed would be interpreted as evidence of weakness rather than of strength, and in his presidential address, without any direct reference to the Conference agenda, he appealed to the members to do nothing to alienate the Trade Union, Co-operative and Temperance movements. On the other hand, in support of the clause it was urged by Leonard Hall and others, that "what was wanted was a fixed, definite and permanent policy having regard, not to the present only, but to the ultimate triumph for which they were working in the future." This, of course, was the very object which it was maintained could best be secured by the less rigid proposal put forward by the National Council. This asked from members the following declaration : "I hereby declare myself a Socialist, pledge myself to sever my connection with any other political party, and to vote in the case of local elections as my branch of the I.L.P. may determine, and, in the case of the Parliamentary elections, as the Conference specially convened for that purpose may decide." This was adopted and is still the election policy of the I.L.P. Yet, curiously enough, at the very first election the Special Party Conference recommended the "Fourth Clause" line of action and inaction.

The opportunity came in July. The Liberal Government was defeated on the question of an insufficient supply of explosive material for the Army—evidently a more serious default than an insufficiency of food or work for the unemployed. The I.L.P. went into the contest with a manifesto to the electors of Great Britain and Ireland, the following extract from which shows the electoral policy advised, but certainly not adopted, by Socialist voters :—

"The I.L.P. has for its object not merely the return

of working men to Parliament, but the entire reorganisation of our system of wealth production on the basis
of an industrial Commonwealth. To accomplish this we
aim at breaking down the system of party government
which is responsible for dividing the great mass of the
people into separate camps, so evenly balanced that the
one neutralises the other, and thus reduces the franchise
to a mockery. So long as we continue to vote for
Liberals and Conservatives, the mockery of government,
of which we have seen so much, will continue.

"In twenty-nine constituencies I.L.P. candidates will
go to the poll, and the Party has decided at a special
conference of delegates from all parts of the country that
in all other constituencies the members shall ABSTAIN
FROM VOTING. For this election we consider this
the most effective method of achieving our object."

The result showed that the workers in most constituencies where there were no Labour candidates did not
act upon this advice. They exercised the franchise and
voted against the Liberal Party, which, through a long
period of deep distress, had proved itself callous to the
claims of the unemployed. The Liberal Party was
badly routed. Some of its leading men, such as Mr.
John Morley and Sir William Vernon Harcourt, were
cast out, chiefly through the intervention of I.L.P. candidates; but in the main the verdict against Liberalism
was an expression of discontent with the Party rather than
of revolt against the system which the Party represented.
The Socialist propaganda had not yet penetrated deeply
enough, and especially, it had not been able to make the
Irish population in the constituencies subordinate their
Nationalist aspirations to their economic needs. It was
the Irish vote in this election which saved the Liberal
Party from utter ruin. And it was the Irish vote that
defeated Keir Hardie in West Ham and returned a Tory

who had not the faintest sympathy with Home Rule, the official Liberals, by countenancing such tactics, making it clear that to them Keir Hardie was a more dangerous adversary than any Tory. A very high compliment indeed, and one that confirmed the I.L.P. contention that there was no fundamental difference between Liberalism and Conservatism.

The Socialists, though not one of their candidates was returned and they lost their single Parliamentary seat, showed not the slightest sign of dejection. They were, indeed, jubilant. They reckoned up their votes and found that they had polled an average of 1,592 votes per candidate. They believed that a proportionate support was waiting for them in most of the other constituencies where they had been unable to put up candidates, and they knew that with these votes they could win Local Government seats in every part of the country.

Hardie wrote a farewell letter to the West Ham electors, concluding in his usual optimistic vein : ''The moral and intellectual power of the community are on our side and those in the end will triumph. I thank my friends for the zeal with which they worked. The triumph of our movement has not been delayed; we have but purified it by purging it of unworthy elements. Let the friends of our cause be of good cheer.''· So ended Keir Hardie's third year's experiment as a lone fighter in Parliament.

There is another aspect of this Parliamentary struggle which should not be lost sight of in forming our estimate of the character of this man. There was no wages' fund from which he could draw an income. He was not the paid servant of any trade union. Payment of Members was still far in the future. During these three years, as always, he had to earn his own living and maintain his home in Cumnock. That he, the self-taught man from the pits, untutored and untrained except in the rough school of perpetual industrial strife, should have been able to do this without the slightest sacrifice of principle, is proof of great capacity and indomitable spirit. It was the recognition of this that won for him the respect of the better section of his opponents, and the trust and affection of his colleagues and comrades in the movement of which he was now the acknowledged leader. Doubtless, during these years there were times when it was well-nigh impossible to make ends meet, either in London or in Cumnock, but of these things neither he nor the good wife at home ever made mention.

Release from Parliament brought the opportunity to realise a long-cherished desire. In the autumn of the previous year he had made plans to visit America, and had actually booked his passage, but at the last moment certain unexplained obstacles intervened—probably financial— and the project had to be abandoned.

Now there came an invitation from the American Labour Day Committee to attend the Chicago Labour Congress on September 2nd. The Chicago Labour Congress was described by H. D. Lloyd (who also wrote pressing Hardie to accept) as "composed of the best elements of the Trade Union movement of Chicago," and it was urged that Hardie's visit would be "a matter of national—and international—importance." He had some hesitation in accepting the invitation, due to the fact that Mrs. Hardie had been for some time in rather poor health. She had, however, recovered considerably, and, said Hardie, "she, with that devotion to the cause which had enabled her to endure so much uncomplainingly in the past, sank herself once more." He regarded the American expedition as part of a much bigger project. "Next year," he said, "I hope to visit Australia or New Zealand and thus get the entire advanced

Labour movement into active speaking contact," a plan which he ultimately fulfilled, though not in the chronological order here indicated. In addition to this high seriousness of purpose, Hardie undoubtedly expected much personal enjoyment from the Transatlantic excursion. He made his preparations with almost boyish zest and enthusiasm, and revelled humorously in the kindly arrangements for his comfort made by numerous friends and comrades. He relates with great gusto how one friend sent him a cigarette case, how another brought him a cigar case, and yet another a box of cigars wherewith to keep it filled; a fourth brought a packet of "Old Gold" and a pipe, and a fifth, "the widow's mite, in the shape of a matchbox made by himself"—a monotonous succession of gifts, due, as Hardie whimsically said, to the fact that he had "only one vice," characterised by one of his friends as an ability "to smoke anything from a cuttypipe to a factory chimney." "At least, I shall have plenty of tobacco for the next seven days."

He celebrated his thirty-seventh birthday quietly at Cumnock, and next morning started off on his travels.

At Liverpool, the port of departure, he was joined by Mr. Frank Smith, who was to be his companion and confidant in this and many other enterprises. Mr. Smith had come into the Socialist movement by way of the Salvation Army, of the social work of which he had been one of the principal organisers, until the futility of patching up an ever-extending evil had driven him to look for a fundamental cure, and naturally brought him to Socialism. Right up to the end Hardie and he were very close friends.

The Merseyside Socialists organised a great send-off demonstration, and, not content with marching in procession to the quayside, chartered a tug on board of which a crowd of enthusiasts attended the Cunard liner right out of the harbour bar, cheering and singing in a way, as Hardie said, "calculated to make every passenger on the 'Campania' discuss Socialism."

The immediate result was an invitation to address the passengers on the subject of "Competition," this title having been suggested by the denunciatory banners displayed from the tug. This was the kind of request which Hardie never refused. Probably no man has ever spoken for Socialism in so great a variety of circumstances. The hillside or the street corner, the church pulpit or the university debating hall, made no difference to him; he delivered his message with as much emphasis and impressiveness to students and professors and aristocrats and millionaires as to colliers and dock labourers and common working folk.

On this occasion he drew his illustrations of the social and industrial world from the classes into which the passengers were divided—the privileged class, the plutocrats, and the common people—and showed "how the two former were sitting on the backs and keeping their hands in the pockets of the latter, robbing them of the land, robbing them of the fruits of their labour, and all in the name of the law and by the means of competition, and so keeping the workers in subjection." Needless to say, the two I.L.P. men and the steerage folk enjoyed themselves, and probably some of the "plutocrats" also.

One personal note of the voyage may be preserved as characteristic. The other passengers were in the habit of putting back their watches an hour each day, so as to be right with New York time on arrival. Not so Hardie. "With that sympathy with Toryism which I am known to possess, I declined to alter my time. By keeping to the Cumnock time I could always tell

exactly what was being done at home—when the
children went to school, when they returned, when
they went to bed, and the rest of it—and found
more to interest me therein than in trying to keep
pace with Daddy Time."

The two companions contributed to the "Labour
Leader" at the time a series of intensely interesting
descriptive articles, which even now might bear reproduction in book form, alike as an extra biographical
memento, and as a means of comparing American labour
conditions of that time with the present. For Hardie
it was a memorable pilgrimage.

His was the kind of mind that never becomes *blasé*
or impervious to new sensations. Every day, almost
every hour, of his journeying brought something of the
thrill of a new adventure. At New York he was most
cordially welcomed and fêted by all sections of the
Socialist and Labour movement, who sank their differences in order to do honour to the fearless agitator from
across the "fish pond." He visited Daniel de Leon,
at that time editor of "The People," whom he describes
as "a fair specimen of the energetic, clear, cool enthusiast. Seen in the editor's den at 184 Market Street, he
recalls the pictures one has seen of the French Communists manning the barricades, in his striped blouse,
white kerchief at the throat, slightly oval face, with full
beard growing grey, and the clear eye and olive-tinted
skin of the South. A man accustomed to give and receive
hard knocks, he has enemies as well as friends, but all
agree that for single-mindedness and purity of aim he
has few equals."

In New York, and through his fifteen weeks' tour,
Hardie noted regretfully the keen, almost fierce antag-
onism between the various sections of the Labour and
Socialist movement, but was gratified to find their

antagonisms fade away, at least temporarily, in the common desire to show him respect and give him a "good time." The travellers were nearly a week in New York before starting West. They spent daylight hours in the "Bowery," and night-time hours in China Town. They contrasted the vaunted Yankee equality with the rigidity of the "colour line." They were the guests of the select Manhattan Club, whose members viewed with disapproval alike the political opinions of their visitors and their preference for ginger ale to burgundy. They dined at Delmonico's where pipes were taboo and cigars the only permissible smoke, and they mingled with the early-morning line of hungry men waiting for a free distribution of bread outside the Vienna Bakery. They penetrated as far as they dared into the social under-world, and, as their motives were higher than mere curiosity, they doubtless succeeded better than most sightseers.

The writer has thought it well, during the course of this narrative, to present Hardie as he appeared to some of his contemporaries. This "New York World" picture of him may not come amiss :

"As a representative of the great class he is undoubtedly more interesting than anything he may say. He is a strong man. His face is strong and his jaw is square; his head is big and well shaped. His hair is fairly long and curly. He is intensely earnest. He has no non-sense about him and no cant. He uses words to express what he thinks, not to sound well. He dresses simply, perhaps too simply, for there is as much affectation in simplicity as in show. His shoes are low-cut and heavy, and his blue shirt and tie match and are sensible. His nose is straight and long. He has a good eye which looks squarely at and into you. His chest is big. He is temperate. He has read more than the average ignoramus who will try to teach him about American institutions. He knows what few men who try original thought ever learn. He knows that he can never hope to learn much or to do much. He realises that he is like a small insect working at the foundations of a coral island. He does not expect to raise society ninety feet into the air in his lifetime. Those who argue with Mr. Hardie will always find one difficulty about him. He knows pretty well what he is talking about." Thus the American pressman measured him up, if not quite accurately, with some superficial shrewdness.

At Chicago his reception was on a bigger scale even than at New York. This was accounted for partly by the fact that his visit coincided with the great Labour Day demonstrations at which he was regarded as the chief speaker, and he was well reported in the press. Here he diverged sixty miles north to Woodstock, where Eugene V. Debs was in prison on a charge arising out of the part he had played in the Pullman strike. Hardie was hugely tickled when Debs himself came down the prison steps with a "walk right in and make yourselves at home." The great labour leader has been in prison since then, and has been under much more rigid surveillance. He is there, much to the disgrace of America, whilst this is being written.

During his brief sojourn at Chicago and Milwaukee he attended a nomination convention and gained some insight into American electoral methods. When he came away it was "with a feeling of regret that so many earnest, wholehearted reformers were engaged in fighting such side issues as the silver question when by going straight for the Socialist ticket they would settle that and many other questions."

The tour took the travellers almost as far west as they could get. They went to Denver, Leadville, "two hundred feet up in the clouds," Colorado Springs, Salt Lake City, San Francisco, and the Montana mining district, Altruria, Santa Rosa, Kansas City, St. Louis, and many other places not in the way of the ordinary tourist.

At San Francisco the travellers ran up against the "Almighty Dollar" on a somewhat big scale. The Mayor of the city, better known as the "Silver King" from the fact that he had amassed millions of dollars out of silver-mining and speculation, was an ardent believer in bimetallism, which was at that time the chief plank in Mr. Bryan's platform as candidate for the Presidency. The Mayor had persuaded himself that if it could be shown that England was falling into line with the American bimetallist campaign it would greatly help Mr. Bryan's candidature, and he put it to Hardie, in the presence of Frank Smith and the Rev. Mr. Scott of the Presbyterian Church, as a business proposition that he should get the I.L.P. to make a declaration in favour of bimetallism, or, failing that, that he should himself make a speech in its favour as Chairman at the I.L.P. Annual Conference in return for which service Hardie would receive a cheque for 100,000 dollars— about £20,000. The Mayor and the minister were both surprised when Hardie and Frank Smith laughed the idea out of court, the Mayor especially being quite unable to comprehend the point of view of a labour leader who could turn down a business proposal of this kind.

There were doubtless many others equally mystified by such conduct. To them it almost seemed as if this inexplicable Scotsman had a contempt for "siller." He had refused the Liberal Party money. He had refused the Carnegie money. He had refused the money from the Edinburgh ladies, and now he had rejected almost contemptuously a fairly substantial fortune in return for a speech.

Forty-eight hours later the two travellers landed in Butte City possessed of a financial equipment of exactly one dollar, ten cents.—about five and sixpence—to find that remittances expected from Chicago had not arrived. The story of how a providential Scottish piper saved the situation afforded Hardie many a reminiscent chuckle in days to come. The local comrades, chiefly Knights of Labour, had placed a buggy at their disposal to enable them to see the sights, and, when returning from a visit to an Indian encampment, their ears were regaled by sounds which set the Scotsman's blood tingling. "Do you hear that music?" he said to the driver. "That ain't no music," was the reply," that's the Scotch pipes." "Drive to where they are being played," said Hardie, and the driver, whose appreciation of Scotch whisky was greater than his knowledge of Scottish music, speedily landed his fares at the door of a wooden drinking saloon whose proprietor, a stalwart Scot of the Macdonald clan, was marching in front of the bar playing reels and Highland dirges, and who, with his drouthy customers, hailed the Labour man from the Old Country with enthusiasm. A meeting in the Opera House was arranged impromptu for the same evening, and, thanks to the rallying power of Macdonald's pipes, a crowded audience heard the Socialist message. Seventy-five dollars were handed to Hardie as the surplus after paying all expenses. "And that," said Keir, when telling the story, "was how Providence came to the rescue at Butte City."

Hardie addressed meetings in most of the important towns, and in the industrial districts. He conferred with the trade union and Socialist leaders and with all kinds of public officials, and in every possible way tried to gain information concerning industrial and political conditions. But he did not delude himself into the belief that he had learned sufficient to justify him in speaking as an authority on American Labour problems. As he said in summing up : "The impressions one gets in hurrying across a great continent are necessarily mere surface impressions, and do not qualify one to dogmatise or even to describe. I like to know, not only what appears to the observation, but the causes which have produced the things seen, and these are not always so easily obtained." "Still," he continued, "I have the feeling that having gone there to learn, the visit in this respect has not been entirely in vain. Of one thing I am certain. The cause of Socialism and the I.L.P. has been benefited, and some fresh links have been forged in the chain which will one day bind the workers of the world in international solidarity. There as here, we found that the common sense of Socialism is a much more powerful argument than its hard, dry, scientific, economic justification. Few people are scientists, but all are human, and the secret of the success of the I.L.P. here at home has been the homely, essentially human tone which has been the chief note of its teaching."

That last sentence is exceedingly illuminative of Hardie's own Socialist inspiration. He was not of the stuff of which doctrinaires are made.

The winter of 1895 was a very distressful one, especially in the west of Scotland, where, in addition to the unemployment consequent upon trade depression, there was a lock-out of engineers which lasted for several months, and of course affected some of the auxiliary occupations. Socialists, as such, were not in a position to intervene, and could only make use of the trouble as propaganda against the capitalist system.

There was no Keir Hardie in Parliament to help to focus political opinion on the industrial question, and the

Tory Government, with no effective criticism from the Liberal Opposition, could afford to let matters drift. During the first few weeks after his return from America, Hardie's domestic affairs, concerning which he was always very reticent, naturally absorbed much of his attention, as also did the affairs of the "Labour Leader." Previous to his departure for America he had found it necessary to appeal to readers and sympathisers to re-double their efforts for an increased circulation and advertisement revenue. There had been a very encouraging response, but the ship was still in troubled waters financially. It is doubtful if it ever fully emerged from this trouble during all the years whilst Hardie was responsible for its guidance. Yet somehow he managed to keep it going.

A statement which he made at this time helps to throw light on another matter which has sometimes been a source of conjecture to friends as well as enemies—his relationship to the movement financially. In response to enquiries as to his terms for lectures he said : "I have endeavoured, not with much success, to clear my out-of-pocket expenses from these talking engagements. Train fares and travel mean money. So does postage. So does the loss of time involved in connection with the work which, in the case of a man who earns his living by his pen, as I do, comes to a serious item. The return journey between Scotland and London costs about £3 10s. in fares and necessary food. To some parts of the Kingdom it costs more; to some less. I found two years ago that a fixed uniform charge of £3 3s. for all meetings in the provinces enabled me to meet all expenses. This charge covers everything, hotel bill, travelling and all other outlays. When I am living in London or Glasgow these places have all the meetings they want, and there is no question of fee or expense." It is quite clear from this statement that the I.L.P. offered no inducement to adventurers in search of fame or fortune. It had neither political preferment nor financial advantage to offer to its adherents, nor any soft jobs. Yet it continued to attract into its ranks many men and women of high attainments.

It must, at any rate, be quite clear that the founder of the I.L.P. was not living luxuriously. As a matter of fact, during his first three years in Parliament, twenty-five shillings a week was the most he was able to remit to Mrs. Hardie in Cumnock, and sometimes not even so much as that.

On December 21st, he presided at a dinner given to "Labour Leader" contributors at the Albion Hotel, Ludgate Circus, London, and paid tribute to the satisfactory service rendered by his co-workers on the paper. This meeting, however, is chiefly memorable because it was the occasion of the last public utterance of Sergius Stepniak, the great Russian Nihilist exile, whose book, "Underground Russia," was the first revelation to the British people of the working of those tremendous unseen forces beneath the surface of Russian society whose effects are now plainly visible to the whole world. Parts of the speech may be quoted as illustrative alike of the characters of Stepniak and Hardie and of the similarity of Socialist conception by which both men were inspired.

"Socialism," said Stepniak, "is now the only force able to inspire men with that boundless devotion, and utter disregard for personal safety which we see constantly exhibited by Socialists in every land. It is remarkable that whenever you have before you a movement which is really like the religious movement at the time of the Reformation, it is Socialism which is behind it. It is so in Russia, France, Germany, America—everywhere." Speaking of the great growth of the Socialist movement in this country, he said : "Although I know that my comrade in the chair does not like signalling out personalities, I feel it is only fair to say that Keir Hardie was the one man in England who did more than most in that great work.   There are points in his programme with which I do not entirely agree, but I cannot help admiring in his individuality, the character, the straightforwardness, the perfect simplicity and unconquerable energy which finds renewed impulse in every obstacle.   Keir Hardie has shown what an Englishman can do.   I can say that in the name of thousands of my comrades in Russia, where Keir Hardie's name is as well known as that of the greatest of Englishmen.''   Two days later Stepniak was dead, having been run down by a passing train while crossing the railway line on his way to a meeting of his co-patriots in another part of London.   The following Saturday there gathered outside Waterloo Station representatives of the world-wide revolutionary movement, to pay tribute to his memory and to renew their vows of devotion to the common cause.   His fellow countrymen, Kropotkin and Volkhovsky; Bernstein, of the German Social Democrats; Malatesta, of Italy; Nazarbeck, of Armenia; William Morris, Keir Hardie, Herbert Burrows, John Burns, of the British Socialist movement, besides many representatives of art and science and literature, and a sad concourse of exiles, mourning the loss of their great brother.

Stepniak, like so many of the Russian revolutionary leaders, was born in the ruling class, and had given all his power and genius to the overthrow of that class.   He had organised secret propaganda and revolt, had found it necessary to meet violence with violence, and—it was believed—had helped to rid the world of more than one of its worst tyrants.   Yet the testimony of all his associates declared him to be one of the gentlest of men, a man of a sweet and a lovable nature.   When the I.L.P. was formed he joined immediately, and between him and

Hardie there had been frequent intercourse. Hardie was also at this time on terms of intimacy with Kropotkin and had spent hours at his home drinking samovar-made tea, and smoking many pipes of tobacco while the apostle of Anarchism paced the floor of his paper-littered room and gave illustration after illustration to prove that parliamentary institutions were "a quicksand in which honesty, manhood, courage, and all else were lost." "Were we all Kropotkins," said Hardie, "Anarchism would be the only possible system, since government and restraint would be unnecessary."

Naturally, communion with these and other strong souls, purified as by fire through persecution and suffering, was not without influence on a mind that, up to the very last, never ceased to expand. His perception of the fact that though many people have the same purpose, they must of necessity approach their problems from different angles and from different circumstances, made him averse to dogmatise as to methods and he was tolerant of Socialists and reformers whose ways were not as his ways. This trait in his character was very evident at the International Congress this year when the place of Anarchists in the Socialist movement became a very vital question.

The Congress, which was held in the Queen's Hall, London, began on Monday, July 27th, and continued for six days. The organising committee responsible for calling it had to be guided by the following resolution passed by the Congress held at Zurich in 1892 : "All trade unions shall be admitted to the Congress, also, all those Socialist parties and organisations which recognise the necessity for the organisation of the workers and for political action.

"By political action is meant that the working-class organisations seek, as far as possible, to use or conquer political rights and the machinery of legislation for the furthering of the interests of the proletariat and the conquest of political power.''

Upon the interpretation and application of this ''standing order,'' so un-English in its dress and form, there was much and heated debate. A considerable number of delegates, especially from Holland and France, had come with credentials from societies that did not include parliamentary action in their programmes. Some of these were trade unions pure and simple which had sent well-known Anarchists as their delegates. There were also ''Free Communists''—all non-parliamentarians. Hardie was in favour of their admission. ''It might be alleged,'' he said, in defining his position at the meeting of the I.L.P. section, ''that if they supported these people's claims they were sympathising with Anarchists. For his part, he was more afraid of doing an unfair thing towards a body of Socialists with whom he did not see eye to eye, than he was of being called an Anarchist.'' Tom Mann took the same point of view, and both supported their positions in the Congress. The I.L.P. delegates were divided on the question, but the German section and the British S.D.F., who largely dominated the Congress proceedings, were united in refusing admission to the non-parliamentarians. In the end, Anarchist delegates were excluded, though many of the prominent Anarchists found entrance as trade unionists. Fundamentally, the question at issue was the same question which had divided Bakunin and Marx in the days of the old International and which in these days still intervenes to prevent the reconstitution of a united international Socialist movement. Modern Socialism is simply the concrete expression of ideas of government which at that time had not passed the stage of being mere formulæ. Hardie did not think it well that the whole movement

J. KEIR HARDIE

should be bound rigidly along a certain fixed pre-
conceived line of development, and he believed that
political and industrial methods were not irreconcilable.

This seems the right place to bring into view Hardie's
opinions on the general strike. He had endeavoured,
without success, to get the I.L.P. to put down a resolution in favour of a general strike for the achievement of
a universal eight-hours' day, and in the "Labour
Leader" he expressed regret that an opportunity had not
been provided for discussing the proposal at the Congress. In this article he declared himself definitely in
favour of it, and adduced arguments which seem more
weighty to-day than they did then, perhaps chiefly
because the objective has changed from an eight-hours'
day to the much bigger one of making an end of war. It
must be remembered that Hardie had been cradled and
reared in the midst of industrial strife, and that though
he was now the foremost advocate in this country of
political action, and was continually advising the miners
that through the ballot box they could achieve their ends
more quickly than by industrial action, he had never
counselled them to let go the strike weapon. Throughout his American tour he had been impressed by the
backwardness of labour political organisation in that
country and by the readiness of masses of the workers
to come out on strike, and he believed that, by a policy
of this kind, the political actionists and the industrial
actionists in Europe might find common ground. He
did not, however, believe in any mere spasmodic lightning strike policy. He recognised that for successful
international action long preparation was necessary. His
suggestion was that the International Congress Bureau
should take charge of the movement, that the date of the
general strike should be fixed four years in advance, and
that the intervening time should be employed in

propaganda and organisation and in the co-ordinating of the labour sections in every part of Europe, America, and Australia. He believed further, that such a movement would force the hands of the international diplomatists, and compel them to agree to the establishment of common labour conditions in all countries. He, in fact, supported the general strike, believing that the more effectively it was organised the less need would there be for putting it into operation, while the preparations for it would tend to unify the forces working for international Socialism. It is not the business of the biographer to discuss these theories and policies, but simply to present as faithfully as may be the mental processes of the man whose life is being portrayed.

During the greater part of this summer, the I.L.P. was engaged in defending the right of free speech. Ever since its formation, the I.L.P. had used the open-air meeting to an extent never attempted previously. Wherever a branch of the party existed, the out-door Socialist meeting became a feature of the public life of the district. Exceedingly capable lecturers addressed these meetings. Assisted by local speakers who were always ready to reinforce the efforts of the more experienced platform orators, J. Bruce Glasier, Mrs. Bruce Glasier, Enid Stacy, Caroline Martyn, S. D. Shallard, Joseph Burgess, Tom Mann, Leonard Hall, Keir Hardie and a host of others, were continually on the move from place to place. In many places large audiences were attracted and Socialist leaflets and pamphlets were widely circulated. Naturally, the more conservative elements in the community did not look upon these signs of active life with favour, and in various localities they sought to invoke law and authority to stop the flood of, what seemed to them, pernicious doctrine. The usual result was to give the new movement a bigger advertisement. The greatest of these fights took place at Manchester. What was known as the "Boggart Hole Clough case" filled the papers for some time and excited every branch of the I.L.P. in the country. It was, however, only typical of what took place on a lesser scale in many other districts.

Boggart Hole Clough is a kind of glen situated in a public park then recently acquired by the Manchester City Council. The I.L.P. had been holding meetings there, and, on the plea that they were causing an obstruction, the Parks Committee decided to prohibit the meetings. The I.L.P. paid no attention to the prohibition, maintaining that there was no obstruction. Their speakers, however, were summoned before the stipendiary magistrate and fined. Two of them, Mr. Leonard Hall and Mr. Fred Brocklehurst, went to prison for a month rather than pay the fine. Week by week the prosecution of speakers and literature sellers continued. But the Party had determined to fight the matter out, and fight it out it did. Week by week the meetings were held and the audiences grew bigger and bigger. The accused persons, amongst whom were J. Bruce Glasier, Keir Hardie and Mrs. Pankhurst— the latter not yet notorious in the suffrage movement— defended themselves in court. Boggart Hole Clough and the Manchester Court House became the two most interesting places in Lancashire, both radiating valuable Socialist propaganda. Notices of appeal to higher courts were intimated, and Boggart Hole Clough threatened to become a national question. The stipendiary began to find excuses for adjourning without passing sentence. The climax came when Hardie intimated that he had four hundred and seventy-three witnesses to call. That finished it. There were no more prosecutions. By-laws were framed which enabled the

Parks Committee to climb down without too much loss of dignity, and the Boggart Hole Clough question ceased from troubling. The general effect was to confirm the British right of public meeting and freedom of speech, a right which not even the exceptional wartime regulations of recent years were able to destroy.

The free speech agitation was good for the I.L.P. At the Annual Conference held at Nottingham, in April, there had been some signs of lassitude, due probably to reaction from the extraordinary electioneering exertions of the previous year. A by-election in May, at Aberdeen, where Tom Mann polled 2,479 votes and reduced the Liberal majority from 3,548 to 430, had helped greatly to re-inspire the rank and file throughout the country with a belief that their movement was very far from being a forlorn hope; and now this struggle for free speech, which, on a smaller scale, had to be maintained in many other places than Manchester, provided just the kind of stimulus required for a party, which, if it were to continue, must be continually fighting and putting itself in evidence in competition with the other parties.

Following quickly upon this stimulus came the opportunity of a by-election at East Bradford, and it was decided to contest the seat, not with much hope that it could be won, but partly to test the strength of the movement in a district which was the birthplace of the I.L.P., and partly to exploit the opportunity for propaganda afforded by a contest which would arrest the attention of the whole country. Hardie himself was chosen as the candidate and entered into the fray with his customary vigour. "Not as one would," he said, "but as one must—that I suppose is the guiding principle, and so I go. We will make a fight of it, and the I.L.P. has never yet had occasion to regret its by-election contests, neither will it East Bradford."

J. KEIR HARDIE

It was a three-cornered contest, and like every other parliamentary election in which Hardie was one of the principals, was conducted with exceeding acrimony on the part of his opponents, the Liberals as usual carrying off the palm for unscrupulousness and making no secret of the fact that they were more concerned to keep Hardie out than to win the seat from the Tories. Three years of him at Westminster had been more than enough for them. In the words of T. P. O'Connor: "Keir Hardie had to be fought." In the end, the Conservative candidate was returned by a majority of 395 over the Liberal, and Hardie received 1,953 votes.

The orthodox political oracles were not slow to appreciate the meaning of the Labour poll. Said the "Times": "The Independent Labour Party seems to have drawn away votes in nearly the same proportion from the ministerialist as from the opposition." Said the "Morning Post": "We have no desire to make little of the Labour vote in Bradford, for it is clear that two thousand electors are ready to support a Labour candidate in both the Eastern and the Western divisions, and such a body might well hope to turn the scale in the event of a contest being confined to a Unionist and a Radical." They need have had no dread of that eventuality. The I.L.P. had no desire to become merely the deciding factor between the two political sections of capitalism. Its aim was to demonstrate the identity of interest embodied in these two sections and to organise the workers for the purpose of fighting both and of destroying the system which they represent. Hardie made this unmistakably clear, both in his "Leader" comments and in an article which he wrote for the "Progressive Review," at that time edited by William Clarke. In this he derided the attempts of Liberal spokesmen to make out that the Liberal Party and the

I.L.P. had common aims and needed each other's help. This article was replied to in the same magazine by Mr. Herbert Samuel, then regarded as one of Liberalism's coming men, a fact which is mentioned here simply to show how definitely the ex-miner was accepted as the exponent of the new political force. They might vilify and abuse and misrepresent him in their party press. They might ridicule and caricature him in their comic papers. But there was one thing they could not do. They could not ignore him. He was an established factor in the political life of the nation, and his influence had to be reckoned with in every move in the game of party politics. It must be said that Hardie never made any attempt to soften the asperities of political controversy. He was well endowed with that aggressiveness which is an essential part of the equipment of any man who seeks to make headway on the political battlefield, and he sought always to accentuate rather than modify the essential antagonisms between the old order and the new. The one thing he feared for the I.L.P. at this time was the possible sacrifice of independence for the sake of some immediate gain or illusory concession, and he seemed deliberately to maintain a situation in which compromise would be impossible.

Nor was it from the capitalist parties only that he had to face criticism. Strange to say, he was suspected by certain sections of the Socialist movement itself, notably, the Social Democratic Federation, which, in its weekly organ, "Justice," ostentatiously dissociated itself from Hardie on the ground that he did not represent the Socialist movement of this country. The chief counts against him were that in Parliament he had muddled the unemployment question, had at the International Congress identified himself with the Anarchists, and had said in the country that Socialism was not a question of economics at all—a series of charges which seemed to show that the capacity for misrepresentation was not monopolised by his capitalist critics. He replied by a statement of facts concerning his parliamentary work and his attitude towards Anarchism, and by a declaration of his Socialist principles, which, while it repudiated the charge of indifference to economics, showed quite clearly that he was not the same kind of Socialist that his critics claimed to be. "I am a Socialist because Socialism means Fraternity founded on Justice, and the fact that in order to secure this it is necessary to transfer land and capital from private to public ownership is a mere incident in the crusade. My contention is that under present circumstances we are under the necessity of keeping this side uppermost, and my protest is against this being considered the whole of Socialism or even the vital part of it." He was exposed to a perpetual cross-fire from capitalists, Socialist doctrinaires and laggard trade unionists, and there was never any danger of his controversial weapons becoming rusty for lack of practice. Intellectual stagnation was not possible for Keir Hardie.

A detailed chronicle of his public activities during these years would probably prove to be monotonous reading, but the experiences of that period were far from monotonous for those who passed through it. It was a period when the struggle between organised labour, nationally and internationally, seemed to grow ever fiercer and fiercer. Such a chronicle would have to tell the story of the long drawn-out Penrhyn quarries dispute, in which the owner of the soil asserted his privilege as a landlord and as an employer, by simply closing down the quarries regardless of the men's right to work, the consumer's demand for the commodity, and the State's overlordship. It would have to tell of the great

Hamburg dock strike, of the help given by the workers of this country and the strengthening of the International Labour alliance thereby. It would have to tell of the historic lock-out of the engineers, which lasted fully six months and revealed itself as a determined attempt on the part of the federated employers to destroy Trade Unionism. It would have to tell of the persecution, imprisonment and torture of Anarchists in Spain, of the consequent assassination of Canovas, the Spanish Prime Minister, and of the outburst of indignation on the part of the workers of all countries against the atrocious methods of the Spanish Government. It would have to tell of the expulsion of Tom Mann from Germany, and Macpherson, the "Labour Leader" correspondent, from France, and it would have to note the slowly gathering clouds of war which finally burst over South Africa and produced in this country a fever of Jingoism which threatened to extinguish the I.L.P. and all that Hardie and his associates had worked for.

To all these events and movements Hardie was in some way, directly or indirectly, related—through the "Labour Leader" and on the platform, giving to the wrongs of the oppressed at home and abroad, that sympathetic publicity withheld by the capitalist press and capitalist governments, raising funds for the relatives of men on strike or locked out, stating the men's case clearly and strongly, not merely in relation to the particular industry immediately affected, but in relation to the general Labour movement, and emphasising always the comprehensive significance of all these troubles as the inevitable outcome of capitalism in its present stage of development, finally curable only through Socialism. In these years Socialists had something more to do than propound theories about value and economic rent, and the people were in no mood either to listen to these theories or to understand them. For many of them the immediate struggle was with the wolf at the door, and the business of the Socialist agitator was to help his class to fight the wolf. It was a serious loss that Hardie was not in Parliament during those years.

His 1897 Christmas message in the "Labour Leader" is not pleasant reading. "I am afraid my heart is bitter to-night, and so the thoughts and feelings that pertain to Christmas are far from me. But when I think of the thousands of white-livered poltroons who will take the Christ's name in vain, and yet not see His image being crucified in every hungry child, I cannot think of peace. I have known as a child what hunger means, and the scars of those days are with me still and rankle in my heart, and unfit me in many ways for the work to be done. A holocaust of every Church building in Christendom to-night would be as an act of sweet savour in the sight of Him whose name is supposed to be worshipped within their walls. If the spiritually-proud and pride-blinded professors of Christianity could only be made to feel and see that the Christ is here present with us, and that they are laying on the stripes and binding the brow afresh with thorns, and making Him shed tears of blood in a million homes, surely the world would be made more fit for His Kingdom. We have no right to a merry Christmas which so many of our fellows cannot share."

It was not often that Hardie wrote with such bitterness, but his words were no more than an expression of the thoughts in many minds at this time.

Not alone did the industrial struggles and their concomitant miseries fill the minds of thoughtful people with fears for the future; there were also the continued outstretching of rival groups of capitalists in search of new markets and the military preparations of the several governments presaging international war.

In his presidential address to the I.L.P. Conference of 1898, at Birmingham, speaking of these ominous portents, he defined the I.L.P. attitude towards war. From this policy the Party has never wavered either before or since. His reference to war expenditure reads strangely in these later days when national indebtedness is computed by thousands of millions. "The terrible spread of the war fever in these closing years of the century," he said, "was to be deplored. The hundred millions of six years ago has become the hundred and six millions of to-day. Naval and military expenditure is for ever increasing, and no year passes without seeing its little expedition setting out with the object of grabbing land which is either of little use to hold or difficult and costly to retain. When every other voice is silent it is necessary that we should make it known that we are opposed to war on principle as well as on account of the cause for which it is now being waged. I do not say we should never fight. As Rider Haggard has said: 'The Almighty has endowed us with life and doubtless meant us to defend it.' War in the past was inevitable when the sword constituted the only court of appeal. But the old reasons for war have passed away, and, the reasons gone, war should go also. To-day they fight to extend markets, and no Empire can stand based solely on the sordid considerations of trade and commerce. This is running the Empire on the lines of an huckster's shop, and making of our statesmen only glorified bagmen."

The time was very near when these principles, so strongly enunciated, were to be put to the severest test, and all who adhered to them were to have their fidelity thoroughly tried.

At this Conference, Mr. John Penny became secretary

instead of Tom Mann, whose energies had of late years been more and more absorbed in the industrial side of the movement, especially those international aspects of it reflected in the Hamburg dock strike and in similar upheavals in the Australian colonies. Tom Mann's services to the I.L.P. in those early years when it was finding itself were undoubtedly of very great value, and Hardie, expressing the feelings of the entire membership, did not fail to pay tribute to them.

It must be stated here that, notwithstanding the optimistic declarations of Hardie and others, the I.L.P. was at this time passing through the most depressing period of its history. It had existed for five years. It had fought numerous by-elections, but had not yet a single representative in Parliament. It had ceased to grow. The number of branches reported year by year remained practically stationary, and many of these branches were merely nominal and consisted in some districts of small groups of die-hards who had no room in their vocabulary for the word defeat. The Party was at this time saved from utter stagnation by the annually recurring municipal elections, which served to maintain the fighting spirit locally, and by the indomitable persistence of its propagandists, of whom its founder and chairman was the chief. Hardie seemed not to know fatigue, or if he did, never showed it. It is not too much to say that it was his tireless efforts, carrying hope and inspiration to the faint-hearted and despondent, that kept the I.L.P. alive. The following itinerary of a fortnight's work set down by himself, will serve to show how fully his time was occupied by this propagandist and organising activity :—

Nov. 17.—Left home, 12 noon; reached London 10.45 p.m.

INDUSTRIAL STRIFE

Nov. 18.—Office work. Open-air meeting in West Ham at night.

„ 19.—Left London 7.15 a.m.; opened bazaar at Halifax at 2 30; spoke at Honley at 8 p.m.

„ 20.—Halifax Labour Church, two meetings.

„ 21.—Opened bazaar at 3; addressed meeting at Yeadon at 8.

„ 22.—Addressed meeting Mexboro'; 3 hours in train.

„ 23.—Mexboro' to Kettering in train 3½ hours. Feet wet trudging through snow. Meeting at 8.

„ 24.—Kettering to London. Meeting in Canning Town.

„ 25.—London to Pendlebury, 5 hours. Two committees.

„ 26.—National Administrative Council, 10 to 5. Conference Social 5 to 11.

„ 27.—10.30 meeting at Eccles; 3 p.m. ditto at Pendlebury; 6 p.m. ditto, ditto.

„ 28.—Meeting at Walkden.

„ 29.—Committee in Manchester at 4. Conference with Oldham branches at 8.

„ 30.—12.45 midnight, started home. Number of letters received and answered, 75.

In addition he had his "Labour Leader" articles to write, varying from four to a dozen columns weekly. How he managed to accomplish this work it is difficult to say. He had long ago acquired the faculty of being able to think and write under almost any circumstances, and much of his journalistic work was done in third-class railway compartments, amongst all kinds of travelling companions; but even so, the mental and physical wear and tear must have been most exhausting, not to speak of the irregularity of meals, and the constant change of sleeping accommodation. Yet he had never a grumble, and every new host or hostess found him cheerful and smiling and ready to adapt himself to every circumstance.

During June of this year he spent several weeks in South Wales. The great strike of the Welsh miners had already lasted thirteen weeks and there were no signs of a termination. The miners' demands were for a twenty per cent. increase, the establishment of a minimum wage, and the abolition of the sliding scale by which in the past their wages had been regulated.

Though discouraged by their own official leader, "Mabon," they had come out on strike to the number of ninety thousand in support of their demands, and there was privation all over South Wales. By a coincidence, the I.L.P. associated itself with the miners' revolt. The South Wales I.L.P. Federation had resolved upon a special organising campaign, and had engaged Mr. Willie Wright, a well-known propagandist, to carry through the work. As it happened, his arrival on the scene synchronised with the outbreak, and as most of the local I.L.P. men were involved in the strike, there was nothing for him to do but throw himself into the struggle.

If he could not form I.L.P. branches, he could form relief committees, help the women and children, stimulate the men, and through the columns of the "Labour Leader" make known to the Socialist movement throughout the country the real nature and consequences of the South Wales dispute. This he did most effectually. A "Labour Leader" relief fund was raised, committees formed to administer it, and many miners' children were thereby saved from absolute starvation.

One fact in connection with this relief fund ought to be mentioned. In response to a letter from Hardie,

INDUSTRIAL STRIFE

Mr. Thomas Lipton—now Sir Thomas—sent a substantial quantity of provisions. Hardie had refused to make use of Mr. Andrew Carnegie's money to advance his own political campaign in West Ham, but when it came to feeding hungry children, no rich man's money was barred, and he was even willing to become a suppliant on their behalf. Nor did he consider his freedom of action restricted thereby. Shortly afterwards he was exposing Lipton as a sweating employer in a series of "White Slaves" articles in the "Leader." On the question at issue he had given his opinion at the beginning of the dispute. His advice was that the men should stand firm for the discarding of the sliding scale, and that they should as quickly as possible join up with the British Miners' Federation, and he spoke scathingly of the Welsh and North of England leaders whose policy kept these districts isolated from each other and also from the main body, thus making a national policy for miners impossible.

When he visited the strike area in June, he found the military there before him, though there had not been the slightest indication of violence or law-breaking on the part of the strikers. At some of his meetings the soldiers were visibly in evidence, while at others they were known to be in reserve and within call at short notice, a state of matters which had an irritating effect upon the workers, especially upon the women folk, and on several occasions very nearly produced the result which the presence of the military was supposed to avert. The absence of rioting during this dispute was certainly not due to any lack of incentive on the part of the authorities.

In his public utterances Hardie did not hide his contempt for what he considered to be the timid and temporising attitude of the miners' representatives in Parliament, who had made no protest against the presence of the soldiers in Wales, and who, in his opinion, had utterly failed to make use of their parliamentary opportunities on behalf of the men on strike. Probably never more than at this time did he regret his enforced absence from the House of Commons. And, certainly, looking back on his activities during the Hull strike, we can easily imagine how, from the floor of St. Stephen's, he would have turned the eyes of the whole country towards South Wales, especially as in this case he would have been fighting for his own craft and speaking of conditions concerning which he had practical knowledge. The Welshmen, for their part, did not regard him as a stranger or outsider. They knew him to be a miner. If they had any doubt, his homely talk soon dispelled it. They had not forgotten his outspoken championship in connection with the Albion colliery disaster a few years previously, while the touch of religious fervour with which most of his speeches were warmed was very much to their liking. He addressed some fourteen or fifteen meetings, mostly in the Rhondda and Merthyr districts, and he has recorded the fact that there was rain at all these meetings, and that nearly every day he got wet through. In the Merthyr district the campaign was organised by the active spirits of the I.L.P., one of the most enthusiastic of these being Llewellyn Francis, of Penydarren, whose barber's shop became the rendezvous for all the most advanced men, whose assembling together provided the nucleus of that organisation which, two years later, sent Hardie once more to Parliament under circumstances which made that achievement seem almost miraculous. That this ulterior result had no place in Hardie's mind will be seen when we come to describe the electoral activities of that time.

The strike ended early in September in the defeat of

the men, who had held out for full six months. But it was not unfruitful politically. When it started there were no more than half-a-dozen branches of the I.L.P. in all South Wales. When it finished there were thirty-one, some of them with upwards of two hundred members.

In the second week of September a Conference of all the I.L.P. branches in the Merthyr, Dowlais, and Troedyrhiew Parliamentary Division was held in the Welcome Coffee Tavern, Merthyr, with David Davies, railway signalman, in the chair. Willie Wright was there also, as witness to the outcome of his labours; also Mr. Robert Williams, F.R I.B.A., an architect of some distinction, resident in London, but always actively interested in the welfare of his native Wales. Mr. Williams was a member of the I.L.P., contributing occasionally to the pages of the "Labour Leader," and had long been on terms of personal friendship with Hardie. During the strike he had rendered assistance, especially in the organising of concerts in London by a Welsh choir on behalf of the relief funds, and his co-operation in the project for the return of a Socialist representative had therefore considerable weight with the miners. At this Conference the resolve was taken that, come the General Election when it might, the Division would be fought for Socialism. From that day onward the preparations for a contest proceeded apace.

That the dissolution of Parliament could not be very far away was the general opinion in political circles, and the question as to what should be the I.L.P. plan of campaign was giving the leaders and the rank and file much concern. There were two possible policies. Either to encourage the branches to contest seats in a large number of constituencies and make the General Election a national propaganda campaign for Socialism, or to

contest a small number of carefully-chosen constituencies with the definite purpose of getting a few I.L.P.
members into Parliament. The N.A.C. favoured the
latter policy and recommended to the Annual Conference at Leeds, in 1899, that twenty-five seats should be
fought and all the finance and electoral machinery of the
Party be directed towards winning these seats. This
was the plan agreed upon, but of course the advocates
of neither the one policy nor the other could foresee the
very exceptional conditions under which the election
actually did take place. Hardie himself had not at this
time been selected for any constituency. He had been
asked to allow himself to be nominated again for West
Ham, where there was every reason to believe he would
be successful, but Will Thorne having signified his intention of fighting the seat, Hardie abandoned it to him,
much to his regret. Thorne was subsequently elected.

This year took place what was known as the "Overtoun Exposure." This, though in perspective occupying
a very minor place in Hardie's life-work, must be
referred to here because of the sensation which it caused
at the time, the heart-searchings which it stimulated
amongst large sections of sincerely religious people, and
the striking illustration which it afforded of the evils
inseparable from modern commercialism. In the month
of April, a strike occurred amongst the labourers in
Shawfield Chemical Works, at Rutherglen, near Glasgow. Had the demands of the men, which were
absurdly moderate, been granted, there would probably
have been no Overtoun exposure. They were refused,
and the workers, who were totally unorganised, solicited
the help of the "Labour Leader" to give publicity to
their grievances. Inquiries were made and revealed
very grievous conditions. It was found that the men
had to work twelve hours a day for seven days a week,

and that without any meal time; that the wages paid were 3d. and 4d. an hour; that the nature of the work in the manufacture of chrome potash was exceedingly injurious to the health of the workers, producing virulent and incurable skin diseases, and affecting devastatingly the respiratory and digestive organs; that there was no attempt by the management to provide adequate protection against these physical evils; and that the sanitary arrangements in some parts of the works were nil, and in other parts limited to the bare minimum enjoined by law.

The head of the firm and virtual owner was Lord Overtoun, a gentleman held in the highest esteem in religious and philanthropic circles for his good works. He had been made a peer in recognition of his "great worth as a moral and religious reformer." His estimated spendings on charity amounted to £10,000 a year. He was a leading light in the councils of the Free Church of Scotland, and was himself a frequent preacher of the "Gospel of Christ." He was a noted temperance reformer. He was opposed to Sabbath desecration, and had headed deputations in opposition to the running of Sunday trams in Glasgow. In politics he was a Liberal and contributed substantially to the party funds. The "Labour Leader," in a series of articles which, because of the controversy created, continued for several months, depicted these two contrasting sets of facts. The circulation of the "Leader" went up by leaps and bounds. The articles were reproduced in pamphlet form and the sale was enormous. Then there came a day when the printer of the "Labour Leader" refused to print any more references to Lord Overtoun, and the paper appeared with a blank page, save for an explanatory note by David Lowe, the managing editor. Another printer was got, and the paper came out the following

week with the Overtoun article included. An inter-
dict was obtained against one of the pamphlets because
of a personal reference to a certain clergyman who had
tried to defend Lord Overtoun. The offending passage
was deleted, and the pamphlet went out to meet a
demand which had only been increased by the attempt
to prevent its publication. And so the interest kept on
growing—likewise the number of Hardie's friends and
enemies, the latter, of course, attributing to him the
worst of motives, and in some cases actually construing
his action as an attack on religion. There was no
possible answer to the exposure except that which placed
religion and business in two separate compartments—
an answer which of necessity proved the contention
of the Socialists that religion and capitalism were
incompatible.

The vindication of the exposure was found in the
fact that as the controversy went on the conditions inside Shawfield Works kept improving. Sunday labour
was reduced to the absolute minimum necessitated by
the nature of the trade, better sanitary arrangements
were introduced and wages in some degree increased.

By the time this local agitation had come to an end,
something had happened which absorbed the attention
of the whole nation, and made it necessary for the
British Socialist movement to define its attitude towards
British imperialist policy. Great Britain was at war
with the two South African Republics.

CHAPTER SEVEN

THE SOUTH AFRICAN WAR—MERTHYR TYDVIL

THE history of the South African War has been written officially from the standpoint of the British Government and also unofficially by various writers who do not all agree in their ascriptions of causes and motives. What we are concerned about here is the attitude of the I.L.P. towards the war and the part played by Keir Hardie during that time. Happily it is possible to set forth the I.L.P. attitude quite clearly without much traversing of ground which is covered by the historians.

On September 9th, 1899, five weeks before the outbreak of war, the National Administrative Council of the I.L.P. met at Blackburn and adopted the following resolution, equivalent to a manifesto, for circulation amongst its branches and for general publication :—

"The National Administrative Council of the I.L.P. protests against the manner in which the Government, by the tenor of their dispatches and their warlike preparations, have made a peaceful settlement difficult with the Transvaal Republic.

"The policy of the Government can be explained only on the supposition that their intention has been to provoke a war of conquest to secure complete control in the interests of unscrupulous exploiters.

"A war of aggression is, under any circumstances, an outrage on the moral sense of a civilised community and in the present instance particularly so, considering the sordid character of the real objects aimed at.

J. KEIR HARDIE

"It is especially humiliating to the democratic instincts of this country that an ulterior and unworthy motive should be hidden under pretence of broadening the political liberties of the Uitlanders. Even if the admitted grievances of the Uitlanders were the real reason of the threatened hostilities, war would be an extreme course quite uncalled for.

"We also protest against the action of the press and the bulk of the leading politicians in strengthening the criminal conduct of the Government by misleading the public and rousing the passion for war, and we express the hope that it may not yet be too late for the manhood of the nation to prevent this outrage upon the conscience of our common humanity."

This, let it be repeated, was five weeks before the outbreak of war. The members present were J. Keir Hardie (in the chair), France Littlewood, J. Bruce Glasier, Philip Snowden, H. Russell Smart, J. Ramsay MacDonald, James Parker, Joseph Burgess and John Penny (Secretary). In thus definitely and uncompromisingly setting forth the I.L.P. conception of the causes of the war and the Party's policy towards it, the N.A.C. took a step which decided, amongst other things, that for several years to come the I.L.P. would be the most unpopular Party and its adherents and leaders the most bitterly abused persons in the country. The Liberal Party escaped this odium by reason of the fact that having no alternative policy, it virtually acquiesced in the war, while criticising the diplomacy which had brought it about. Some few men there were in both of the orthodox parties who rose above party and even above class interests. Sir Edward Clarke, Q.C., one of the ablest of Tories, and destined in the ordinary course of events to reach the Woolsack, openly opposed the Government policy and sacrificed the remainder of his political life rather than be a consenting party to what he described as an absolutely unnecessary war caused by diplomatic blundering, the real responsibility for which, he declared, "rested upon Mr. Chamberlain and Sir Alfred Milner." On the Liberal side, Sir Robert Reid (now Lord Loreburn), Mr. James Bryce, Mr. John Morley, Mr. Lloyd George and Mr. John Burns spoke out strongly, but their utterances were more than counterbalanced by the Imperialistic declarations of Lord Rosebery, Sir Edward Grey and Mr. Asquith, the real mouthpieces of official Liberalism. Sir William Harcourt and Sir Henry Campbell-Bannerman at the beginning blew neither hot nor cold. Inside the House of Commons, the only definite opposition came from the Irish Party. Outside in the country, the only British political parties opposing the war policy were the I.L.P. and the S.D.F., parties without a single representative in Parliament. The press, with the exception of the "Morning Leader," the "Manchester Guardian," the "Edinburgh Evening News," and Mr. Stead's monthly, "Review of Reviews," was wholly with the Government, and soon succeeded making the war thoroughly popular with the masses and in creating an environment of intolerance in which free speech was well-nigh impossible. To Hardie and the other I.L.P. leaders it was a source of satisfaction to find that they had the support of the rank and file membership. Indeed, it is not too much to say that the membership of the I.L.P. constituted the only section of the community that was well informed concerning the questions at issue. South African affairs had received special attention in the "Labour Leader," and latterly, a series of articles signed "Kopje," which was the *nom de plume* of an exceedingly capable South African journalist, provided the readers of Hardie's paper with an account of the doings of the Chartered Company's agents and officials as viewed through other glasses than those of the Imperialist or the gold seeker, and described the development of the Cecil Rhodes' policy as it affected the natives, the Boer farmers and the Chartered Company's white employees, otherwise known as Uitlanders. Other writers in the same paper had turned a somewhat piercing searchlight upon the share lists of the Chartered Company and De Beers Ltd., and upon the manner in which influential members of these companies with high social status in this country were in a position to influence the colonial policy of the Government, itself well impregnated with Imperialist tendencies. I.L.P. members were therefore quite able to distinguish between the ostensible and the real causes of the war. They did not believe that it was a war to right the wrongs of the Uitlanders. They did not believe that the military power of Great Britain was being used merely to establish franchise rights in the Transvaal which had been refused to the people at home for half a century and were still withheld from womenfolk in this country. They *did* believe that already the process of fusion between the Dutch settlers and the British incomers had begun, and would, in course of time quite measurable, complete itself through intermarriage, social intercourse and mutual interest. They knew something about the diamond mines and the gold mines, the De Beers' compounds and the forced native labour, and they believed with their National Executive that the war was a "war of conquest to secure complete control of the Transvaal in the interests of unscrupulous exploiters." When Hardie, Glasier, MacDonald, Snowden and the other leaders declared wholeheartedly against the war, it was with the knowledge that they had their people behind them, few in numbers comparatively, but dependable and stout of heart.

To the I.L.P., however, the struggle raised a question much greater than whether Boer or Briton would rule in South Africa. It involved matters materially affecting the process of world development towards Socialism. Hardie expressed this view with much clearness. "In the transition stage," he said, "from commercialism to Socialism, there must needs be much suffering. All new births are the outcome of pain and sorrow. It was so when England passed from the pastoral into the commercial stage. So, too, when the machines began to displace the hand, and the factory the cottage forms of industry. For two generations there were want and woe in the land. So, too, must it be when the change from production for profit to production for use is made. A great and extended Empire lengthens the period required for the change and thus prolongs the misery, and it follows that the loss of Empire would hasten the advent of Socialism. The greater the Empire the greater the military expenditure and the harder the lot of the workers. Modern imperialism is, in fact, to the Socialist, simply capitalism in its most predatory and militant phase."

Such reasoning was incomprehensible to a populace whose mentality seemed to be well expressed by Lord Carrington, when he said : "We must all stop thinking till the war is over," a condition of mind certainly very essential to the maintenance of the war spirit. The British nation, however, was not allowed to stop thinking for long. This war, like all other wars, did not go according to plan. It began in October. By Christmas Day Methuen had been defeated at Modderfontein. An entire British regiment had laid down its arms. General White was besieged in Ladysmith. Cecil Rhodes, in whom was personified the capitalist interests at stake, was in danger of capture at Kimberley, and General

J. KEIR HARDIE

Roberts was on order for the seat of war (with Kitchener soon to follow), and ever more troops were being drafted out.

In face of these realities the jingo fever temporarily cooled down, and in the slightly saner atmosphere other people than the Socialists began to consider whether a movement for peace could not now be started. On Christmas Eve, Silas Hocking, the novelist, writing from the National Liberal Club, sent out the following letter to the press :—

"Sir,—There are many people who think, with myself, that the time has come when some organised attempt should be made by those who believe in the New Testament to put a stop to the inhuman slaughter that is going on in South Africa—a slaughter that is not only a disgrace to civilisation, but which brings our Christianity into utter contempt. Surely sufficient blood has been shed. No one can any longer doubt the courage or the skill of either of the combatants, but why prolong the strife? Cannot we in the name of the Prince of Peace cry 'Halt!' and seek some peaceful settlement of the questions in dispute? As the greater, and as we think the more Christian, nation we should cover ourselves with honour in asking for an armistice and seeking a settlement by peaceful means. We can win no honour by fighting, whatever the issues may be. In order to test the extent of the feeling to which I have given expression and with a view to holding a conference in London at an early date, I shall be willing to receive the names of any who may be willing to co-operate."

Canon Scott Holland, preaching in St. Paul's Cathedral, sounded an even higher note. "We should humiliate ourselves for the blundering recklessness with which we entered on the war, and the insolence and arrogance which blinded us so utterly. Let there be no more vain-glory, no more braggart tongues, and let us at the beginning of the New Year find our true understanding." As an immediate result of these appeals and the conference which followed, the "National Stop-the-War Committee" was brought into existence. This, with its auxiliary committees throughout the country, organised huge peace demonstrations in most of the big centres of industry during the winter. In nearly every case these demonstrations had to fight against organised hooliganism stimulated by the jingo press and the jingo music halls, and inflamed to delirious passion as the tide of war began to turn and the news of British victories came across the wires.

The I.L.P. naturally associated itself prominently with this Stop-the-War movement, and its leaders, especially Hardie as the recognised "head and front of the offending," had directed against them, not only the virulence of the war press, but frequently the unrestrained violence of the mob—unrestrained, at least, by the official maintainers of Law and Order, though voluntary bodyguards were soon forthcoming, and the physical force patriots learned, some of them to their cost—as they were taught again some years later—that the advocates of peace were, on occasion, capable of meeting force with force. In spite of all the brawling intimidation of the war party, many successful demonstrations were held. At Leeds, Manchester, York, Birmingham, Glasgow, Edinburgh and various other places, the advocates for a peaceful settlement on honourable terms were able to get a hearing, and the very violence of the opposition secured for them some press attention, which, though mostly derisive, advertised the purposes of the movement. The Glasgow meeting was probably typical of the others. It was organised by a local committee of which David Lowe, of the "Labour Leader," was secretary. The chairman was Baillie John Ferguson, of the Liberal Association. The speakers were Mr. Cronwright Schreiner, of the Cape Parliament, Mr. Lloyd George, and Mr. K. J. Wilson.

Keir Hardie, Robert Smillie, Joseph Burgess, W. M. Haddow and prominent local I.L.P. men were present, not as speakers, but as directors of the defending forces. The preparations were as for a pitched battle. Before the doors were opened to the public, the hall was nearly filled with assured supporters. Outside there was an expectant mob of many thousands, conspicuous amongst them being University students and habitués of Glasgow Clubland, and when at last the doors were opened there was a mad rush as of stampeded wild cattle. Only a limited number got through the defences, and many heads were broken in the attempt. Inside the hall, the meeting went on. In the stairways and corridors, and at the back of the area, the battle raged. The police, whose headquarters were next door, held aloof with a serene impartiality equivalent to an encouragement to riot, until towards the end, by orders of the Sheriff, and to save the hall property from being wrecked, they were compelled to come into action. The meeting, however, was held. Lloyd George escaped unscathed, thanks to Socialist protection, and, as history tells, lived to become the War Spirit's most blind and excellent instrument. The following week at Dundee and Edinburgh similar scenes were enacted, and Hardie, who was the principal speaker, was only saved from maltreatment by a Glasgow bodyguard that attended him at these places. It was a fine, exhilarating fighting time.

But Hardie at this time was doing better work than

at peace demonstrations. He was wielding his pen with a skill and prowess such as he had never exhibited before, and with the possession of which he has not even yet been credited, so much has it been the habit to regard him either as a mob orator or as a parliamentary extremist. A perusal of the files of the "Labour Leader" for this period will reveal Hardie as a writer, the reverse of declamatory and devoid of those florid superficialities common to controversial journalism.

An article under the heading of "A Capitalist War," which he contributed to "L'Humanité Nouvelle," and which was reproduced in the "Leader," is perhaps as fine an example of compressed but accurate historical writing as is to be found anywhere. It traces, step by step, the development of South Africa from the first Dutch settlement down through the successive treks, the founding of the Dutch Republics, the discovery of the gold fields, and the consequent incursion of the speculators and exploiters, involving the British Government in their adventures, and steadily as fate driving the Boers into a corner in which they must either fight, or surrender their national existence. He verifies all his statements, produces his facts and authorities, draws comparisons between ancient and modern imperialism, and sums up his argument with a literary skill all the more effective because it is unaffected and does not pretend to be literary. This was his conclusion: "The war is a capitalist war. The British merchant hopes to secure markets for his goods, the investor an outlet for his capital, the speculator more fools out of whom to make money, and the mining companies cheaper labour and increased dividends. We are told it is to spread freedom and to extend the rights and liberties of the common people. When we find a Conservative Government expending the blood and treasure of the nation to extend the rights and liberties of the common people, we may well pause and begin to think." The latent unforced sarcasm of that last sentence is characteristic of a literary style which is not dependent upon expletives or invective for its strength.

At this high level he kept writing all through the war, reviewing Bryce's "Impressions of South Africa" or J. A. Hobson's "The War in South Africa," criticising the supineness of the Liberal Party, examining the Government's defence of its policy and exposing its evasions, and commenting upon the incidents of the war with a wealth of argument, illustration and appeal, directed always to the one conclusion, that the war must. be stopped. The pity of it was, that all this fine work was limited in its effect, and never reached the people who could have most profited by it.

The "Labour Leader," of course, shared in the unpopularity of its editor and its party, and the circulation declined, thereby circumscribing the scope of its influence. The lack of a newspaper press capable of competing with the lavishly financed journalism of the vested interests has always been the chief handicap of the Socialist movement. Had Hardie been possessed of a publicity organisation such as has always been at the service of the leaders of other political parties, his worth would have been recognised much earlier, his influence in his lifetime would have been greater, and some more important person than the present writer would be at work on his biography. It was the same lack of a publicity medium that made it necessary for the I.L.P. to have its anti-war manifesto placarded on walls throughout the country. There was no other method of proclaiming its views on a national scale, and even this was not very effective, as in many places the bills were torn down almost as soon as they were posted.

LABOUR PARTY

Amid all this war controversy and tumult, the political education and organisation of labour moved quietly forward. This year was formed the Labour Representation Committee, which became the Labour Party of the present day, and now challenges the other political parties for control of the government of the nation. The first step was taken in Scotland. On Saturday, January 6th, 1900, what was described as "the most important Labour Conference ever held in Scotland," met in the Free Gardeners' Hall, Picardy Place, Edinburgh, when two hundred and twenty-six delegates came together for the purpose of agreeing upon a common ground of political action and of formulating a programme of social measures upon which all sections of the workers might unite. Robert Smillie was in the chair, and amongst those on the platform were Keir Hardie of Cumnock, Joseph Burgess and Martin Haddow of Glasgow, Robert Allan of Edinburgh, John Carnegie of Dundee, John Keir of Aberdeen, with John Penny, Bruce Glasier and Russell Smart holding a watching brief for the I.L.P. National Council. As this meeting is, in a sense, historical, it may be well to place on record its composition. Trade Unions sent one hundred and sixteen delegates. Trades Councils twenty-nine, Co-operative organisations twenty-eight, Independent Labour Party branches thirty-four, Social Democratic Federation branches nineteen. The acting Secretary was George Carson of Glasgow, whose activities in the formation of the Scottish Trades Union Congress, in 1897, had brought him in close touch with every section of organised labour in Scotland, and this connection he now utilised in getting the present Conference together. Smillie, in his brief remarks as Chairman, went as usual straight to the root of the matter. "They had had enough of party trimming and

J. KEIR HARDIE

sham fighting, and were determined to be done with that once for all and have Independent Labour representation." The following resolution was adopted : "Recognising that no real progress has been made with those important measures of social and industrial reform that are necessary for the comfort and well-being of the working classes, and further recognising that neither of the two parties can or will effect these reforms, this Conference is of the opinion that the only means by which such reforms can be obtained is by having direct independent working-class representation in the House of Commons and on local administrative bodies, and hereby pledges itself to secure that end as a logical sequence to the possession of political power by the working classes."

An amendment to strike out the word "independent" was defeated by a large majority, as was also another amendment to define the object of the Conference as being "to secure the nationalisation of the means of production, distribution and exchange." The Conference, it will thus be seen, while breaking completely with the political traditions of the past, refrained from identifying itself with Socialism. It was a Labour Representation Conference, that, and nothing more. There is no need to detail the other proceedings of the Conference, as its decisions and the organising machinery which it outlined were, for the most part, incorporated in the programme and constitution of the larger national Conference which was held in London in the following month, but it will be agreed that an account of the Labour Party movement would be incomplete, if it failed to take note of this rather notable Scottish gathering.

The date of the British Conference was February 27th, 1900, the place of meeting the Memorial Hall, London. It was the outcome of a resolution passed by the Trades

Congress the previous year, which itself was the culminating sequel to the many debates initiated by Hardie on
the floor of the Congress in bygone years.   On this
occasion, however, the Congress, instead of remitting
the matter to the Parliamentary Committee, had
instructed that Committee to co-operate with the Independent Labour Party and other Socialist bodies.   This
joint Committee was duly appointed, and requested
J. Ramsay MacDonald to draft a constitution for the new
Party—a wise proceeding which enabled the Conference,
with the minimum amount of friction, to achieve the
purpose for which it had been called.

The proceedings of this memorable meeting are chroni-
cled in the official report and also in A. W. Humphrey's
admirable "History of Labour Representation." What
we are concerned with here is the part which Hardie
played in the Conference.   He was perhaps more deeply
interested in its success than any delegate present.   It
was for this, the political consolidation of organised
labour, that he had given the greater part of his life,
and although he knew well that this was not the end,
but only the essential means to the end, namely, labour's
conquest of political power, for that very reason he was
keenly alive to the possibility of failure at this particular
juncture.   Against any such mischance he was watchfully
on guard.   The danger of a breakdown lay in the
different, almost antagonistic, conceptions of what should
be the composition and function of a Parliamentary
Labour Party held by certain Trade Union sections and
by certain Socialist sections.   The question of the formation of a Labour group in Parliament was the danger
point. Against a proposal by James Macdonald of the
S.D.F. that Socialism be adopted as a test for Labour
candidates, an amendment by Wilkie of the Shipwrights
making a selected programme the basis and leaving the

members free outside the items which it contained, had been carried after a somewhat acrimonious debate.

This was altogther too loose and indefinite, and Hardie intervened with a resolution in favour of establishing a distinct Labour group in Parliament, which should have its own whips and agree upon a policy embracing a readiness to co-operate with any party which, for the time being, might be engaged in promoting legislation in the distinct interest of Labour, and, conversely, to associate itself with any party in opposing measures having an opposite tendency; and further, no member of the Labour group should oppose a candidate whose candidature was promoted by any organisation coming within the scope of Resolution No. 1. Wilkie withdrew his proposal and Hardie's resolution became the finding of the Conference. Its virtue lay in the fact that it committed the delegates, Socialist and Trade Unionist alike, to the formation of an Independent Parliamentary Labour group, and also provided that temporary alliances with other parties should be determined, not by the individual members, but by the group itself acting as a unit. Probably these disciplinary implications were not fully grasped by some of the Trade Unionists, but that was not Hardie's fault. He never at any time wilfully left his meaning in doubt, either to the one section or the other. He was a Socialist, but this was not a Socialist Conference, and even if it had been possible by a majority vote to make it so, that would have been an unfair departure from the purpose for which it was called. The one thing to do at that moment was to make Labour Representation a fact. "The object of the Conference," he said, referring to the S.D.F. resolution, "was not to discuss first principles, but to ascertain whether organisations representing different ideals could find an immediate and common ground of

action, leaving each organisation free to maintain and
propagate its own theory in its own way; the object of
the Conference was to secure a united Labour vote
in support of Labour candidates and co-operation
amongst them on Labour questions when returned."
In this way, and on that basis, the L.R.C., as it was
familiarly called, came into being.

The first Chairman was F. W. Rogers, of the Vellum
Binders' Union, who will be chiefly remembered for his
persistent pioneering of the Old Age Pension movement. The first Treasurer was Richard Bell, of the
Railway Servants. The I.L.P. delegates on the first
Executive were Keir Hardie and James Parker. The
S.D.F. were represented by Harry Quelch and James
Macdonald, and the Fabian Society by E. R. Pease.
Thus all the Socialist sections had a place in the
councils of the new Party, though the S.D.F. seceded
later. The Secretaryship was placed in the capable
hands of J. R. MacDonald, to whose appointment was
undoubtedly due the immediate recognition of the
L.R.C. as a new vital force in British political life.

Easter week brought the Eighth Annual Conference
of the Independent Labour Party (held this year in
Glasgow), an event which has its chief biographical
interest in that it marked Hardie's retirement from the
Chairmanship which he had held uninterruptedly since
the formation of the Party. The delegates seized the
opportunity to mark their high esteem and deep affection for the man whom all recognised as their leader.
During the session the business was suspended in order
to present him with an address wherein it was sought
to express "with gratitude and pride our recognition of
the great services he has rendered the Independent
Labour Party and the national cause of Labour and
Socialism." J. Bruce Glasier, his successor in the

J. KEIR HARDIE

Chairmanship, in moving the resolution, made a speech which is here reproduced because in some measure it reflects characteristics common to both men, and also because it indicates, in a manner which no amount of biographical detail can equal, the character of the work which had gained for Hardie so abiding a place in the hearts of the rank and file of the Party. "I have claimed of my comrades of the N.A.C.," said Glasier, "the privilege of moving this address as one of Keir Hardie's oldest personal friends and colleagues in the Socialist movement, and also as a fellow-Scotsman. It is with some emotion that I look back on the early days of my association with him, and consider how much has happened since then to forward the Socialist cause in our country. In those early days many of us doubted the wisdom of his political policy as we have not infrequently since had occasion to differ from him, but in most instances events have shown that his wisdom was greater than any of ours. In connection with the political issues before our Party and the country, Keir Hardie has displayed a truly marvellous insight, I would almost venture to say second-sight, for indeed I do not doubt that Keir Hardie is gifted with at least a touch of that miraculous and peculiarly Scottish endowment. In the House of Commons and in the country he has established a tradition of leadership which is one of the greatest possessions of the Socialist and Labour movement in Britain. His rocklike steadfastness, his unceasing toil, his persisting and absolute faith in the policy of his party, are qualities in which he is unexcelled by any political leader of our time. He has never failed us. Many have come and gone, but he is with us to-day as certainly as in the day when the I.L.P. was formed. By day and by night, often weary and often wet, he has trudged from town to city in every corner of the land bearing witness to the cause of Socialism and sturdily vindicating the cause of Independent Labour Representation. He has not stood aloof from his comrades, but has constantly been in touch with the working men and women of our movement as an every-day friend and fellow-worker. He has dwelt in their houses and chatted by their firesides, and has warmed many a heart by the glow of his sympathy and companionship. The wear and tear of these many years of propaganda have told somewhat on the strength of our comrade, but he has never complained of his task nor has he grown fretful with the people or their cause. On the N.A.C. his colleagues are deeply attached to him. He is always most amenable to discussion with them. They do not always agree with his views, but they have been taught by experience to doubt their own judgment not once, but twice and thrice, when it came into conflict with his. But I must not detain you with this ineffectual effort to express what I feel. I shall venture only one word more. Hardly in modern times has a man arisen from the people, who, unattracted by the enticements of wealth or pleasure and unbent either by praise or abuse, has remained so faithful to the class to which he belongs. His career is a promise and a sign of the uprising of an intensely earnest, capable and self-reliant democracy. He is a man of the people and a leader of the people."

These words, be it remembered, were spoken when the I.L.P. was passing through its darkest hours, when its teachings were unpopular and its adherents marked down as political Ishmaelites, and when militarism was rampant in the country; and their utterance at such a time indicates that not only Keir Hardie, but his colleagues and followers, were endowed with great faith and great courage, and explains how it is that the I.L.P. has survived through all the succeeding years. Hardie, of course, remained on the National Council, and his personality continued to reflect itself in every phase and aspect of the movement.

This Conference, which was the first since the outbreak of war, confirmed and reaffirmed absolutely the anti-Imperialist policy of the National Council, already spontaneously approved and supported by the branches. The Conference also issued a strong protest against all forms of conscription, and expressed "deep sorrow at the terrible famine that had fallen upon the toiling people of India," which, it declared, was to a great extent the result of the heavy taxation placed upon the people and the expropriation of their slender resources by the existing Government and capitalistic occupation of India.

To focus public attention upon this latter question was indeed impossible. The people of this country were so preoccupied by affairs in South Africa as to be incapable of realising the calamitious condition of India. The I.L.P. protest was like a very still small voice, yet some people heard it in that far away oppressed land, and appeals came to Hardie and MacDonald asking them to come and see for themselves how India was governed—appeals which, though they could not be responded to then, did not go unheeded.

A general election was now near at hand. The finish of the war, though still distant, was thought to be within sight. The trained British forces, two hundred and fifty thousand strong, were gradually overmastering the small volunteer armies of the Republics, and the tactical question for the Government was whether it would wait for, or anticipate, the final victory before going to the country. For the opponents of the war policy it did not matter which. They had little hope of coming out on top in existing circumstances, whilst the

Liberal Party, as Laodicean in its attitude on the terms
of settlement as it had been towards the war itself, had
no lead to give the people. Whether the election came
soon or late the return of the Salisbury-Chamberlain
Government was a foregone conclusion.

In an open letter to John Morley, Hardie made a
strong appeal to that statesman to cut himself adrift
from the Rosebery-Grey-Asquith section of Liberalism
and give a lead to democracy. "A section of very
earnest Liberals are thoroughly ashamed of modern
Liberalism and anxious to put themselves right with
their own consciences. Working-class movements are
coming together in a manner, for a parallel to which
we require to go back to the early days of the Radical
movement. Already, two hundred and twelve thousand
have paid affiliation fees to the Labour Representation Committee. What is wanted to fuse these elements
is a man with the brain to dare, the hand to do, and the
heart to inspire. Will you be that man?" Mr. Morley
did not respond. Probably Hardie did not expect him
to do so. But the nature of the appeal indicates the
existence of possibilities which might have considerably
changed the course of parliamentary history in this
country, and of Britain's international policy.

Hardie was specially desirous that in the forthcoming
election all the anti-Imperialist forces should work in
unison with each other, and, in the "Labour Leader,"
he invited opinions as to whether or not the I.L.P.
should issue a white list of candidates other than Labour
Party nominees, who, because of their consistent opposition to the war policy, should receive the support of
I.L.P. electors. He declared himself strongly in favour
of such a course, and specially mentioned such "unbend-
ing individualists as John Morley and Leonard Court-
ney," together with some Socialists like Dr. Clark and

J. KEIR HARDIE

Lloyd George. The latter name classified as Socialist, sounds strange to-day, but was certainly justified by some of the Welsh politician's utterances, publicly and privately, on social questions at that time.

The election came before the Party had made any decision regarding the suggestion, but there can be no doubt that it was acted upon, and that the anti-war candidates got the Labour vote.

The Special Election Conference held at Bradford on September 29th, decided: "That the full political support of the Party be given to the candidates of the S.D.F. now in the field, also to the Labour and Socialist candidates promoted by local branches of the I.L.P. in conjunction with other bodies, and to all candidates approved by the Labour Representation Committee; and that in all other constituencies, each branch be left to decide for itself what action to take, if any, so as best to promote the interests of Labour and Socialism."

Hardie was not present at this Conference, having already entered upon a fight in two separate constituencies, Preston and Merthyr. John Penny, the General Secretary, was also absent, acting as election agent at Preston. So rapidly did events move that the same issue of the "Labour Leader" which reported the Conference gave the result of the Preston election, Hardie being at the bottom of the poll with 4,834 votes as against nearly 9,000 given for each of the two Tory candidates.

It was a tremendous task Hardie had undertaken in contesting simultaneously these two seats, so far apart from each other, not only geographically, but industrially and politically. Yet the double contest somehow typified Hardie's personal attitude towards both political parties. Preston was a double constituency represented by two Tories. Merthyr was a similar constituency represented by two Liberals. It was as if they had been specially selected to exemplify his hostility to both parties, yet, when the dissolution of Parliament came, he had been selected for neither, and his course of action was undecided.

For months previously his colleagues on the N.A.C., desirous that, whatever happened to the other candidates, he should get back to Parliament, were on the look-out for a seat which would give him a reasonable chance of success—a seemingly hopeless quest in the feverishly patriotic state of the public mind. Merthyr, in view of his work amongst the miners, seemed the most promising. As early as March 21st, we find John Penny writing to Francis, who has been mentioned already, and who was now secretary of the Penydarren I.L.P., asking for an accurate and exhaustive report upon the advisability of running an I.L.P. candidate for Merthyr. The answer seems to have been indecisive yet encouraging, and, on July 25th, Bruce Glasier wrote the following letter, which is illustrative alike of the N.A.C.'s anxieties in the matter and of Hardie's personal disinterestedness where the welfare of the movement was concerned :—

"Chapel-en-le-Frith,

"*via* Stockport.

"Dear Francis,—Kind remembrance and hearty greetings to you. The N.A.C. meets on Monday at Derby, when we shall have to take the Parliamentary situation into most careful consideration. Among the most important things that we shall have to come to some conclusions upon, is the constituency which Keir Hardie ought to be advised to contest. We all feel that Hardie has a claim to the best constituency that we can offer him, and we also feel that it is of the utmost importance to the Party that he should be returned. Hardie himself does not view his being returned to Parliament as a matter of much moment, and he is only anxious that at least he should fight where a worthy vote could be obtained. But I am sure you will agree with us that if any single man is to be returned, that man should be Hardie. I am therefore going to ask you to kindly inform me as frankly as possible what you think would be Hardie's chances were he to contest Merthyr, and especially what you think would be the attitude of the Trade Unionists and miners' leaders. Hardie has himself a warm heart towards a South Wales seat—or rather, if you will, contest—but I am anxious that there should be at least a reasonable hope of a very large vote, if not actual success, before we consent to his standing. I am sure, therefore, you will give me your sincere opinion upon the matter. You might let me have a reply c/o Tom Taylor, 104 Slack Lane, Derby, not later than Monday morning."

Francis, upon whose judgment much reliance was placed, must have replied favourably, so far as the I.L.P. was concerned, but doubtfully with regard to the official Trade Union attitude, and raising questions as to financing the candidate, for the following week, on August 2nd, Glasier again wrote, explaining that "a strong election fund committee had been nominated, but that in most cases the local branches held themselves responsible for the expenses." In the case of Merthyr, if Hardie were adopted by the Trades Council, and the N.A.C. finally approved the candidature, the N.A.C. would, he was sure, contribute towards his expenses. If the Trades Council declined to be responsible for his candidature, and the I.L.P. agreed to run him with the approval of the Trades Council, the N.A.C. might constitutionally take the entire responsibility (with, of course, the utmost local help) of running him. "Hardie, if returned, would support himself by his pen and by lecturing, as he did when formerly in the House. There would be no difficulties on that score." The following passage is noteworthy for various reasons : "The election fund will be an entirely above-board affair. The money will be collected publicly, and we expect that many well-known advanced Radicals will subscribe. A. E. Fletcher, Ed. Cadbury, A. M. Thomson ("Dangle"), Arthur Priestman, etc., will probably be on the committee."

Still the negotiations proceeded leisurely and indecisively, due doubtless to the difficulty of bringing the official Trade Unionists into line, and probably also to the belief that the election could not come till the spring of next year. As late as September 19th, we find C. B. Stanton, miners' agent—whose strong support of Hardie at this time stands out in strange contrast to his violent jingoism fourteen years later—urging Francis, Lawrence, Davies and others, to attend a conference at Abernant on the following Saturday, to deal with the question of a Labour candidature; and on September 21st, John Penny wrote from Cardiff to Francis as follows : "This morning's London 'Standard' reports that at the conclusion of the meeting at Preston, Hardie promised to give his final decision on Monday next. Let me know if you expect him in Merthyr, and if he comes through Cardiff, you might let me know the time of his arrival so that I could meet him at the station and have a talk. I see that he is booked up to be at the Paris Conference next week. So, if he goes, there will not be much time for fighting. It is now honestly, Preston or Merthyr. My advice is go in and win. Saturday's conference must invite Hardie and so leave the onus of decision with him." And, finally, on the same date, Hardie himself wrote this note, also to Francis :—

"Dear Comrade,—Many thanks for your letter. *I have decided to accept Preston.* It is not likely now that Merthyr will succeed in putting forward a Labour candidate. Your wisest policy would be to defeat Pritchard Morgan, and thus leave the way open for a good Labour man at the next election. He is one of the most dangerous types the House of Commons contains.—Yours faithfully,

"J. KEIR HARDIE."

Merthyr seemed now completely out of the running, but the following day, September 22nd, the Abernant Conference adopted him and decided to go on, no matter what happened at Preston. Hardie, of course, did not go to the Paris International Congress. He addressed huge meetings at Preston, and immediately after the vote counting (the result of which has already been given) passed into Wales just one day before the polling, to emerge triumphantly as the junior Member for Merthyr, to the great bewilderment of the newspaper-reading British public, who had already seen his name in the lists of the vanquished.

The victory was practically won before he arrived on the scene, so enthusiastically did the local men throw themselves into the contest. The N.A.C. despatched Joseph Burgess to act as election agent, with S. D. Shallard as his assistant. Both of these worked with a will in systematising and co-ordinating the committees in the various districts and in addressing public meetings, but it was the people on the spot who had been looking forward to and preparing for this day during many months, and who by the most Herculean efforts brought every available Labour voter to the polling booths. It was they who won the victory. Their energies were directed wholly against Pritchard Morgan, characterised by Hardie as a "dangerous type." They did not expect, and, indeed, did not desire, to defeat D. A. Thomas, the senior member (known in later years as Lord Rhondda), who was one of the few Liberals definitely opposed to the war, and had thereby preserved the pacifist tradition of the constituency whose greatest glory was that it had sent to Parliament Henry Richard of fragrant memory, known as the Apostle of Peace and pioneer of arbitration in international disputes. Of Pritchard Morgan nothing need be said here, except that he was by profession a company promoter, and doubtless regarded a seat in Parliament as a valuable aid to his speculative activities.

Hardie only spoke three times in the constituency; once in the open-air at Mountain Ash, once at Aberdare, and once in Merthyr (indoors), and all on the same day. If there were any doubts as to the result, his appearance in the constituency at once dispelled them. Yet, coming on the back of his Preston exertions, the one day's labour amongst the Welsh hills in an atmosphere of intense excitement must have strained his powers of endurance to the utmost. Writing reminiscently when it was all over, he says : "I have dim notions of weary hours in a train, great enthusiastic open-air crowds in the streets of Preston, and thereafter, oblivion. Jack Penny tells me that my opening performance in one afternoon included almost continuous speaking from three o'clock till eight, with a break of an hour for tea." Yet he was defeated at Preston and victorious at Merthyr, though he only spent eleven waking hours in the latter constituency previous to the opening of the poll—eleven hours of "glorious life," with victory cheering him on.

J. KEIR HARDIE

And then that last tense experience as the votes were being counted. "The Drill Hall; the general presiding officer; the anxious faces of the watchers at the tables as the voting urns were emptied and their contents assorted. Joe Burgess, confident from the start; St. Francis, strained to a tension which threatened rupture; Di Davies, drawn 'twixt hope and fear; the brothers Parker, moved to the cavernous depths of their being. Di Davies looked up and nodded, whilst the shadow of a smile twinkled in his eyes. At length came the figures, and Di found vent for his feelings. St. Francis was not so fortunate. Who can measure the intensity of feeling bottled up in the unpolluted Celt? A great cheering crowd. A march to a weird song whilst perched on the shoulders of some stalwart colliers, I trying vainly not to look undignified. A chair helped considerably. That night, from the hotel window, in response to cries loud and long-continued, I witnessed a sight I had never hoped to see this side of the pearly gate. My wife was making a speech to the delighted crowd."

The desire to be near her husband at this time of crisis; perhaps even an intuition of victory, had drawn the hame-loving Scots guidwife all the way from quiet Cumnock to this scene of excitement, and probably here, for the first time, came to her some real revelation of the insistent call which kept her man so much away from his ain fireside. It was certainly a great gratification to Hardie to have his wife sharing in his triumph; a pleasure equalled only by his sense of the thrill of pride with which the great news would be welcomed by his old mother in Lanarkshire, from whom he had inherited the combative spirit that had kept him fighting from boyhood right up. To her was sent the first telegram announcing the result.

MERTHYR TYDVIL

The election figures were :—

D. A. Thomas ...	...	8,508
J. Keir Hardie ...	...	5,745
W. Pritchard Morgan ...		4,004
Majority for Hardie	...	1,741

He took no rest, but passed immediately into the Gower constituency to assist in the candidature of John Hodge, of the Steel Smelters, and it was not until the General Election was completed that he got home into Ayrshire to meet the eager, almost boisterous, greetings of his old associates.

Very happy weeks these undoubtedly were for Hardie. A natural man always, he made no secret of the pleasure he derived from the congratulations that were showered upon him at this time; but most of all he took satisfaction from the expressions of delight on the part of those who had been associated with him in his early struggles on behalf of a political Labour movement. At Cumnock, where he was fêted in the Town Hall, he found himself surrounded by the men who had shared with him the rough spade-work of twenty years before. James Neil, who had led many a picketing expedition, was in the chair. George Dryburgh was also there, and William Scanlon of Dreghorn, and many other veterans of the Ayrshire miners' movement. A speech by Alex. Barrowman so comprises almost in a single paragraph the whole philosophy of Hardie's career up to that time, that a reproduction of it is more valuable than whole chapters of minute biographical detail would be.

"Their townsman," he said, "had he cared to turn his talents to personal advantage, might to-day have been a wealthy man. Liberalism or Conservatism would have paid a big price for his services had they been for sale, whilst he might have found an easy life as a writer for the ordinary press. But he was not built that way. He had all his life been creating agencies through which the spirit of democracy might find expression, and had been content to sow that others might reap. Twenty years ago he might have found a snug berth as secretary to some old-established Union, instead of which, he came to Ayrshire where the men were not organised, and established a union that had now nine thousand members. Not finding any newspaper representative of his opinions, he had started one, and the 'Labour Leader' was now a recognised power. Seeing through what he conceived to be the hollowness of political parties, he set to found a Party of his own, and had succeeded, for the Labour Party was now a reality. Shallow people might say it was Mr. Hardie's perversity and masterfulness that made him do these things. In reality, they were the outcome of his intense earnestness, combined with his extraordinary energy and ability."

In truth, an admirable summing of Hardie's work and its impelling motives, and, accustomed as he was to misrepresentation, it was a joy to know that he was understood and appreciated by those who knew him best.

A poem addressed to him by an anonymous local poet, exemplifies, whatever may be its poetic merit, how far from being merely materialist was the appeal which his life had made to his comrades in Ayrshire.

"Brave Soul! From early morn till darksome night,
For ever leading in the fitful fight.
Come for an hour into our social room
And, heark'ning to our cheers, let fall the gloom
From off thy wearied face. Lay off your sword,
And laugh and sing with us around the board.
And when the night is done, your armour don,
And face again your fierce foes all alone—
Strong in the faith that Right at last will be
The mightiest factor in Society."

The Glasgow movement also organised a big congratulatory demonstration in the City Hall, where only eight months before he had been in some danger of physical assault.

The chairman of the Glasgow District Council of the I.L.P., W. Martin Haddow, presided, and on the platform, in the balconies, and in the area of the hall, Socialists, Trade Unionists, Co-operators, Irish Nationalists, besides men and women of every shade and section of advanced political thought, joined, as one press writer said, "to do honour to the man in whose triumph they seemed to see the foreshadowing of ultimate political victory for that democratic principle which concentrated the aims of them all." The Merthyr victory was indeed one of the great events of his life, bringing to him a sense of real personal achievement, and it was recognised as such by the people for whose appreciation he most cared. He enjoyed it thoroughly and made no attempt to disguise his pleasure. The following Sunday he spoke at a meeting similar to that at Glasgow in the Free Trade Hall, Manchester. During the next week he was banqueted by the London City Socialist Circle, and made a run into Wales for what proved to be a triumphal tour through his constituency, and then back into Ayrshire for a few weeks' much-needed rest and quietude in the companionship of his own household.

The children were now grown up and of an age to understand and take some pride in the work in which their father was engaged. The eldest boy, James, had just finished his apprenticeship as an engineer, the youngest, Duncan, was making a start at the same trade, and the daughter, Agnes—known familiarly as Nan— had also left school, and was assisting her mother in the housekeeping duties. Doubtless as they gathered

171

round the fireside they found much to interest them in
the tales their father had to tell of the big world in
which he had travelled so much; of what he had seen
in the American Wild West; of his visits to France,
and of the varied contrasting scenes of life in London
Town, and of the House of Commons and the strange
animals that frequented that place, to which he was now
going back again. He was a good story-teller, given
the right kind of audience, and what better company
could there be than his own young folk amongst whom
to fight his battles and live his life over again during
these few weeks of restfulness? And for them, too,
there was some compensation for having such an absentee
father. December 3rd saw him back at Westminster
taking his stand once again as a "one-man Party."

CHAPTER EIGHT

WHEN the new Parliament met, Hardie was the
only one of the six hundred and seventy
Members who put in an appearance without
being summoned to attend. All the others had, according to usage, been summoned by their respective party
leaders, Conservative, Liberal and Nationalist. The
Liberals even claimed Richard Bell, the other L.R.C.
representative. Hardie had no leader, and only
nominally had he a colleague. Yet he was not unwilling
to have one, as the following utterance shows: "I am
told there is a publication called the 'Gazette' in which
notices concerning Parliament appear, but never having
seen the publication I cannot vouch for the truth of the
statement. Leaders of parties, it seems, send out
notices to their followers concerning when Parliament
is to meet, and the fact that John Burns has not yet
taken to fulfilling this part of his duties accounts for my
having been unsummoned. It may be further noticed
that as the Labour Party has not yet appointed its Whip,
I am an unwhipped Member of Parliament. Does the
House contain another?"

There is here more than a hint that he would have
been willing to recognise John Burns as his leader, and
also a suggestion that the time was opportune for the
Trade Union Members of Parliament to cut themselves adrift from the Liberal Party and form a distinct

Labour group. The hint was not taken, and all through his second Parliament, as in his first, Hardie was condemned to "plough a lonely furrow." He did, indeed, continue for some months hoping that the working-class members would group themselves together at least for the purpose of taking common action on industrial questions, and it was certainly no blame of his that this did not take place. Again and again, at this time, he went out of his way to make public his appreciation of Burns's high debating powers, and his belief in the possibility of forming a parliamentary party under his leadership. But the hour had not come, and even if it had come, John Burns was not the man. Hardie himself was the man, but he had to await the hour—and the followers. In this House of Commons he was still an Ishmael. It was well for him that, in addition to his faith in the movement, he possessed what many persons did not credit him with, a lively sense of humour. The whimsicality of the whole situation gave him food for much quiet laughter.

A general election had just been held. The whole public life of the nation had been convulsed, and the result was a House of Commons in which the only new feature was Keir Hardie. The Salisbury-Chamberlain Government was in power as before. The Liberal Party was in opposition, and, as before, impotent and practically leaderless. The Nationalists were, as before, at the tail of the Liberal Party. It seemed as if the general election had been held for the sole and express purpose of getting Hardie back into Parliament. That, at least, was all it had achieved. In his present mood, Parliament and all its appurtenances seemed to him like a grotesque joke. Reference has already been made to his faculty for literary expression. If ever, as a supplement to this memoir, there should be pub-

lished a selection of his fugitive writings, there will
surely be included his impression of the opening of
this Parliament. It is replete with genial, yet caustic
sarcasm, of which a mere extract cannot possibly convey
the full flavour. After explaining the preliminary mum-
meries and their Cromwellian origin, he says, "new
members in the lobby are astonished at the procession
they now behold approaching. First comes a police
official, a fine, burly, competent-looking man; behind
him follows a most melancholy-looking old gentleman
who would make the fortune of an undertaker by going
out as a mute to funerals. He wears black cotton gloves,
his hands are crossed in front of his paunch, and he
moves sadly and solemnly behind the police officer. It
might be a procession to the scaffold so serious does
everyone look. Behind the mute comes 'Black Rod.'
He is gorgeously arrayed, not exactly in 'purple and
fine linen,' but in scarlet and gold lace. He moves for
all the world like an automaton worked by some
machinery which is out of gear. If ever you have seen
a cat, daintily picking its way across a roadway on a
wet day, you have some idea how General Sir M. Bid-
dulph approaches the House of Commons." And so
on, through all the proceedings down to the final exit
of the Lord Chancellor from the House of Lords, "a
squat little man, with a pug nose, trying to look dignified." Finally, we have Hardie's serious comment on
the whole ridiculous tomfoolery, which, as he sees it,
is "quaint without being impressive." "Times and circumstances have changed during the last thousand
years, but the forms of these institutions remain
practically as they then were, *which is typical of much
that goes on inside these walls.*"

A week or two later he was writing in a very different
mood, describing the naval and military pageantry,

attendant upon the funeral of Queen Victoria. The Queen died on January 21st, and it is significant that in the "Labour Leader" the following week, his reference was not to that event, but to the death of another—a comparatively obscure woman—Mrs. Edwards, of Liverpool, the wife of John Edwards, the founder of the "Reformers' Year Book." She had been one of the many intimate friends he had made during his travelling to and fro among the comrades. Of her he wrote : "She was the most kindly and unselfish creature that ever trod the earth. Her tact and her cleverness, her energetic spirit, and, above all else, the great soul, big enough, noble enough to forgive and sweep aside the faults of everybody and search out the kernel of goodness that is so often hidden by the hard covering of one's defects." Yet the omission of any reference to Queen Victoria's death was probably not deliberate. He was at the time in the North of Scotland, addressing anti-war meetings in Dundee, Aberdeen and Inverness, and in the midst of this work the news of the passing of his friend would affect him more nearly than the passing of the monarch.

Next week, he paid his tribute to the departed Queen. "It is as the pattern wife and mother, the embodiment of the virtues upon which the middle-class matron bases her claim to be considered the prop and mainstay of the race, that Queen Victoria was known and respected. The pomps and ceremonies of her station do not seem to have had any charm for her, whilst her manner of dressing was plain, almost to dowdiness. The quiet retreat of Balmoral, far removed from the turmoil and intrigue of fashionable society, had for her a charm which few can appreciate. The pomp and panoply of martial life was as far removed from such a life as anything well could be.

IN PARLIAMENT

"There are tens of thousands of loyal British subjects who loved to honour the Queen, who in their hearts resent the association of her memory with the military life of the nation, and in their name, as well as in my own, I enter my protest against the barbarous display of the bloodthirsty implements of war, amidst which the remains of a peace-loving woman will to-day be laid to rest."

The "barbarous display" took place in due course, and Hardie, in a very powerful description of it, which cannot be reproduced here, laid bare what seemed to him to be the sinister meaning and purport of it all; the militarisation of the very spirit of the nation, and the subordination of the true idea of citizenship. "In a constitutionally governed country, Parliament, not the monarch, is the real seat of authority. The soldier is the servant of the State. On this occasion the soldier was everything, the civilian nothing. The Members of Parliament, the chosen of the people, the real rulers of the nation—they came not to take part in the funeral, but stood upon the purple cloth-covered seats, and gazed like so many school-children upon the military thirty yards away. The administrative councils of the nation were totally ignored. The cadets of the Duke of York's Military Training College had a stand; the servants at Buckingham Palace had one; but there was no room in all the streets of London, nor in the public parks through which the procession passed, for a stand for the members of the London County Council.

"As for the seats of learning, the Christian Church, Science, Art and Commerce—they were all ignored. Having joyfully placed their necks under the heel of the soldier, they are each receiving their meet reward."

Thus, bitterly and prophetically did Hardie read the lesson of Queen Victoria's military funeral, the precursor of many a similar pageant, deliberately planned, as he believed, to overrule the naturally peaceful tendencies of the common people. Hardie was a Republican, but never obtrusively so, and on this occasion it was not so much the monarchy that was the object of his attack, as the aggressive militarism which sought to pervert the national respect for the departed monarch to its own sinister ends.

A few months later his views on the monarchical institution itself found an opportunity for expression when the revised Civil List, consequent upon the succession of King Edward to the throne, came up for discussion in Parliament. He had previously, on the King's Speech, endeavoured to add an amendment, which after thanking the King for his speech, expressed regret that the monarchy had not been abolished, which the Speaker had gravely, and without any apparent perception of the covert humour of the proposal, ruled out of order. He had also intervened in the debate on the expenses of the late Queen's funeral in a manner not pleasing to some of the Tory members whose unmannerly interruptions drew from him the remark that "honourable members sitting opposite are evidently not in a condition to behave themselves," a reference to the after-dinner boisterousness of the said honourable Members which the Speaker declared to be "offensive."

On the question of the Civil List he was not to be turned aside. Under the new proposals the provision for the Royal Family was increased from £553,000 to £620,000, but although, as a matter of course, Hardie objected to this increase and challenged every detail, it was on the ground of his "objections to monarchical principles" that he opposed the entire Civil List and divided the House, taking fifty-eight members into the Lobby along with him, John Burns acting as his fellow-

teller in the division. Of the fifty-eight, only four were
working-class Members. The other fifty-four were of
the Irish Party. The "Leeds Mercury's" description of
Hardie's deportment on this occasion may be quoted as
an aid to our general conception of the kind of man
he was, and also as a corrective to the widespread
misrepresentation of him as a mere self-advertising
demagogue. "Mr. Keir Hardie," said the "Mercury,"
"delivered a speech on frankly Republican lines. He
drew cheers from the Tories by admitting that the working class were now favourable to Royalty, and provoked
their laughter by adding that this was because the
working man did not know what Royalty meant. But
he quietly stuck to his point. The hereditary principle
whether in the Legislature or on the Throne, was, he
maintained, degrading to the manhood of the nation,
and it was the clear duty of men like himself to try to
get the nation to recognise the fact. This, and many
other things, he uttered in smooth, dispassionate, fault-
lessly fashioned phraseology. He is, in fact, one of the
most cultured speakers the present House of Commons
can boast. His doctrines are anathematised by some,
contemptuously laughed at by others, but he has a
Parliamentary style and diction that may put the bulk
of our legislators to shame."

These events and discussions extended over several
months, with much else in between, but are here grouped
consecutively, as the most effective means of setting
forth Hardie's views and attitude towards Royalty. He
never at any time went out of his way to attack the
Monarchy, but simply availed himself of the opportunities to do so, as they arose. His aim, of which he never
lost sight, was the building up of a Labour Party for the
realisation of Socialism. To this purpose, all other
questions were subsidiary or contributory. He recog-

nised very clearly that in his present situation, without the support of an organised party in the House, the only use he could make of Parliament was as a propaganda platform, and even that was determined, to some extent, by his power of arresting the attention of the capitalist press. And this he certainly succeeded in doing. The British people were never allowed to forget that there was a man in Parliament called Keir Hardie, or that he belonged to the dangerous fraternity of Socialists.

Right in the middle of this discussion about Royalty he found an opportunity for putting Socialism in the centre of the stage, so to speak, though only for a brief moment. April 23rd, 1901, is an historic date for the British Socialist movement. Hardie, in the private members' ballot, had been lucky enough to secure a place for that particular date, but unlucky enough to be last on the list. He put down the following resolution, which, as it is the first complete Socialist declaration ever made in the British House of Commons, must have a place in this account of the life of its author: "That considering the increasing burden which the private ownership of land and capital is imposing upon the industrious and useful classes of the community, the poverty and destitution and general moral and physical deterioration resulting from a competitive system of wealth production which aims primarily at profit-making, the alarming growth of trusts and syndicates, able by reason of their great wealth to influence governments and plunge peaceful nations into war to serve their own interests, this House is of opinion that such a state of matters is a menace to the well-being of the Realm and calls for legislation designed to remedy the same by inaugurating a Socialist Commonwealth founded upon the common ownership of land and capital, production for use and not for profit, and equality of opportunity for every citizen."

His presentation of this resolution was certainly a most remarkable parliamentary performance. It was half-past eleven before the preceding business was disposed of. At twelve o'clock the House must stand adjourned. At twenty-five minutes to twelve Hardie rose to put the case for Socialism to an audience mostly comprised of its enemies. Arthur Balfour was there, drawn, as one writer said, "by the metaphysical curiosity of the Scot, to amuse himself hearing what a brother Scot had to say on Socialism." John Morley was there, the parliamentary embodiment of individualist philosophy. The young Tory bloods were there, their hostility, for the moment, submerged in their curiosity. The Liberal commercialists were there, interested, but critical and incredulous. The Irish members were there, sympathetic and encouraging in their demeanour.

How skilfully Hardie performed his difficult task, let the capitalist press again bear witness. Said the parliamentary writer for the "Daily News" : " Mr. Keir Hardie had about twenty minutes in which to sketch the outlines of a co-operative commonwealth. He seemed to me to perform this record feat of constructive idealism with remarkable skill, and indeed it would be difficult to imagine a creation of human fancy that would produce more deplorable results than the society from which Mr. Hardie in his vivid way deduced the China Expedition, the South African War, and the London slums. Mr. Balfour, coming back from dinner, smiled pleasantly on the speaker, doubtless calculating that things as they were would last his time."

The closing sentences of Hardie's speech are worth preserving because of the prophetic note in them, which indeed was seldom absent from any of his utterances.

J. KEIR HARDIE

"Socialism, by placing the land and the instruments of production in the hands of the community, will eliminate only the idle and useless classes at both ends of the scale. The millions of toilers and of business men do not benefit from the present system. We are called upon to decide the question propounded in the Sermon on the Mount, as to whether we will worship God or Mammon. The last has not been heard of this movement either in the House or in the country, for as surely as Radicalism democratised the system of government politically in the last century, so will Socialism democratise the industrialism of the country in the coming century."

And as he said, so it is coming to pass. The new century to which he pointed is still young, but the democratising of industry proceeds apace. Shop stewards, workshop committees, Industrial Councils, Socialist Guilds, and in Russia, the Soviet system as a method of government, are all re-creating society on Socialist models. Many of the elements making towards the democratic control and direction of industry are now in operation, and so Hardie's prediction is in course of being fulfilled. Truly, it was not without reason that many of his associates ascribed to him the qualities of a seer.

Meantime, outside Parliament, the movement continued to move. The Labour Representation Committee had held its first Annual Conference, and was able to report an affiliated membership of 470,000 workers. All the Socialist bodies, I.L.P., S.D.F., and Fabian Society, were represented, and although the Conference rejected a resolution moved by Bruce Glasier on behalf of the I.L.P. declaring for an "Industrial Commonwealth founded upon the common ownership of land and capital," it adopted one brought forward by the Dockers, demanding "the passing of such laws as will put an end to a system under which the producer of wealth has to bear an enormous burden in the shape of rents and profits, which go to the non-producers."

The I.L.P. also, at its Annual Conference, held this year at Leicester, was able to report considerable progress, but naturally found its chief cause for self-congratulation in the fact that Hardie was once more in Parliament, his election being, in the opinion of the Executive, "a signal of battle, not only for the I.L.P., but for the entire Labour and Socialist movement of the nation." A proposal by the N.A.C. for the establishment of a "Payment of Members' Fund," having for its object to pay him £150 a year as "a compensation for the extra expenses and loss of time entailed upon him as a working Member of Parliament," was endorsed by acclamation, and on this modest allowance, raised by voluntary subscription, Hardie became, for the first time, a paid Member of Parliament. It is very doubtful if this sum ever covered his expenses. It certainly made provision for no more than very "plain living" to which happily he was well inured.

In the industrial world, also, events were shaping in a way calculated to impress even the most conservative sections of the workers with a sense of the need for parliamentary action. The Taff Vale decision, which rendered trade unions legally responsible for the actions of their least responsible officials, together with other decisions making peaceful picketing a criminal offence while leaving employers free to organise blackleg labour under police protection, struck at the very life of the industrial labour movement and converted to the policy of the I.L.P. thousands who could not be reached by street corner or platform agitation. Naturally, Hardie, MacDonald, Snowden, and the other Labour

Party advocates did not fail to exploit the situation to the advantage of their cause.

In the midst of all this work he contributed to the Co-operative Annual for 1901 an article, informative and suggestive, on Municipal Socialism, in which he summarised comprehensively the results achieved up to that time. The facts and figures have, of course, been superseded by new facts and figures, but his argument, based alike upon historical continuity and upon common sense, has not been superseded.

"The battle now being waged around Municipal trading is but the renewal of a struggle carried on for two hundred years against king, cleric, and lordling ere yet there was a Parliament in being. The issues remain the same, however much the methods may have changed. As the burghers triumphed then, so will they now. Already property of the estimated value of £500,000,000 has passed from private to public ownership. The citizens of our time are beginning to realise the benefits which follow in the train of common ownership. On every side can be seen the dawning of the idea that were the means of producing the fundamental necessaries of life—food, clothing, shelter—owned communally, as many of the conveniences already are, the problem of poverty would be solved."

In this way he sought to make it plain that Municipal Socialism was simply through Local Government administration an application of the co-operative principle.

About this time, and in all the following years, he was much in request as a lecturer by the Co-operative Educational Committees which were being formed throughout the country, largely as the result of permeation work by Socialist members of the various societies. To these requests he responded as often as his other duties would allow. His name invariably drew audiences composed not of co-operators only, but of the general public, brought by curiosity to see and hear the notorious agitator under non-political and therefore non-committal auspices. On these occasions he usually put party politics aside and devoted himself to co-operative propaganda.

Frequently, in illustration of the practical value of co-operative effort, he recalled how, in the early days of the Miners' Trade Union movement the establishment of the Co-operative shop in a district had enabled the miners to free themselves from the grip of the "Company's Stores," and had thereby given that self-reliance upon which their fight for better working conditions depended; a practical illustration which was easily understood, and paved the way for an exposition of the more far-reaching possibilities of co-operation.

He believed that the co-operative movement must in course of time, and of necessity, join hands with the Trade Union movement for the attainment of political power, but refrained from urging this too strenuously, lest premature action should be hurtful rather than beneficial to both movements. The co-operative movement has seldom had a more judicious or a more sincere advocate than Keir Hardie.

In July of this year, while Parliament was still in session, Hardie had his first touch of illness, and had to remain in bed for upwards of a week, a new experience to which he did not take at all kindly. The surprising thing to his friends was that he had not broken down sooner. He had, as one of them said, "been doing the work of several ordinary mortals." His correspondence itself was enormous, and he had no private secretary. His advice was sought by all sections of the Labour movement. Every day brought its committees, deputations, interviews and visitors from far and near; while every week-end found him on the propaganda platform in some part of the country, sometimes far distant from London. This entailed long, wearying train journeys. He recovered quickly, but it might have been better if he had taken warning from this first indication that his powers of endurance were being overstrained. He was immediately as busy as ever, both inside and outside of Parliament, but especially outside amongst the I.L.P. branches and trade unions, stimulating them to get ready with their candidates and organisation for the next general election which he was convinced would see a Labour Party very strongly entrenched at Westminster.

It must be said, however, that such opportunities as occurred for testing the grounds for this optimism did not give much encouragement. A three-cornered by-election contest in North-East Lanark found Robert Smillie once more at the bottom of the poll, and at Wake-field, in the spring of the following year, Philip Snowden was defeated by the Conservative candidate in a straight fight. Yet these seeming rebuffs notwithstanding, pre-parations for the election went on steadily, and the movement continued to grow in strength. These by-elections were regarded as merely experimental skir-mishes, and not symptomatic of the probable results in a general election fight.

Speaking at Clifford's Inn under the auspices of the Metropolitan Council of the I.L.P., Hardie said, "There were subtle causes at work which were hasten-ing the movement, and amongst them might be instanced such decisions as that recently given by the House of Lords in the Taff Vale case. The power of the trade unions through the strike had been immense, but their power through the ballot-box was immensely greater, and it was only necessary for their members to learn to vote as they had learned to strike, to secure their victory.

There was reason for looking forward with absolute confidence to the future."

In the midst of all this public activity Hardie was not free from the casual and inevitable cares and difficulties of family life which in some circumstances may be mitigated, but in none can be evaded. In January, 1902, his daughter Agnes, now verging into early womanhood, was taken dangerously ill, and for several weeks hovered between life and death. For the whole of that period the father was absent from Parliament and from the public platform. He was in Cumnock by the bed of sickness, nursing the girl, comforting the mother and hiding his own fears as best he could. In the first week in February, he was able, in the "Labour Leader," to assure enquiring sympathisers that the invalid was making fair progress towards recovery. "She is still weak, but with care that will pass." As a matter of fact, this trouble left effects behind from which she could never entirely shake herself free, and caused him to be always more tenderly solicitous for her than for the two boys who had inherited his own sturdy constitution.

In the last week of the following April came another trial, more inevitable, but none the less wrenching because it was inevitable. "On the night when Mr. Balfour gagged discussions regarding the Bread Tax, I found Hardie," wrote one of his friends, "in the inner lobby watching for a telegram. 'If I get a wire,' said he, 'I must leave for Scotland by the midnight train,' and at the time when the House was dividing he was going northward." He had been summoned to the deathbed of his mother and father. The two old people passed away within an hour of each other, and it could be said of them literally that "in death they were not divided." The now famous son, of whom they were so proud, was in time to bid them good-bye. A strange parting that must have been.

"Fear of death," wrote Hardie afterwards, "must have been an invention of priestcraft. He is the grim king for those who are left to mourn, but I have not yet seen a deathbed, and I have seen many, where the White Herald has not been welcomed as a friend and deliverer. These two talked about death as if it were an every day incident in their lives. They did so without emotion, or excitement, or interest of any kind. They were dying together, whereat they were glad. Had it been a visit to Glasgow, three miles distant, they could not have been more unconcerned. In fact, such a journey would have been a much greater annoyance to father. They never even referred to any question of the Beyond. As Socialists they had lived for at least twenty-five years, and as such they died and were buried. They had fought life's battles together, fought them nobly and well, and it was meet that they should enter the void together."

At their cremation a few days later, Hardie himself, amidst a gathering of mournful friends and relations, spoke the last parting words in the building where thirteen years later he himself was to be carried. Outwardly he was calm, inwardly he was deeply moved. "Henceforth," he wrote, "praise or blame will be even less than ever an element in my lifework. Closed for ever are the grey eyes which blazed resentment or shed scalding tears when hard, untrue things were spoken or written about me or my doings. Silent is the tongue which well knew how to hurl bitter invectives against those who spoke with the tongue of slander, and stilled are the beatings of the warm, impulsive heart which throbbed with pride and joy unspeakable when any little success came her laddie's gait." And with this sense of an irreparable void in his life, he turned to work once more.

When he returned to London he found it necessary to make another change in his way of living. The friendly household wherein he had been accustomed to sojourn during the Parliamentary session, had been broken up, also through death's visitation, and he had to look for a new home in London—a home which, in point of rental, would not be too expensive. He found it, after some weeks' house-hunting all over London, in Nevill's Court, Fetter Lane, off Fleet Street, at 6s. 6d. a week. Within a stone's throw of the "Labour Leader" London office, and twenty minutes' walk of Westminster, it was certainly quite near his daily work, and yet as remote from the bustle and turmoil of modern city life as if it were a survival of mediæval times round which the new world had built itself—indeed, it was such a retreat. It was a tumble-down structure of the fifteenth or sixteenth century, built of timber and plaster, and of a most uninviting exterior. Inside, it was better. The floor of the room had been kept clean by honest scrubbing, and a match-board partition had been put up so as to convert the large room into a sitting-room, bed-room and kitchen. There was a garden, "thirty inches wide and fifteen feet long," wherein he could grow, and actually did grow, Welsh leeks, and primroses and gowans transplanted from Cumnock. In a short time, artist and craftsman friends having come to his aid, "the gnomes were driven out and the fairies took posses-sion and transformed this corner of slumland into a very palace of beauty." "I would not," he said quaintly, "exchange residences with his most gracious majesty Edward VII, nor deign to call the King my cousin"; and here he settled down for that part of the remainder of his life which had to be spent in London. Hither, from

J. KEIR HARDIE

all parts of the country, aye, from all parts of the world, came those special and intimate friends who were of the Keir Hardie fellowship. Collier folk from Wales and from Scotland up to see the sights of London; poets and painters; sculptors and literary folk; exiles from Russia; home-returning travellers from Australia or America, came. An Indian prince at one time, a Highland crofter at another, and, of course, his colleagues of the I.L.P. Council and his own family folk from Cumnock and Cambuslang. Never was any notoriety-hunter or newspaper gossip-monger able to break into this sanctuary reserved for himself and his intimates, and sometimes for himself alone. For it was for him one of the attractions of this retreat that he could, when he chose, be alone with himself and his own thoughts. "More than irksome, it is demoralising to live always under the necessity of having to speak and be spoken to, to smile and look pleasant. Companionship is good, but solitude is best." In this abode, right in the heart of the hurly-burly, he could find solitude.

There are readers of this book who will be grateful for the following picture of Hardie in his London retreat as limned by himself on one of his nights of solitariness when he had it all to himself. Incidentally, also, it is somewhat self-revealing. "These jottings are made this week" ("Labour Leader," June 21st, 1902) "in the silence and solitude of my London mansion, which is the envy of all who have seen it. Outside, the barking of a dog is the only sound which disturbs the clammy night air. Despite an eighth of an acre of sloping roof, the Toms and Tabbies keep a respectful silence. Within, a fire burns cheerily, and the kettle sings on the hob. The flickering candlelight throws on to the walls quavering shadows from the tall, white-edged and yellow-breasted marguerites (horse gowans), the red seeding stalks of the common sorrel, the drooping yellow buttercups and the graceful long grasses which fill two graceful gilt measures and a brown mottoed beer jug. Here and there big purple bells and ruby roses lend a touch of needed colour. From the top of the tea caddy in the middle shelf within the deep recesses of the ingle nook, the dual face of Ralph Waldo Emerson, fashioned by the skilful hands of Sydney H. Morse, farmer, philosopher, sculptor, Socialist, looks sternly philosophic from his right eye across at Walt Whitman—a plaque containing a perfect replica of whose features from the same master-hand hangs opposite—whilst with his left eye the genial philosopher winks roguishly at Robert Burns in his solitary corner near the window. Florence Grove lives in the two pictures which adorn the wall, as does Caroline Martyn in the transparency for which I was long ago indebted to our energetic comrade, Swift, of Leeds, whilst big, warm-hearted Larner Sugden's presence can be felt in the little oak table with its quaint carvings. Yes, my mansion is perfect. The spirits of the living and the dead whom I revere are here. Let the scoffers and the Dyke Lashmars sneer (referring, of course, to the character of that name in Gissing's book). To me it is as much a fact that this room was built for me hundreds of years ago as if Robert Williams had drawn the plans to my orders, and A. J. Penty superintended the erection of the building. From which it will be inferred that the primitive instincts of the race are still strong in me. And now, as Big Ben has tolled one, and the dog has ceased to bark, I will smoke one pipe more, and then to bed.''

The beginning of June brought the end of the South African War, which had lasted nearly three years instead of the two or three months which it was expected would be sufficient for the subjugation of the Boers.

Hardie, and with him the I.L.P., had never swerved
in opposing the British policy, and week by week, both
by speech and pen, he had supported the Boers in their
resistance to the superior military power of Great
Britain. He regarded such resistance not only as
patriotic from the Burghers' point of view, but as a
service to humanity in its necessary struggle against
capitalist Imperialism, and he was fain to discern in the
terms of settlement some guarantee for the development
of a united democracy in South Africa. Whether or not
his hopes have been justified, or will yet be justified,
does not lie within the province of this book to say. That
chapter of history is not closed even yet.

With the end of the war there came a marked abate-
ment in the jingo-fostered prejudice which had prevented Hardie and his colleagues from getting, even
amongst the working classes, a fair hearing for their
advocacy of the principle of Labour representation.
They were not now so frequently assailed with the epithet "pro-Boer," and even that epithet, when applied,
had come to have a less malignant interpretation in the
minds of men who were beginning to perceive that under
the new regime South Africa was not likely to become
the paradise for British labour which had been promised
The importation of cheap Central African native labour,
and the whisperings already heard of the possible introduction of even cheaper and more servile Chinese
labour, helped to confirm the contentions so persistently
urged by Hardie and his colleagues on hundreds of
platforms, that the war was a capitalists' war, fought in
the interests of mineowners and financiers.

There was, for a time, a decided falling away of
patriotic fervour on the part of the working classes,
accelerated by a steady increase in the number of unemployed, accompanied, as usual, by an equally steady

decrease in wages. To many it seemed as if the employing classes had utilised the war distractions to consolidate and strengthen their own position. New combinations of employers had been formed, alike in the coal trade, the steel trade and the textile trade, which, taken together with the law-court attacks upon the workers' right of combination, had all the appearance of deliberate and well-conceived class war. In this atmosphere of chronic discontent the argument for the attainment of political power became more and more acceptable to organised labour, while the indifference of both the Liberal and the Tory Parties convinced many that such power could only be achieved through the Independent Labour Party. The unopposed return of David Shackleton, of the textile workers, at the by-election at Clitheroe was the first electoral expression of a change of outlook on the part of trade unionists, the textile workers having been hitherto amongst the most conservative sections of the workers. Shackleton was not a Socialist, but he stood definitely as an independent L.R.C. candidate, and there was significance in the fact that the only opponent whom the Liberals could even venture to suggest was Mr. Philip Stanhope, who had been an out and out opponent of the war. There was good reason for regarding this election, not only as a victory for Labour, but as symptomatic of a reaction from Imperialism.

Hardie continued to be active both with speech and pen, and did not seem to reckon with the effects of the emotional and mental strain which recent events had imposed upon him. Probably economic considerations as much as anything else prevented him from taking the rest which was now due, for the "Labour Leader," though again increasing in circulation, was not prospering financially, and he had difficulties in making ends meet which were not revealed except to very close confidants whose lips were sealed on these matters. A prize drawing, originated by some friends to aid the funds of the paper, was not very successful, and only served to show that all was not well.

In September, with Mrs. Hardie, he took a short holiday in the West Highlands, the rest-value of which he spoilt by addressing a meeting at Ballachulish, where a long drawn out dispute between the quarrymen and their employers was in progress, the details of which had been written up in the "Labour Leader" by the present writer. In November he was medically advised that the only alternative to a serious breakdown was that he should go away for a complete rest. He went for a week or two to the Continent, where he had some experiences which were anything but restful. He was present at a duel in Paris in which M. Gerault Richard, Socialist deputy and editor of "La Petite Republique," was one of the principals. He found excitement in the ferociously elaborate preparations, and much amusement in the innocuous outcome thereof. He was persuaded to visit the opera, and, to satisfy Parisian etiquette, borrowed a friend's dress suit, probably his first and last appearance in such apparel. In Brussels, he was arrested on suspicion of being an Anarchist and detained for several hours until he could show that he was a Member of the British Parliament and in no way connected with the underworld individual who had recently exploded some blank cartridges in the vicinity of the King of the Belgians. It was a good holiday with plenty of change of air, scenery and circumstance, but decidedly not restful.

He got back to London just before the Christmas rising of the House, and signalised his return by endeavouring to have the question of the unemployed discussed on the motion for adjournment. He was prevented, however, from doing so by the Speaker's ruling, a decision which he characterised as an infringement of "the unquestioned right of members of the House of Commons from time immemorial." Before going to bed he wrote a long letter to the press which appeared in "The Times" and several other London papers the next morning. In this he demonstrated from Board of Trade statistics and trade union returns that the number of unemployed workers in the country was not less than half-a-million, and that the consequent wide-spread distress called for immediate remedial measures by Parliament. And so ended a year which, for him, had been full of stress and distress, but not without hope and encouragement for the cause he had at heart.

With the opening of the New Year there came a change in the staff of the "Labour Leader" which must be noted. David Lowe ceased to be assistant editor, a position which he had held almost ever since the paper ·was started as a weekly. Hardie said, in a farewell note : "His graceful writings and his business capacity have done much to win for the 'Leader' such measure of success as it has attained." David Lowe, alike by his distinctive quality as a writer and his close connection with the "Leader" in its early years of struggle, has his rank among the personalities of the British Socialist movement. His place on the "Leader" was filled by another Dundee man, Mr. W. F. Black, a journalist of experience, who, having become a convinced Socialist, found it impossible to continue as sub-editor of the Liberal "Dundee Advertiser," the more especially as he had been recently selected as Labour candidate for Dundee.

As the weeks passed, the unemployed problem

assumed more serious dimensions, the discharged soldiers from South Africa helping to swell the already formidable army of workless folk. On Friday and Saturday, February 22nd and 23rd, an Unemployed Conference was held at the Guildhall, London, attended by 587 delegates from town councils, corporations and Labour organisations, testifying to the nation-wide concern created by the existing distress. At the various sessions of the Conference the chairmen were Sir Albert Rollit, M.P., Mr. Wilson, Lord Mayor of Sheffield, and Keir Hardie, no longer standing isolated and alone, as in bygone years. At this Conference, Sir John Gorst first mooted the idea of local labour employment bureaux, with a central clearing house, now so familiar as a part of our administrative mechanism. It should be said, however, that Sir John suggested these only as palliatives, and declared that "though the symptoms of social disorder were periodic, the disorder itself was chronic"—which was equivalent to saying that it was inherent in the capitalist system.

Hardie, as was his custom when there was a chance of getting some practical work done, refrained from much speaking. He moved "that the responsibility for finding work for the unemployed should be undertaken jointly by the Local Authorities and by the Central Government, and that such legislation should be introduced as would empower both central and local authorities to deal adequately with the problem." Other resolutions along the same line were adopted, including one by George N. Barnes, which, if it had effectively materialised, might have given the Conference some real and lasting value. "That a permanent national organisation be formed to give effect to the decisions of the Conference, and that the Provisional Committee be re-appointed with power to add to its number"—so it ran.

This Conference was important chiefly as a symptom—

J. KEIR HARDIE IN HIS ROOM AT NEVILL'S COURT, LONDON

The Union Jack flag was captured from the Jingo mob which attacked his meeting at Johannesburg

Copyright

a sign that the "condition of the people" question was at last troubling society. Parliament remained wholly unresponsive, and this period of distress, like so many of its predecessors, had to find its only amelioration in soup kitchens, stoneyards, and local relief works, which, as hitherto, provided a minimum of useless work at pauper wages. Such bodies as the Salvation Army and the Church Army found a vocation in distributing charity.

Even in this work Hardie took a hand, and he has related pathetically and with a kind of sad humour, some of his experiences delivering Salvation Army tickets in Fleet Street and on the Embankment. Not infrequently he spent his two hours beyond midnight, after the House had risen, assisting at one or other of the Salvation Army shelters, thus repeating, under more heart-breaking conditions, the kind of work he had performed in his own Lanarkshire village, twenty-four years earlier. The worst thing about it was the fatalistic patience of the sufferers. In Lanarkshire, the men and women were at least fighting. These crowds of helpless atoms had no fight in them.

All this time he was toiling like a galley-slave on the propaganda platform. Thus, on one Friday in March, we find him speaking in Browning Hall, London, on Saturday attending a National Council meeting in Manchester, the same night addressing a Labour Church social meeting in Bolton, on the Sunday speaking in the open air at Farnworth (in March, remember) and at night in the Exchange Hall at Blackburn. On the Monday he was present at a joint committee in Westminster on the new Trade Union Bill, and, in the evening, he addressed a meeting in Willesden. And he was not in good health. He was literally giving his life for the cause. Besides, in the "Labour Leader" he was writing more than ever before.

J. KEIR HARDIE

At the I.L.P. conference, held at York, several changes occurred in the National Council. J. Bruce Glasier retired from the chairmanship, having held the position for three years, and Philip Snowden was unanimously elected in his place. Isabella O. Ford found a place on the Council, the Party thus expressing in a practical way its belief in sex equality. John Penny, who was entering into business on his own account, retired from the secretaryship, having given invaluable services to the Party through an exceedingly critical period of its history. His place was filled subsequently by the present secretary, Francis Johnson.

It may be well to note the complete personnel of the N.A.C. at this juncture: Chairman, Philip Snowden; Treasurer, T. D. Benson; members of Council, J. Ramsay MacDonald, J. Keir Hardie, J. Bruce Glasier, James Parker, Isabella O. Ford, and Fred Jowett. All, save Hardie and Glasier, are still, at the time of writing, alive, and all except Parker have remained loyal to the I.L.P. T. D. Benson retired from the treasurership only last year. It was due largely to his wise counsel and business-like handling of the Party's finances that it was able with such limited resources to do so much effective work in the political field. He guided the Party more than once through a veritable sea of financial troubles. The friendship between him and Hardie was something more than a mere political comradeship and seemed to be the outcome of a natural affinity between the two men.

Though Parliament did not respond legislatively to the claims of the unemployed, it would not be true to say that these claims found no reflection in the political world. In March, Will Crooks was returned for Woolwich, and in July, Arthur Henderson was elected for Barnard Castle, and in both contests the unemployed problem was a prominent, if not a determining, factor. Both·candidates had signed the L.R.C. declaration, and their success, in the one case against a Tory and in the other against both a Liberal and a Tory, was decidedly disconcerting to the orthodox party politicians, who, with a general election once more in view, had to find some kind of a political programme applicable or adaptable to the social conditions.

The great fiscal controversy re-emerged out of the discontents of the people and the opportunism of the statesmen. Mr. Chamberlain produced his scheme of colonial preference, and in doing so provided both his own party and the Liberals with a cause of quarrel calculated to distract the attention of the electorate from the new Labour Party organisation, and re-establish the old party lines of division. Before the end of the year there had developed a raging, tearing platform war between Liberals and Unionists on the old "Protection *versus* Free Trade" issue, by means of which both parties hoped to rally the workers behind them. Mr. Chamberlain urged—we must believe with all sincerity—that in his proposals lay the guarantee against that foreign competition which was supposed to be the main cause of dull trade and therefore of unemployment, and that with this security of employment would come good wages. He suggested further that the Tariff imposts would provide funds for Old Age Pensions. On a question of this kind, the new Labour Party could not by reason alike of its economic principles and of its hopes for international goodwill, avoid taking the Free Trade side, and the danger was that by doing so it would lose its identity and become merged in the Liberal Party. Hardie was quick to descry both the Chamberlain fallacy, and the Free Trade tactical pitfalls. "I am no fetish worshipper of Free Trade in the abstract," he said, "but I know enough of economics and of history to convince me that the only outcome of Chamberlain's proposals would be to add enormously to the cost of living, without any prospect whatever of wages getting correspondingly advanced. The dislocation of trade that would follow any attempt to set up a Zollverein would throw large masses of men out of employment, which again would react in the lowering of wages. Protection may protect rent and interest, but for the worker, under a competitive system, there is no protection save that which the law gives him. It is to be hoped, all the same, that organised Labour will not be led into a mere Free Trade campaign at the heels of the Cobden Club. A constructive industrial policy is demanded, and the opportunity is one that should not be wasted of proving that Labour can be creative in legislation as well as destructive in criticism."

Naturally, it was left to the I.L.P. to formulate and give publicity to Labour's alternative constructive policy, which, as was to be expected, took the form of a series of definitely Socialist proposals of a practical kind. An extensive platform campaign was arranged and successful demonstrations held in all the large towns and industrial centres, at which were emphasised the failure of protection in other countries to relieve or extenuate the poverty of the workers, and the equal failure of Free Trade in this country to give security of employment or improve social conditions. The workers were asked "to assist in returning Labour Members to Parliament for the purpose of promoting legislation to nationalise the mines, railways, and other industrial monopolies, in order that the wealth created may be shared by the community, and not be for the advantage of the rich and idle classes."

MacDonald (who had written for the Party a book

ILLNESS

critically examining the Chamberlain proposals for an Imperial Zollverein) Snowden, Jowett, Barnes, Glasier, and most of the leading men and women of the I.L.P. took part in these meetings, but, alas, Hardie was not amongst them. By the time the campaign commenced he was out of the firing-line. Whilst in Wales amongst his constituents, he was taken dangerously ill. The long-threatened, long-evaded collapse had come, and he had to give in.

The trouble was diagnosed as appendicitis, and the doctors decided that an operation was necessary if his life was to be saved. He himself well knew that loss of life might be one of the consequences of the operation, and though he took it quite calmly, the same knowledge sent fear into the hearts of all his friends and right throughout the Socialist movement in this country and in other lands. The highest surgical and medical skill was secured, and there was something like a sigh of relief when it was made known that the operation had been successful. Nor was the expression of sympathy confined to the Socialist movement. People of every shade of political opinion, and in every grade of society, found ways and means of showing their good-will. The messages of sympathy included one from Major Banes, his former opponent at West Ham, and one from King Edward, who had recently undergone a similar ordeal. For the time being political enmities were—with some few vulgar exceptions—forgotten, and it was generally recognised that this Labour leader was in some respects a national possession whose character and work reflected credit, not only upon the class from which he had sprung, but upon the nation of which he was a citizen. A prominent Liberal official wrote, on the eve of the operation : "Forgive me if I seem to be impertinent in forcing myself upon your notice at a time when you

have more than enough of vastly more important matters
to fill your mind and time. But I am sincerely anxious
that all will go well with you to-morrow. Never was
there a moment in the recent history of our country when
your great powers were more needed in the field of active
strife than now. I heartily pray that the operation may
be in every way successful." John Burns's letter was
characteristic :—

"Dear Hardie,
"I am pleased to hear you have come through the
operation successfully. This illness ought to be a warning to you, and to others similarly engaged who do not
realise the wear and tear of such a life as ours. Get
well, take a rest, and when recovered 'tak a thocht and
mend.' With best wishes for your speedy recovery, the
forcible expropriation of your pipe, a freedom from
articles, and an immunity from 'Marxian' for three
months.
                              "Yours sincerely,
                                      "JOHN BURNS."

The process of recovery was very slow, and was not
accelerated by his own haste to get on his legs again.
He spent several seemingly convalescent weeks in a
nursing home at Falmouth, and managed to get home
to Cumnock for the New Year. "Marxian," of the
"Labour Leader," who met him in London on Christmas Eve, wrote : "All Keir's genuine friends should still
insist that he should continue his rest from active work
until at least the return of spring. He ought really to
be banished to the Mediterranean till July next. As it
is, he is going on to Scotland and he talks of doing some
platforming before the end of January. Anyone who is
aiding and abetting this sort of thing might be more
eligibly employed stopping rat holes."

ILLNESS

His Christmas message in the "Labour Leader" was of the nature of an official farewell as editor and proprietor. In the first week of the New Year the paper passed into the control of the I.L.P. and became the official Party organ, thus fulfilling the original intention of its founder, though the date of the transference was doubtless determined by his illness. "From the first," he wrote, "it has been my intention that the paper should one day become the property of the Independent Labour Party. That, however, I thought would be when I was no more. The thought of parting with it is like consenting to the loss of a dearly loved child. But circumstances are always bigger than personal feelings. I have no longer the spring and elasticity of a few years ago, and that means that the pressure of work and worry must be somewhat relaxed. But, and this is really the deciding factor, the interests of the Party require that it should possess its own paper. The events of the past twelve months have borne this fact in upon me with irresistible force. And so, subject to the fixing of a few unimportant details, the 'Labour Leader' will pass with this issue into the ownership and control of the I.L.P. Time was when this would have been a risky experiment. Now, with the Party organised and consolidated as it is, the risk is reduced to a minimum. For the I.L.P. is no longer a mixed assortment of job lots. It is an organisation in the truest sense of that much misused word."

Running through this good-bye note there is a discernable a note of regret that the good-bye should have been necessary. The "Labour Leader" was one of his tangible achievements. Something concrete, something he could lay his hands upon and say, "this is of my creation." He had put the stamp of his own character upon it, and his whole soul into it. "What it has cost me to keep it going no one will ever know, and few be able even to remotely guess. But it has kept going, and now the Party takes it over as a self-supporting, going concern. I am proud of the fact." He paid full tribute to those who had helped. So numerous were they that only a few could be singled out—"Marxian," "who has never quailed, and even now would like to see the thing go on on personal lines"; W. F. Black, "who, before he joined the staff, gave much valuable voluntary help, and came on to the paper at considerable pecuniary sacrifice"; his brother David, "who has been literally a pillar and a mainstay. Had he not been there, the main actors would long ago have had to succumb"; David Lowe, "whose services and talents were freely given at a time when they were much needed"; William Stewart (Gavroche), "who has made his sign manual a passport to the close attention of every thoughtful reader."

Of course, the change did not, by any means, involve his complete severance from the direction of the affairs of the paper. As a member of the N.A.C., he had his share with the others in the control of its policy, and his counsel had, naturally, much weight. He still continued to be its most valued contributor, and through all his remaining years he found in the "Labour Leader" his chief medium for the expression of his convictions on all public questions. At this particular juncture, relief from editorial and financial responsibility was the best thing for him that could have happened. His recovery was slow and rest was imperative. During the early months of 1904, he spent most of his time at home in Cumnock, with occasional visits to Glasgow and Edinburgh. On these occasions he was to be found either amongst the second-hand bookshops adding to his collection of Scottish Ballad literature, or in companionship with congenial friends whose doors and whose hearts were always open to him. William Martin Haddow and Alexander Gilchrist in Glasgow, the Rev. John Glasse and Mr. John Young in Edinburgh, and many others besides, had each their fireside corner ready for "Keir," and he, on his part, had never any difficulty in making himself as one of the family.

At home in Cumnock he had his family around him as he and they had never been before. He had his books, and his garden, and his dog, and, of course, his pipe, and when the weather favoured his strolls through the collier "raws," he could fight the early battles over again amongst old comrades. Occasionally there was a day's tramp across the moors towards Glenbuck, or over the hills towards Dalmellington. But, withal, he rallied back to health very, very slowly. He had been too near death's door, and the winter weather in Scotland is not favourable to convalescence.

So, as the spring advanced, he, with some reluctance, agreed that a complete change of air and scene was essential. Thus it came about that early in March he was *en route* for the Riviera, *via* France and Switzerland, with J. R. MacDonald as his companion on the first stages of his journey.

It was his first holiday free from political or propagandist objective, and he enjoyed it thoroughly, especially the last month, spent entirely at Bordighera, which he described as "the most charming spot in the Riviera," an impression due perhaps in some degree to the human companionship which he found there.

"At Bordighera I was met by the Gentle Prince of the Golden Locks, and conducted to his marble-pillared palace, with its beautiful arched and vaulted ceilings and tiled floors. There I met the Boy Corsair of the Kaurie Hand—a stalwart viking, a true son of the sea—and the Bold Brigand of the Mountains, to all of whom I owe much. In plain language, they are two young artists and a poet, all striving after the real and true in life and living. There also came Africanus Brown, the Good Physician, who literally brought healing in his presence. The memory of Bordighera and its warm hearts will long remain fresh and green with me."

Week by week during these three months he contributed to the "Labour Leader" descriptive sketches of his experiences and impressions which, of course, cannot even be summarised here. They would still bear reproduction in book form. There are "men of letters" whose literary fame is built upon foundations almost as slender.

At Mentone he had an interview with the exiled ex-President Kruger and "was impressed with the stately dignity of the man, an exile from the land he loves so well and from the people whom he has welded into a nation."

June had begun when he returned home, much the better for his holiday, but even then not fully restored to health. "Keir Hardie," one parliamentary correspondent wrote, on June 24th, "is back again this week, but though he looks well, we are all sorry to hear that he is not so well as he looks."

Nevertheless, he had come back to work, though for the next two years more outside of the House than inside.

For the first time since the I.L.P. was formed, he was absent from its annual conference, held this year at Cardiff. There was universal and sincere regret for his absence, but also general agreement that in the circumstances the Riviera was a better place for him than South Wales. He was, as a matter of course, re-elected to the N.A.C. Mrs. Pankhurst was also amongst the successful candidates, thus adding one more forceful personality to a body already fairly well equipped with such. Mrs. Pankhurst, who had been a member of the Party since its formation, was now beginning her special activities in the Women's Suffrage movement and made no secret of her intention to subordinate all other aims to its furtherance. Subsequent developments make it necessary to note this fact.

CHAPTER NINE

THE CLASS WAR IN THEORY AND PRACTICE

BEFORE many months were over, Hardie was back again on the Continent, not this time in search of health, but to play his part in the International Congress at Amsterdam. It was said at the time that the Amsterdam Congress would be historical because of the great debate on international Socialist tactics. That is true, but not in the sense anticipated. Probably, the real historical interest in the Amsterdam Congress lies in the fact that it revealed deep schisms within the "International" itself which rendered that body wholly impotent when the supreme testing time came ten years later. These divisions were most evident amongst the delegates from France and Germany, the two countries where Socialism had been most successful in its efforts for Parliamentary representation.

In France, one section, led by Jaurès, on the ground that the Republic was in danger and that clericalism was an ever-active menace to democracy, had been supporting the Anti-Clerical Ministry, though Jaurès himself never took office. Another section, led by Jules Guesde, was opposed to any appearance of alliance with the Government. In Germany, the critical examination of Marx by Bernstein had been causing trouble, and the German Party at its annual conference in Dresden the previous year, had by an overwhelming vote condemned what it called Revisionist tendencies. At the Amsterdam Congress the German Party and the French

THE CLASS WAR

Guesdists joined forces to make the German resolution international and applicable to Socialists in all countries without regard apparently to differing circumstances, political, economic, or historical. In reality the resolution was aimed at Jaurès and his section. It declared the class war to be ever increasing in virulence and condemned Revisionist tendencies and Jaurès' tactics. Bebel, Kautsky, Jaurès, Adler, Vandervelde, MacDonald, all took part in this debate. It was a veritable battle of giants, and for that reason, memorable to those who were present. We are only concerned, however, with the attitude of Hardie and the I.L.P. towards this question of Socialist tactics. The I.L.P. was, in its own tactics, as much opposed as the Germans and the Guesdists to Socialist participation in capitalist governments, but it had never affirmed that such tactics should be universally applicable nor, even in any one country, unalterable. In the case under debate, its delegates to the Congress held that the Socialist movement in each country must decide what its tactics should be, that any attempt by the International Congress to prescribe a given line of action would settle nothing, and that, indeed, in any country where Socialists themselves were strongly divided on the matter, such an attempt would only tend to deepen the division. As a matter of fact, there was a strong desire amongst the rank and file of the French Socialists for unity, and Jaurès having been defeated by but the smallest majority, no resentment was caused by the debate and vote. The immediate result was to unite the French Party and make possible for it those years of political success with which the name of Jaurès will be for ever associated. The result in Germany was nil. The controversy between the orthodox Marxian and the Revisionist continued and produced barrenness.

Moreover, the I.L.P. had never accepted the class war as an essential dogma of Socialist faith, and its delegates could not support a resolution embodying that dogma. In the British section, which comprised delegates from the I.L.P., the L.R.C., the S.D.F. and the Fabians, and over which Hardie presided, all this had to be debated with a view to deciding on which side the votes of the section would be cast, and there were stormy scenes within the section as well as in the Congress. In the end, there was some kind of compromise, and the vote of the section was given in favour of an amendment by Vandervelde, of Belgium, and Adler, of Austria, which, whilst affirming the whole doctrine of Socialism and accepting the Kautsky resolutions as determining the tactics of the movement, left out those portions which condemned revision. This amendment was defeated, but, as was afterwards pointed out, by the votes of nations which either had no parliamentary system, or no strong Labour Party in Parliament. The only European nations having parliamentary institutions which voted against it were Germany and Italy. "This," said Hardie, "is a fact of the first significance and indicates clearly what the future has in store for the movement." Some part of that future has already disclosed itself. The attempt to find a common measure of tactics for countries so widely separated in industrial and political development as Russia and Germany, or Russia and Great Britain, is doomed to failure. Tactics must be determined by circumstances and events.

There were two incidents in connection with this Conference of perhaps even greater significance than the debate on tactics. One was the public handshaking of the delegates from Japan and Russia, whose countries were at that time at war. The other was the appearance for the first time at an international congress of a representative from India, in the person of Naoroji, who delivered a strong indictment of British methods of government in India.

A sequel to the Congress was the necessity which it imposed upon Hardie of stating more clearly than ever before his views on the question of political tactics, and also on the question of the Class War. On the former, it will be best to give his own words. The following quotation from an article which he contributed to the "Nineteenth Century" will serve the purpose : "The situation, as revealed by the voting at Amsterdam is this. Wherever free Parliamentary institutions exist, and where Socialism has attained the status of being recognised as a Party, dogmatic absolutism is giving way before the advent of a more practical set of working principles. The schoolman is being displaced by the statesman. No hard and fast rule can be laid down for the application of the new methods, but generally speaking, where the Socialist propaganda has so far succeeded as to have built up a strong party in the state, and where the ties which kept the older parties together have so far been dissolved that there is no longer an effective Reform Party remaining, there the Socialists may be expected to lend their aid in erecting a new combination of such progressive forces as give an intellectual assent to Socialism, and are prepared to co-operate in waging war against reaction and in rallying the forces of democracy. When this can be done so as in no way to impair the freedom of action of a Socialist party, or to blur the vision of the Socialist ideal, it would appear as if the movement had really no option but to accept its share of the responsibility of guiding the State. Then, just in proportion as Socialism grows, so will the influence of the representatives in the national councils increase, and the world may wake up some morning to find that Socialism has come."

Complementary to the foregoing statement must be taken his almost simultaneous declaration in the "Labour Leader," that he could not conceive of any set of circumstances as likely to arise in his lifetime which would lead him to agree to an alliance with any Party then existing. "In Great Britain, for the present, there is no alternative to a rigid independence."

This declaration occurred in "An Indictment of the Class War," which extended through two articles in the "Leader." In this "indictment" he maintained that to claim for the Socialist movement that it is a "class war" dependent upon its success upon the the "class consciousness" of one section of the community, was doing Socialism an injustice and indefinitely postponing its triumph. It was, he said, in fact, lowering it to the level of a faction fight. He objected to the principle of Socialism being overlaid by dogmatic interpretation. He agreed, of course, that there was a conflict of interests between those who own property and those who work for wages, but contended that it was the object of Socialism to remove the causes which produced this antagonism. "Socialism," he said, "makes war upon a system, not upon a class," and one of the dangers of magnifying the class war dogma was that it led men's minds away from the true nature of the struggle. "The working class," he said, "is not a class. It is a nation"; and, "it is a degradation of the Socialist movement to drag it down to the level of a mere struggle for supremacy between two contending factions." He quoted Belfort Bax as saying that "mere class instinct which is anti-social, can never give us Socialism," and he referred to Jaurès as declaring that out of 49,000,000 people in France, not 200,000 were class-conscious Socialists, and to Lieb-

THE CLASS WAR

knecht as saying the same thing about Germany, and he queried, "When are the proletarians to become class conscious?" He deduced from these facts, and from the philosophic arguments of Bax and Morris, that "Socialism would come, not by a war of classes, but by economic circumstances forcing the workers into a revolt which will absorb the middle class and thus wipe out classes altogether."

Speaking of the "Communist Manifesto," upon which the class war dogma is said to be based, he quoted the statement of Engels, one of its authors, that "the practical application of the principles of the manifesto will depend on the historical conditions for the time being existing," and he recalled that the famous document was written in 1847, "when Europe was a seething mass of revolutionary enthusiasm."

Of the manifesto itself, he contended that, however correct it might be as a form of words, it was lacking in feeling and could not now be defended as being scientifically correct, inasmuch as the materialist theory therein expounded made no allowance for the law of growth or development. He agreed that the emancipation of the working class must be the act of the working class itself, but contended that in this country the workers had already politically the power to free themselves, and that it was the ignorance of the workers which hindered the spread of Socialism. That ignorance we were now called upon to attack with every weapon at our command, and it was because the class war dogma led the workers to look outside themselves for the causes which perpetuated their misery that he opposed its being made a leading feature in Socialist propaganda. That Socialism was revolutionary was indisputable, but he maintained that reformative improvements in the workers' conditions did not necessarily

weaken the revolutionary purpose of Socialism. He
denied that revolution required the violent overthrow
of the bourgeoisie by open war. "No revolution can
succeed which has not public opinion behind it, and
when that opinion ripens, it, as we have seen over and
over again, breaks down even the walls of self-interest."

Naturally, this "indictment" provoked a storm of
controversy within the movement. In this controversy
Hardie did not again intervene. He had defined his
attitude towards the class war theory, and he left it at
that. Theoretical disputation amongst Socialists was
distasteful to him. He was always more in his element
fighting the avowed enemies of Socialism than in
quarrelling with its friends. Even in fighting its enemies
his desire was, if it were possible, to make friends of
them, and in this he was not always unsuccessful.

There was no lack of problems, political and social,
calling for immediate attention—problems the equitable
solution of which meant the removal of obstacles in the
path towards Socialism. Amongst these, the question
of political sex-equality was one of the most important,
and was now nearing the stage when Parliament could
not neglect it much longer. This question illustrated,
though he never used it in that way, Hardie's contentions concerning the class war. The vote was demanded,
not for working women only, but for all women,
irrespective of class. It is true that a strong argument
in its favour was the large place now occupied by
women in the industrial field, their share in the staple
trade of Lancashire being specially cited as proof of
their right to the vote, but sex equality was and has
always been the basis of the demand for women's suffrage. Political equality with men had been demanded
not on the grounds of special industrial or social
service, but as a common citizen right. Yet in the very

fact of agreement on this fundamental principle, there lay the germs of a disagreement out of which arose much confusion and friction within the suffragist movement itself. Political equality with men, but how? By pressing for "adult suffrage," which, of course, included both sexes, or by demanding the franchise for women on the existing basis for men, namely, household franchise.

The I.L.P., of course, favoured both, political equality being inherent in its conception of social equality, and the National Council, with a view to securing legislation which would not only enfranchise women as householders, but also entitle them to equality with men in any future extension of the franchise, had drafted a Women's Enfranchisement Bill to be introduced by Hardie at the first opportunity. As this is a matter of historical interest the text of the Bill may be given. It was as follows :—

"In all Acts relating to the qualification and registration of persons entitled to vote for the election of Members of Parliament, whatever words occur which import the masculine gender, shall be held to include women for all purposes connected with and having reference to the right to be registered as voters, and to vote in such election any law or usage to the contrary notwithstanding."

There was division of opinion as to the wisdom of this line of advance both within the women's movement and within the I.L.P. The Women's Social and Political Union, in which Mrs. Pankhurst was the dominant force, favoured the policy embodied in the above Bill, which came to be known as the Limited Suffrage Bill. The Adult Suffrage League, which included amongst its leading members Margaret Bondfield and Mary Macarthur, stood, as its name implies, for nothing short of adult suffrage. Hardie, knowing well that neither proposal would be carried without great opposition, favoured the "limited" proposal, chiefly for agitational purposes. "If," he said, "the women have a Bill of their own, short, simple, and easily understood, and they concentrate upon that, even though it should never be discussed in Parliament until the general Adult Suffrage Bill is reached, they would, by their agitation, have created the necessary volume of public opinion to make it impossible for politicians to overlook their claims." In the main this was the view held by the Party, and adhered to throughout the subsequent stormy period of agitation for women's rights. This storm, however, was as yet only brewing.

More immediate were the threatenings of trouble from the growing hosts of unemployed workers. In September, Hardie, in Parliament, had called the attention of the Government to the fact that the unemployed problem could not be much longer ignored, and had, as usual, been assured by Mr. Balfour that "there was no evidence of exceptional distress." Almost immediately, as if in answer to this assertion, the unemployed themselves contradicted it with a degree of violence reminiscent of the times of the Chartist movement. In Manchester, Birmingham, Leeds, Liverpool, Glasgow and most of the big towns, not only were there large processions of workless people demanding that the civic authorities should take action for their relief, but also daily gatherings of these people in public places. At Leeds, during one procession, windows were broken all along the line of march. On the whole, however, the demonstrations were orderly, and, thanks largely to the local I.L.P. organisations, which usually took control, the unemployed agitation began to assume an organised and cohesive character such as had been lacking in previous periods of trade depression. Hardie was much in evidence both in the outside agitation and in Parliament, and it looked as if the very imminence of trouble and the call for leadership had restored him to full health and vigour. He declared—referring to the trouble at Leeds—that "if Parliament deliberately rules these men as being outside its ken, they are justified in refusing to be bound by laws made for the protection of well-to-do people."

By the middle of October, the Government had slightly changed its tune, and Mr. Long, the President of the Local Government Board, had called a conference of the Guardians and Borough Councillors of the Metropolitan area to consider the situation. This was immediately followed up by Hardie with a memorial signed by fourteen Members of Parliament asking for a special session, and with a pamphlet in which he dealt comprehensively with the unemployed problem, detailed the powers already possessed by local authorities and Boards of Guardians, and made suggestions for their immediate utilisation. He also considered the larger question of what the Government itself could do if it were willing, and proposed the creation of a new State Department with a Minister of Industry, and a new set of administrative councils, to initiate work and take in charge lands and foreshores, afforestation, building harbours of refuge, making new roads, and so on—in fact, a practical programme of remedies, just falling short of Socialism but leading inevitably towards it, and proving that he was no dreamer but simply a very practical man far in advance of his time. Upon this programme the November Municipal Elections were fought, and resulted in a considerable increase in the number of Labour representatives on Town Councils throughout the country, a result which was taken as foreshadowing what was likely to happen at the first Parliamentary general election.

All through the winter the agitation continued, and contrary to the usual experience, did not slacken off in the spring. In April, the Government produced its "Unemployed Workmen Bill," and in so doing conceded for the first time the principle for which Hardie had fought ever since 1893, the principle of State responsibility for the unemployment problem. As was to be expected, the measure was not of a very drastic character. It followed the lines of Mr. Long's suggestions of six months previously, and authorised local Councils to set up Distress Committees and Relief Committees to be financed by voluntary subscriptions and by a local rate not to exceed one penny in the pound of assessed rental. Unsatisfactory as the Bill was, Hardie recommended that it should be accepted, and as far as possible improved in Committee. He knew well that its very shortcomings would give rise to further discontent and intensify rather than allay the outside agitation upon which he mainly relied for forcing the local authorities to do something practical, and for exposing the insincerity of the Government. The Liberals, when in power, he constantly reminded his audiences, had been quite as futile as the Tories in their dealings with unemployment. Hardie was undoubtedly, before everything else, an agitator, and in this respect was a continual puzzle to the Continental Socialists, who found difficulty in reconciling his professed rejection of the class war theory with what seemed to them his ever militant application of it, and when in the autumn the Government threatened to withdraw the Unemployment Bill, and Hardie made such an uproar in the House as compelled them to go on with it, and arrested the attention of the whole country, the Continental Socialist press was unstinted in its praise of his courage and of his tactics, albeit somewhat mystified by the apparent inconsistency of his parliamentary practice with his congress professions. He was, in fact, doing as he had always done, facing the immediate issue and utilising the circumstances of the moment for the purpose of far reaching propaganda.

Agitation with Hardie was almost a fine art, and always led on to more agitation, with an objective ever beyond. In the present case the objective was the coming general election. It was to this end that he created scenes in the House of Commons over the Unemployed Bill and the bludgeoning of unemployed demonstrations, rousing to anger the jeering back-bench Tories by describing them to their faces as "well fed beasts." It was to this end that he, with the I.L.P., projected a great series of demonstrations in support of the Bill to be held simultaneously all over the country. "Public opinion," he said, "is a manufactured article, and represents that amount of agitation and education which any given cause has been able to exert upon the community." The devoted and tireless members of the I.L.P. had been supplying the agitation and education for years. He believed that public opinion was now in existence which would establish a substantial Party in Parliament at the first opportunity, and he was looking forward hopefully to that event. Already he had a glimpse of what might be possible with such a Party. In these latter months he was no longer fighting single-handed and lonely. The new Labour Members, Henderson, Crooks, and Shackleton had been co-operating with him loyally and steadily, and his parliamentary work had been more congenial than ever before. His hopes were high, and he radiated optimism throughout the movement.

J. KEIR HARDIE

The Unemployment Bill passed, but was rendered practically ineffective by the accompanying "Regulations" and by the reluctance of local authorities to put it into operation, and, as Hardie anticipated, the general working-class discontent was intensified.

CHAPTER TEN

THE end of the year brought the opportunity for which he and his colleagues had been waiting and working. The Government resigned in December, and the Liberals accepted office with Sir Henry Campbell-Bannerman as Prime Minister. As soon as his Government was formed, he dissolved Parliament, and the long hoped for General Election took place.

Concerning the new Government and its personnel, Hardie had some observations to make which, in view of subsequent history, are not without interest. Of the Prime Minister, he said, "The most lasting impression I have of him is when as chairman of the Unemployed Committee of 1893, he so engineered the proceedings as to get the winter through without doing anything for the starving out-of-works. It may be, however, that he has repented of the apparent callousness which the exigencies of party forced upon him in those days, and is prepared to atone for the past by his good deeds in the future." From the democratic point of view the most interesting appointment was that of John Burns to the Local Government Board. "In his early Socialist days," said Hardie, "he fought magnificently, but he has not shown himself the man to lead a forlorn hope or to stand alone in a crisis. He is a hard worker, and that fact alone will create a stir in his department and may lead to surprising results." Hardie coupled Burns with

J. KEIR HARDIE

Morley in this sarcastically back-handed way: "The most prominent Radical in the Cabinet whose distrust of the people is only equalled by that of John Burns. In temperament no two men are wider apart than our brace of 'Honest Johns.' Morley is philosophic, timid and pedantic; Burns headstrong, impulsive and dashing, but they are one in their lack of faith in the democracy." On the other hand, of Sir Robert Reid, the new Lord Chancellor with the title of Lord Loreburn, he declared, "There is no man in politics with a cleaner record or a more democratic spirit." High praise indeed coming from Keir Hardie. Lloyd George, also making his first entrance into officialdom, he described as "a politician with no settled convictions on social questions. He will go all the length his party goes, but hitherto social questions have lain outside the sphere of his orbit. As a hard-working lawyer and rising politician he has enough to do to keep abreast of the fighting party line without wandering into the by-ways of social reform." Asquith and Haldane he characterised as "cold-blooded reactionaries of the most dangerous type. With professions of Liberalism on their lips, they are despots at hearts, and as they are the strong men of the Cabinet and are upholders of the Roseberian interpretation of Liberalism, they can be reckoned upon to see that this view is well upheld in the inner councils of the Cabinet." Lord Portsmouth he summed up as "a Tory who has left his party on the Free Trade question." Lord Crewe was "a recent convert from Unionism," whilst "a big majority of the others are Unionists in all but name. They are all representatives of the landed interests and they certainly have not joined the Government to press forward either land nationalisation or the taxation of land values." "Labour folks," he said, "will note without enthusiasm that there are seventeen land-owning peers, and sixteen place-hunting lawyers in the new Government." He had no illusions. He was building no high hopes for democracy on the advent of the new Liberal Government. His hopes lay in an Independent Parliamentary Labour Party which would act as a spur to the Government and fight it when necessary, and for the realisation of this hope he now plunged himself body and soul into the general election turmoil.

The L.R.C. had fifty-two candidates, ten of whom were I.L.P. nominees, while thirty-two of the others nominated by trade unions were members of the Party. Hardie took part personally in nearly every one of these contests, and during the next three weeks he was working literally morning, noon and night, in the roughest of weather, travelling backwards and forwards from one end of the country to the other, speaking sometimes in crowded halls and stifling schoolrooms, sometimes in the open air, and beyond doubt contributing immensely to the success which the final results revealed. He went everywhere but into his own constituency. There was some doubt as to whether he would be opposed, and as he regarded the general success of the Labour movement as being of more importance than his own individual success, he could not allow himself to be tied up in Merthyr waiting for an opposition which was problematical. Besides, he had reason to believe that his position in Merthyr was now so secure that no eleventh-hour opposition could possibly endanger it, a belief justified by the result, though some of his local supporters were not so confident, and were, indeed, considerably alarmed by the nomination of a shipowning Liberal named Radcliffe, whose candidature in the absence of Hardie, semed to be making rapid progress. As at previous elections, however, the local stalwarts, Francis, Davies, Morris, Barr—an Ayrshire man settled in

Merthyr—Stanton, Stonelake of Aberdare, and a host of
others poured into the constituency, fought the campaign
with vigour and enthusiasm, and Hardie's arrival on the
scene, worn and exhausted, just two days before the
polling, and the inspiration of victories in the country
finished their efforts. The election figures were :—

Thomas (Liberal)	...	13,971
Hardie	...	10,187
Radcliffe (Liberal)	...	7,776
Majority for Hardie	...	2,411

It was the crowning glory of a great campaign. For
Hardie it was even more than that. It was the realisation of all those hopes which had sustained him through
long years of toil and troubles. A Labour Party, twenty-
nine strong, entered Parliament as the result of this
election, and thus another stage in his life-work had been
reached.

He was well pleased, of course, but not unduly elated.
The first Parliamentary Labour Party had been returned,
but it had yet to be tried, and he knew well that its membership comprised some men who, though their sincerity
might not be questioned, were restricted in their political
outlook by their trade union training and environment,
and in some cases by life-long association with party Liberalism; they might be amenable to influences against
which he had been impervious. Better than any of them
he knew the temptations which would beset them. His
greatest satisfaction was derived from the fact that
amongst the men returned were MacDonald, Snowden,
and Jowett, all of them by majorities which seemed to
ensure their permanent presence in Parliament. Often
and often, in private conversation with comrades throughout the country, he had anticipated the return of these

colleagues, and had extolled the special qualities which would enable them to make their mark in Parliament, and confound the enemies of Labour. With such men as these he felt assured that whatever might be the ebb and flow of loyalty inside or outside of the House, an Independent Parliamentary Labour Party would be maintained. He was now in the fiftieth year of his life, the greater part of which had been devoted to the uplifting of his class. The presence of that class now in Parliament as an organised force was the proof that his life had not been without some achievement. Whatever the future might hold in store for him, the past had been worth while.

In the interval between the election and the assembling of Parliament, Hardie spent a week in Ireland along with George N. Barnes, who was also one of the victors in the recent contest, having signally defeated Mr. Bonar Law at Blackfriars, Glasgow. The Irish visit was meant as a holiday, but, like most of Hardie's holidays, it involved a lot of what other politicians would call work. They visited the Rock of Cashel and Killarney and some of the natural and architectural beauties of Ireland, but they also had public receptions and made speeches at meetings arranged impromptu by the Nationalist M.P.s, who hailed as allies the new Parliamentary Labour Party and were sincerely anxious to honour Hardie for his own sake. They also investigated, as far as possible, the social conditions of the districts through which they passed. Hardie was loud in his praise of the operations of the Congested Districts' Board, which he declared to be, "in fact, the most sensible institution I have ever known to be set up by law, and, with adaptations to meet differing conditions, forms the model upon which I should like to see an Unemployment Committee constituted."

Very remarkable are his observations on the Sinn Fein

movement, at a time when its significance was realised by few people in this country, much less the proportions to which it would grow. "It appears to be," he said, "Fenianism adapted to modern conditions. It is anti-political and anti-English. Its supporters tell you that the people are being ruined by being taught to look to the English Government for reforms; that instead of developing a dependence upon the English Government for reforms and waiting upon English capital to develop Irish industries, the Irish people should set about doing things for themselves. Up to a certain point they are individualists of a very pronounced type, but, unlike the old Manchester school of Radical economists, they have no fear of State action, except in so far as it tends to undermine the spirit of the people. I speak with all reserve as to the present strength of the movement, but Mr. Barnes and I, from what we saw and heard, formed the opinion that the Sinn Fein movement was bound to play an important part in the development of Ireland." That prediction has certainly been fulfilled.

With the entrance of the Labour Party into the House of Commons, Hardie's Parliamentary career assumes a new phase. His personality becomes to a certain extent, though never completely, merged in the Party organisation. There still remained questions, as we shall see, upon which he would find it necessary to take a line of his own, but on the main purpose, that of developing and maintaining a definite and distinct Labour policy, he was to be subject to the will of the majority. This was a condition of things very welcome to him. It had always been irksome to him to have to take action in any sudden political emergency without a body of colleagues with whom to consult. In the last year of the previous Parliament, it is true, the co-operation of Henderson, Crooks and Shackleton had somewhat lessened his burden of personal responsibility, but even that was vastly different from having a well-disciplined Party in the House with an assurance of support outside.

Naturally, he was appointed chairman of the new Party, which carried with it leadership in the House. There were other aspirants for the position, but a sense of the fitness of things prevailed, and the honour and duty of leading the first Parliamentary Labour Party fell, after a second ballot, to the man who, more than any other, had made such a Party possible.

The achievements of the Party during the next few years need not be detailed here. The passing of the Trade Disputes Act; the final and definite legalising of the right of combination; the struggle for the feeding of school children, resulting, at least, in the feeding of those who were necessitous; the determined and continuous pressing for the right to work, ultimately compelling the Liberal Party to look for a way out through Unemployment Insurance; the forcing of Old Age Pensions—these and many other seemingly commonplace achievements, yet all tending to raise the status of the workers and increase their sense of self-respect and of power as a class, are recorded in various ways in the annals of the Labour movement. They are part of the history of the nation and are to a considerable extent embodied in its institutions and in the daily life of the people. This was the kind of work that was naturally expected from the new Labour Party. Readers of this memoir do not want recapitulation of Hardie's share in that work.

But it must not be assumed that either he or the other leaders of the I.L.P. allowed their conceptions of political activity to be limited by the immediate struggle for these tentative though essential measures of reform. They were Socialists, representing a Socialist organisation, and to them a true Labour Party must have an international outlook and an international policy in clear contradistinction to the Imperialist policy of the two capitalist parties.

This wider outlook found significant expression in a resolution passed at the instance of the I.L.P. by the Labour Party Conference held in London immediately following this famous General Election. This was a resolution expressly approving the better feeling between Britain and France, desiring *its extension to the German people*, and declaring for a general international understanding that would lead to disarmament. Could it then have been possible to have introduced the spirit of this resolution into British international policy, there would have been no European War in 1914. Already the sinister implications of the *Entente Cordiale*, involving as it did an alliance not only with Republican France, but with Czarist Russia, and the division of Europe into two hostile camps, were troubling the minds of thoughtful, peace-loving people, who could not help connecting the new militarist plans of the War Office with the schemings of the diplomatists.

Hardie's distrust of the Liberal Imperialist group as a reactionary influence within the Government has already been referred to, and from his point of view it very soon found confirmation. Mr. Haldane, the War Minister, foreshadowed the coming strife when he declared his intention to popularise the idea of "a nation in arms," and the inevitable development of his schemes for the creation of a territorial army, voluntary at first, but, as Hardie declared, likely to become conscriptive in its working. "There we have," he said, analysing Haldane's scheme, "a set of proposals which will require the most careful watching and the most unflinching opposition from all friends of peace. By force of social pressure or other form of compulsion, the youth of the nation are to be induced to undergo military training as volunteers. Thereafter they are to be returned into a reserve force which is to be available as a supplement to the regular army when required for service abroad. At a time when continental nations are growing weary of conscription and agitating for its abolition, we are having it introduced into this country under the specious disguise of broadening the basis of the army. When it was proposed to tax food, that was described as broadening the basis of taxation. Now, when an attempt is being made to popularise universal military service, it is a similar phrase which is used to conceal the true meaning of the proposal. In fighting Protection we had the aid of the Liberal Party. Now, apparently, it is the same Party which is to be used to foist a thinly-disguised form of conscription upon the nation."

Readers with war-time experience can now judge for themselves whether this analysis of Haldane's Army Reform proposals was correct or not. The only difference between Haldane and Lord Roberts, Hardie declared, was that "the former, being more of a politician, carefully avoids the hateful word 'compel,' but evidently has imbibed Lord Roberts' ideas down to the last dot." He combated strenuously the theory that the best way to prevent war was to prepare to make war. On the contrary, he held that "the means to do ill deeds makes ill done," and that a nation in arms was an aggressively warlike nation, whose very existence made the maintenance of international peace difficult, if not impossible. This was more especially the case if it were a nation like Great Britain, Imperialist and Commercialist in its world policy. "Militarism and all that pertains to it is inimical to the cause of progress, the well-being of the people, and the development of the race."

This may almost be said to have been the keynote of
his appeal during the remainder of his life, for even then,
to him and to others, there was discernible the cloud no
bigger than a man's hand that was eventually to outspread
and darken the political skies and burst in disruptive
disaster upon the world. To avert this catastrophe the
I.L.P. devoted much of its energy and resources during
the ensuing years, opposing all militarist developments,
whether it was Haldane's Territorial Army scheme, or
the demands for an increase of naval and military armaments, conducting anti-militarist campaigns right up to
the eve of the great tragedy, and hoping always that the
International Socialist movement might so increase in
strength as to be able to preserve the peace of the world.

Doubtless Hardie had this thought uppermost in his
mind during his visit to Brussels the following month as
a member of the International Socialist Bureau to prepare for the next year's Congress at Stuttgart. He had
with him as his colleague on this occasion Mr. H. M.
Hyndman, of whom he said, "a more charming and
agreeable companion no wayfarer ever had," which
causes the reflection that if these two could have been
in close companionship oftener much mutual misunderstanding might have been avoided.

Meantime, while the hidden hands of diplomacy and
finance were busy in European politics, and while the
Labour Party in Parliament was steadily finding its feet
and becoming a force in the shaping of industrial legislation, the Women's Suffrage movement was attracting,
not to say distracting, attention in the country. The
past attitude of party leaders and politicians generally,
the I.L.P. always excepted, had been to ignore it loftily,
to assume that it was a manufactured agitation, the pro-
duct of a few enthusiastic cranks, and that there was
really no demand for the vote by any numerous section

of women. The ethics of political equality did not, of course, trouble these *status quo* politicians. The Women's Social and Political Union set itself out to shatter this serene aloofness, and did so very effectually, shattering some other things in the process. At a Liberal demonstration in Manchester the previous year, at which Mr. Churchill was the chief speaker, a number of suffragists, incensed by the refusal of the platform to answer their questions, set up such a din that the police were called in to eject the women, and a kind of miniature riot took place. Miss Adela Pankhurst and Miss Annie Kenney, two young but very vigorous ladies, were arrested, but no prosecution followed. Immediately after the General Election, a deputation of women sought an interview with the Prime Minister at his residence in London, and on being refused admittance created a disturbance. Three women were arrested on this occasion but were also released without a prosecution. Thus this phase of the movement began.

Hardie did not identify himself with nor express approval of these demonstrations, but he did what was better. Being fortunate in the ballot, he made himself sponsor for a resolution in Parliament which, if it had been carried, and of this there was tolerable certainty, would have advanced the women's cause by several years. The women had been very active during the General Election, and had pledged a majority of Members of the House of Commons to support their demands. Hardie's resolution was designed to enable these gentlemen to redeem their pledges, and thereby secure a majority vote which would in effect have been a mandate to the Government. The resolution was as follows : "That in the opinion of this House it is desirable that sex should cease to be a bar to the exercise of the Parliamentary Franchise." Hardie, knowing that time was valuable, spoke briefly and persuasively. It was known that, as usual, an attempt would be made to talk the resolution out, but precedents were clear, and the Speaker would no doubt have given the closure. Some suffragists in the Ladies' Gallery who were not well acquainted with procedure, seeing the clock fingers creep round to the closing hour, believed that everything was undone, and made a demonstration. That ended the matter and defeated all hope of the closure. The resolution was talked out, or it might be more accurate to say, screamed out. Hardie uttered no word of disapproval of the demonstration, and indeed, to some extent defended the action of the women, but he would have preferred that it had not occurred. He believed that it would have been possible to get the debate closured in time for a division, in which case the resolution might have been carried by a substantial majority. Whether or not his hopes would have been realised can, of course, never now be determined.

Thus ended the famous "grille scene," the precursor of many much more violent demonstrations at public meetings throughout the country, in some of which Hardie himself was destined to be a sufferer. So indiscriminate is fanaticism, even in a good cause.

These events happened in his jubilee year. In response to the suggestion that the occasion should be signalised by some public manifestation, he characteristically advised that it should take the form of a special fund for organisation. Having regard to the recent heavy demands upon the rank and file for election finance, this was not at the moment considered feasible, though it was not lost sight of, as we shall see. What was decided upon was a public reception and presentation. This took place on October 24th in the Memorial Hall, London, which was crowded to overflowing with men and women representative of every phase and section of the Labour and Socialist movement, desirous of celebrating, as one Welshman with a fine spiritual perception put it, "Keir Hardie's fifty years on earth." There were telegrams of congratulation from four hundred and forty-nine branches of the I.L.P. and also from numerous other Socialist and Trade Union organisations, besides messages of goodwill from many distinguished people outside the Socialist movement. As showing how completely he had lived down misunderstanding, for the time, the message from the Social Democratic Federation may be quoted. "This Executive Council of the S.D.F. congratulate Comrade Keir Hardie on the attainment of his fiftieth birthday, express their admiration of his independent Parliamentary career and his outspoken advocacy of Socialist principles as the object of the working-class movement, and wish him many years of life in which to carry on his work for the people." Hardie himself arrived on the scene late, for the characteristic reason that he had been in Poplar speaking on behalf of the Labour candidates there. Philip Snowden presided, and Bruce Glasier made the presentation, which consisted of an inscribed gold watch with fob and seal, subscribed for by the N.A.C. and a few intimate friends, and a gold-mounted umbrella for Mrs. Hardie. Modest gifts, but for that very reason precious to the recipients. Hardie was very proud of his gifts for another reason, quite unknown to the donors. "I've aye wanted to hae a gold watch," he said naively to the present writer, thus confessing to an ambition that was very common amongst douce Scots working men in the days when gold watches were rare possessions. He did not possess his treasure long, nor was he able to hand it on as an heirloom. At the by-election in Bermondsey a few years later the watch was stolen and was never recovered.

Hardie's fiftieth year found him at the height of his mental powers; clear of vision, resolute of purpose, practical and tolerant in the Council room, vigilant in Parliament, persuasive and idealistic on the platform, and with the never-resting pen of a ready writer. He stood out at the time, beyond all question, as the greatest of working-class leaders. His physical appearance also seemed to reflect his mental and spiritual attributes. There had grown upon him an unaffected dignity of bearing, which, with hair and beard greying almost to whiteness, endued his personality with a kind of venerableness, inducing involuntary respect even from strangers. He looked much older than fifty years, except when the light flashed from his eyes in friendly laughter or in righteous anger. Then he looked much younger. Always, even to his intimate friends, there was something mystic, unfathomable, about him. He was at once aged and youthful, frankly open and reticently reserved. The explanation may perhaps be found in some reminiscently introspective words written by himself about this time. "I am," he said, "younger in spirit at fifty than I ever remember to have been. I am one of the unfortunate class who have never known what it was to be a child—in spirit I mean. Even the memories of boyhood and young manhood are gloomy. Under no circumstances, given freedom of choice, would I live that part of my life over again. Not until my life's work found me, stripped me bare of the past and absorbed me into itself did life take on any real meaning for me. Now I know the main secret. He who would find his life must lose it in others. One day I may perhaps write a book about this." The book was never written, more's the pity. It would most certainly have been personally reminiscent and biographical, and the present writer's task would have been unnecessary.

In December of this year he had a surprise for his colleagues of the National Council which took the shape of an offer of £2,000 which had been placed at his disposal and which he desired should be utilised as an organising fund on condition that a similar sum be raised by the Party within a month. The offer was, of course, accepted and the conditions prescribed complied with, the result being a great revival of organising and propaganda activity throughout the whole of the I.L.P. movement. It was disclosed afterwards that the Edinburgh ladies already referred to had taken this method of showing their interest in Hardie's jubilee celebrations.

It may be noted here, and will save any further reference, that these two ladies continued to assist in the same practical way during the remainder of their lives, and in 1913, when Miss Jane Kippen, who had survived the other sister by some years, died, it was found that by her will, the whole of her real estate, approximately £10,000, had been left jointly to Keir Hardie and John Redmond as trustees for the I.L.P. and the Irish Nationalist Party respectively.

The Labour Party—this was the title now adopted by the Labour Representation Committee—held its annual Conference in January, 1907, at Belfast. Both at this Conference, and at the Conference of the I.L.P. at Derby in April, the Woman's Suffrage question caused serious trouble, and, in the first case, very nearly created a breach between Hardie and the organisation which he had brought into existence. At Belfast, the trouble arose out of an amendment to a resolution urging "the immediate extension of the rights of suffrage and of election of women on the same conditions as men."

The amendment, which was carried by 605,000 to 268,000, declared that "any suggested measure to extend the franchise on a property qualification to a section only, is a retrograde step and should be opposed."

The carrying of this amendment was tantamount to an instruction from the conference to the Parliamentary Labour Party not to proceed with its Franchise Bill extending the vote to women on the same qualification as at present ruled for men. Hardie was chairman and leader of the Parliamentary Party. He was, moreover, a firm believer in the policy involved in the limited Bill, a policy which he had supported alike in the House, on the platform, and in the press, and he was keenly disappointed with the conference vote, though he was well aware that the policy of the militant women themselves had helped to bring about that result by prejudicing the delegates against them.

Only a few days before there had appeared in the press what purported to be an official statement from the W.S.P.U. ostentatiously flouting the Labour Party, and declaring that: "No distinction is made between the Unionist and the Labour Parties." There was therefore some ground for resentment on the part of the Conference, and this doubtless expressed itself in the adverse vote. Hardie deplored these manifestations on the part of the women, which he ascribed "to excess of zeal," but they did not shake his adherence to the policy of the immediate political equalisation of the sexes. "We have to learn to distinguish between a great principle and its advocates," he said, and the adverse vote of the Conference came to him as a kind of challenge which he felt bound to meet at once, and before the Conference closed. In the course of moving a vote of thanks to the Belfast Trades Council and the press, he asked leave to make a statement on the matter. The statement will bear recording here, alike for its historical and its biographical interest. It is contributory to our general estimate of the character of the man who made it.

"Twenty-five years ago this year," he said, "I cut myself adrift from every relationship, political and otherwise, in order to assist in building up a working-class party. I had thought the days of my pioneering were over. Of late, I have felt with increasing intensity the injustices that have been inflicted on women by the present political laws. The intimation I wish to make to the Conference and friends is that, if the motion they carried this morning was intended to limit the action of the Party in the House of Commons, I shall have to seriously consider whether I shall remain a member of the Parliamentary Party. I say this with great respect and feeling. The party is largely my own child, and I could not sever myself lightly from what has been my life-work. But I cannot be untrue to my principles, and I would have to be so, were I not to do my utmost to remove the stigma upon the women, mothers and sisters, of being accounted unfit for political citizenship."

This statement, which was quite unexpected, created something like consternation among the delegates, and for the first time in its history, the Labour Party Conference ended in a note of depression.

Though there was much resentment against Hardie within the Labour Party for the line he had taken, which showed itself when he stood again for the chair, and the opposition continued to smoulder, needless to say, the separation did not take place. The decision of the Conference, of course, could not be set aside. What was decided upon, mainly on the suggestion of Arthur Henderson, was that individual members of the Party were left free to support a Woman's Franchise Bill should it be introduced. As a matter of fact, such a measure was introduced during the session by Mr. Dickinson, a Liberal member, and supported in a speech by Hardie, and by the votes of most of the Labour Members.

The trouble at the I.L.P. Conference arose in a different way, though it was essentially the same trouble. Unlike the Labour Party, the I.L.P. was nearly unanimous in its support of the limited Bill, but when in addition to that support, the Standing Orders Committee accepted an emergency resolution, congratulating the suffragists in prison, there was a strong protest against distinguishing preferentially these women from the others who were working loyally for the general objects of the Party. Amongst the most emphatic of the protesters were Margaret MacDonald, the wife of the chairman, and J. Bruce Glasier, whose remarks illustrate vividly the intensity of feeling that was being evoked within the Party by the tactics of the W.S.P.U. "This telegram," he declared, "virtually committed the Party to the policy of the Women's Political Union. It expresses warm sympathy with a special kind of martyrdom. He wished, like Mrs. MacDonald, to express sympathy with and stand up for our own women who had stuck faithfully to the Party. He was all for the women's cause, but not for the Women's Political Union." Hardie, who was mainly responsible for the idea of sending the telegram, and also for its wording, appealed for a unanimous vote, on the ground that as a large proportion of the women who were coming out of prison that week were members of the Party, it would be a graceful act to send the telegram, and that it "should go forth wholeheartedly, without expressing an opinion on the question of tactics, that we have an appreciation for those who have the courage to go to prison in support of what they believe to be right." Notwithstanding this appeal, the motion to refer the telegram back to the Standing Orders Committee was only defeated by eight votes, there being 188 in its favour and 180 against, a striking indication of how evenly the Conference was divided on the matter. Even in the subsequent vote as to whether the telegram should be sent, there were 60 against it. The message was sent, but certainly not wholeheartedly.

The position must be made clear. The I.L.P. was in favour of Women's Suffrage. It had always been. It was in favour also of the W.S.P.U. method of obtaining the vote, namely, by equalising the franchise for the sexes, whatever the basis of qualification might be. But it was not inclined to subordinate every other social question to the advancement of the women's movement, nor to allow itself to be committed to methods of agitation upon which it had never been consulted, nor, in electioneering matters, to be placed in the same category with other political parties who had always opposed the women's claim.

Hardie evidently did not think these dangers were involved in the sending of the sympathetic telegram; or perhaps he thought the Party was big enough to take the risk. The fact that in this matter he was at variance with Glasier and MacDonald and some of the other leaders was very disquieting to many of the members of the Party and a source of satisfaction to its enemies. Evidently the "Woman Question" had disintegrating potentialities, which, if these leaders had been small-minded men, might have worked very great mischief to the movement. To all concerned it brought a good deal of pain, accentuated in Hardie's case by the fact that he was conscious of the symptoms of a recurrence of that physical trouble from which, since the operation, he had never been wholly free, and which a month later resulted in his serious breakdown.

Amidst all these activities Hardie had found time to write a book for the "Labour Ideal Series" projected by George Allen, and published about this time. The title of the book, "From Serfdom to Socialism," indicates its subject and scope. Despite the author's depreciatory foreword, it is one of the most compact and vivid statements of the case for Socialism that has ever been written, comprising in some four thousand words a survey alike of the philosophic and the economic developments towards the Socialist State, not as a finality but as the natural and necessary environment for a future Communist society. "Mankind when left free has always and in all parts of the world naturally turned to Communism. That it will do so again is the most likely forecast that can be made, and the great industrial organisations, the Co-operative movement, the Socialist organisations and the Labour Party are each and all developing the feeling of solidarity and of mutual aid which will make the inauguration of Communism a comparatively easy task as the natural successor to State Socialism."

The charm of the book lies in its lucidity and in the complete avoidance of that technical and turgid terminology which looks scientific, but, for the ordinary reader, is only befogging; and it was for the ordinary reader that the book was written.

A short extract from the chapter on "Socialism" will give some idea of its arguments and method. "The State is what the people make it. Its institutions are necessarily shaped to further and protect the interests of the dominant influence. Whilst a landed nobility reigned supreme, the interests of that class were the one concern of the State. Subsequently with the growth of the commercial and trading class, which, when it became strong enough, insisted on sharing the power of the State with the landed aristocracy, many of the old laws passed by the landlords in restraint of trade were modified. Now that the working class is the dominant power, politically at least, it logically and inevitably follows that that class will also endeavour so to influence the State as to make it protect its interests. As the political education of the workers progresses, and they begin to realise what are the true functions of the State, this power will be exerted in an increasing degree in the direction of transforming the State from a property-preserving to a life-preserving institution. The fundamental fact which the working class is beginning to recognise is that property, or at least its possession, is power. This is an axiom which admits of no contradiction. So long as property, using the term to mean land and capital, is in the hands of a small class, the rest of the people are necessarily dependent upon that class. A democracy, therefore, has no option but to seek to transform those forms of property, together with the power inherent in them, from private to public possession. Opinions may differ as to the methods to be pursued in bringing about that change, but concerning its necessity there are no two opinions in the working-class movement. When land and capital are the common property of all the people, class distinctions, as we know them, will disappear. The mind will then be the standard by which a man's place among his fellows will be determined.''

The book had a wide circulation. It was essentially a propagandist document and ought again to be utilised for that purpose.

A reference made by Hardie at this time to the Irish question should be here noted. It is not inappropriate to the present situation. It was made in answer to a statement by the Rev. R. J. Campbell, who was at this period making approaches to Labour, and who, in an article on "The Labour Movement and Religion," had declared that, as an Ulsterman by origin, he had "an objection to handing the whole of Ireland over to the Roman Catholic majority without proper safeguards." "I often wonder," wrote Hardie, "why it is that Ulstermen oppose Home Rule for the land of their birth. If there is one fact in the future more certain than another, it is that in an Irish Parliament Ulstermen would wield influence greater than any of them have ever dreamed of hitherto. They are at present cut off from their fellow Irishmen because they hold themselves as a sect apart, and are, in consequence, powerless to influence their country's development. One session in the House of Commons would cure Mr. Campbell of the last remnants of the old prejudice against his fellow-countrymen which he probably drank in with his mother's milk and which still clings to him." Hardie's diagnosis of the individual Ulsterman's prejudice was probably correct, though his proposed cure had no guarantee in actual fact. There are Ulstermen who have passed many sessions in the House of Commons, and have become all the more bigoted. It is to be feared that the Ulsterman does not want to be cured of his prejudice and shrinks from the Home Rule experiment for that very reason.

Mr. Campbell shortly afterwards affirmed his belief in Socialism and joined the I.L.P. mainly as the result of discussions with Hardie. After a few years, however, he slipped out, and has not been heard of politically since.

In February of this year, Hardie had the experience of being "ragged" at Cambridge, whither he had gone to address a meeting at the invitation of student and working-class Socialists. He went through the ordeal without coming to any harm, thanks to well-organised protection on the part of the local sympathisers, who took the brunt of the physical abuse meant for the plebeian agitator. A contemporary press comment may be quoted, especially as it supplies contrasting pictures of Hardie's experience as a propagandist and social worker.

"On Saturday night last, Keir Hardie was hooted and mobbed by the students at Cambridge University. There is much varied experience crammed into the working day of the Socialist agitator. At one o'clock in the morning of the same day Keir Hardie was present at quite a different function from the Cambridge one. He was with a few companions on the Thames Embankment, a looker-on at the dispensing of charity to some of London's destitute waifs by the Salvation Army officials. I know not what other experience filled in Mr. Hardie's day between the Thames Embankment and Cambridge University, but in the beginning and ending of it there was surely contrast enough. The bottom dog at the one end and the top-cur at the other; poverty and ignorance on the Embankment; riches and ignorance at Cambridge. The results of our social system epitomised in two scenes." And for both, there was deep sympathy in the heart of Keir Hardie.

Up to the moment of his breakdown in health he was engrossed in work, and in the very week in which he was compelled to give up, he submitted a report on Mr. Haldane's Army Bill which he had prepared at the request of the Parliamentary Labour Party. There was never anything slipshod or superficial about Hardie's methods, and his analysis of the Army Bill was exceedingly searching and thorough. Upon the basis of that analysis he recommended that the Bill should be opposed, root and branch, for the following amongst other reasons :—

"(a) Because it introduces militarism in our public schools amongst boys at their most impressionable age and ere they have arrived at years of discretion.

"(b) Because the method by which officers are to be secured bars out the working class and creates an army of workers officered by rich men.

"(c) Because it introduces the military element into industrial and civil relationships in a way hitherto unknown.

"(d) Because we are not convinced of the need for turning Britain into an armed camp.

"Employers and workmen," said the report, "will alike be inconvenienced by the provisions of the Bill, and in the end it will almost certainly lead to compulsory military service."

On the lines indicated by this report, the Labour Party, led mainly by MacDonald and Snowden, fought the Bill, clause by clause, unsuccessfully of course, the Tory Party being just as militarist as the Liberal Government. Hardie himself, to his deep regret, was unable to take part in a fight into which he would have thrown every atom of his energy. He had already, during the debate on the Army Estimates, in a searching and lofty-toned speech, denounced the measure as "repugnant to all that is best in the moral and civil traditions of the nation." The passing of the Bill is a matter of history, as is also the continued preparation for Armageddon on the part of the rival nations.

That same week, Hardie was laid prostrate and had to be removed to a nursing home for examination. He was loath to believe that the attack was of a kind that would necessitate anything more than reorganisation of his work.

"One thing is certain," he wrote to his friend Glasier, "I won't be able to do any speaking this side of Whit week. The doctors here have been most kind. There were three of them called in for consultation the day I was brought down, and all three have since visited me in their human rather than their professional capacity. I don't know whether they have been talking amongst themselves, but at least they have all harped upon the one thing—that another attack, which they say may occur at any moment, would be a very serious thing, necessitating an operation. They say that by taking things easy and, by observing ordinary gumption in the matter of food, rest, and the like, I may not only go on all right for years, but the trouble may heal up."

Taking things easy was the one thing this man could not do, but on this occasion he had no alternative but to go for a very complete rest, and, somewhat reluctantly, he bowed to the inevitable.

Writing in the train on the way home to Cumnock, he said, "I begin to fear that the process of restoration is likely to be somewhat slow. One part of the internal economy has broken down. I have no desire for food, nor will anything solid lie; whilst even liquids cause a good deal of uneasiness. But I now know this, and have resolved accordingly, and my friends may rely upon it, that I shall be docile and tractable. For the moment there is to be no operation. Nature and more gentle and soothing measures are to have their chance first."

He had got to the point of making good resolutions for the future, and, recalling Liebknecht's reflections on the effect which night work and overwork had upon the naturally strong constitution of Karl Marx, he said, "I

R   245

shall try to remember it after I am well, but there is so much to do, and so few to do it. I pray that the end may be sudden when it comes, a lingering illness must be dreadful." Thus chafingly did he submit to the ordeal of rest.

Several weeks' treatment at the Wemyss Bay Hydropathic brought him relief from pain but did not restore him to vigour, and it became apparent that his complete recovery would be long delayed. "The doctors tell me that to return to active work now means in all likelihood another collapse at an early date. But I cannot remain idle, nor, I feel certain, could I school myself into taking it easy at work. I have never done so. I can idle when idling, but I cannot work like an automaton. It was the same in the pits and in the quarries in my earlier days. I don't like the prospect of another experience like the last few weeks, and I know that the doctors are right. A sick dispirited man is not only of no use in the front rank of our movement—he is apt to be a nuisance to himself and others. Courage, initiative, energy, hope, are all needed, and these the ailing have not got, and cannot give." An unusually despondent mood this, for him, and one that was the surest proof that he was really very ill. And so, gradually, it was borne in upon him that he must accept the advice given by the doctors and by many friends, and go for a long sea voyage.

"I came here," he wrote again from Wemyss Bay, "to try and get well, and settled down to the task as I would to the fighting of a by-election. Six and seven times a day I have dressed and undressed to undergo treatment of one kind and another. To leave the job unfinished would, I feel, be neither fair to myself nor to those who look to me for guidance. The sea voyage idea is not quite settled, but I give it thought as it has begun to shape itself in my mind."

ROUND THE WORLD

When at last the sea voyage was determined upon, the first proposal was for a visit to the Australian Colonies *via* Canada, but finally a voyage round the world was arranged, and as this, of course, included India, that fact altered, as we shall see, the whole complexion of the enterprise. He was the more easily reconciled to the prospect of a long absence from home by the knowledge that he was leaving the movement healthier than it had ever been, both in Parliament and in the country. His friend, Pete Curran, had just won a signal by-election victory at Jarrow, and Victor Grayson was starting out to contest Colne Valley with high hopes of success. In the House, the Labour Party was holding steadfastly together, and its leading men earning distinction alike as practical legislators and as opponents and critics of the Government. It should be noted here that MacDonald was at this time vigorously besetting the Government with demands for information regarding the nature of the agreements being entered into with Russia, which, if it had been given and so made public, might have changed the whole course of future diplomacy. It was certainly through no lack of vigilance on the part of the Labour Party that the nation became involved in international entanglements from which it could not get free without going to war, and which created war conditions in the whole of Europe.

Before sailing, Hardie wrote one article on the political situation, in which he scathingly indicted the Government for shelving all its social legislation to make room for Haldane's Territorial Army Bill. "Everything else had to stand aside for this conscription-made-easy proposal," rendered all the more ominous by the fact that the Government "was making treaties and bargains with Russia, whilst the hands and garments of its rulers drip with the blood of the victims who are daily being done to death for demanding for the Russian people a say in the government of their country."

He sailed from Liverpool on July 12th, having first to undergo the ordeal of big send-off demonstrations in Glasgow, Manchester and Liverpool. In an "Au Revoir" message to the "Leader," he outlined his prospective journeyings as follows: "In Canada and South Africa, Australia and New Zealand I hope to meet again friends of the long ago, and to learn how our movement progresses. Japan and China will be touched in passing, that, and little more. We want all the cohesion possible in our great world-wide movement, and even a handshake in passing may not be without its value in bringing the forces of Labour in closer touch. India was an afterthought. At present a lying press campaign is being waged to bias the people of this country against the nations of that far-off land and to make it difficult for the Government to do anything to break down the official caste under which we hold them in the bondage of subjection. By seeing and hearing on the spot what the actual facts are, I may, on my return, be able to let in a little light upon the dark places of Indian government."

The "afterthought" had thus become the main object of his journey, and the friends at home, who could not see much rest for him in such an enterprise, had to console themselves with the knowledge that he would perforce have to spend at least fifteen weeks at sea.

Throughout Canada he was received with great cordiality and he sent home interesting but none too optimistic impressions of the social conditions prevailing in the Dominion and of the state of Labour and Socialist organisation. Here, as everywhere during his tour, in conference with Trade Union and Socialist leaders, he broached the idea of a world-wide Labour Federation, as a practical and effective supplement to the Socialist International, not with any hope of its materialising quickly, but simply by way of sowing seed that might bring forth fruit in the future. He derived much benefit in health from his brief sojourn in Canada and did not meet with any hostility of any kind.

From the moment, however, of his arrival in India it became evident that those interests to which it was not suitable that "light should be let in upon dark places" had made preparations to prejudice him as a witness for the truth in the eyes of the British people. The fact that there was grave discontent among large sections of the people of India, arising out of the recent partition of Bengal, made it easy for the people at home to accept as true the luridly coloured pictures of Keir Hardie as a fomenter of that discontent. By the end of September, sensational reports, telegraphed through Reuter, of his sayings and doings in India began to reach this country, and were given great prominence and wide circulation in the press.

He was described as going about influencing the minds of the Bengalis, fomenting sedition, and undermining British rule. He was reported to have said that "the condition of Bengal was worse than that of Russia," and that "the atrocities committed by officials would, if they were known, evoke more horror in England than the Turkish outrages in Armenia." "Whereupon," said a friendly commentator, "the Yellow Press was seized with a violent eruption. It vomited forth volumes of smoke and flame and mud, and roared at Keir Hardie like a thousand bellowing Bulls of Bashan, and even journals less tainted with insanity felt extremely shocked and took upon themselves to administer censure upon

the author of this 'scandalous utterance.'"   Even
"Punch" joined in the vituperation with a cartoon by
Mr. Linley Sambourne, which showed Britannia gripping
the agitator by the scruff of the neck and apostrophising
him : "Here, you'd better come home. We know all
about you here—you'll do less harm." At the time that
this disgraceful attack was being made, the Indian
authorities were writing home appreciative accounts
of his doings. For a full fortnight Hardie was
the most violently detested man throughout the
English-speaking world, for, of course, this mighty
noise had its reverberations in every corner of the
Empire, and also in America. Knowing full well
that his colleagues at home would have some difficulty
in withstanding the storm of misrepresentation, he sent
a cablegram to the "Daily Mail" giving a brief review
of the economic conditions and political situation in
Bengal, and concluding with the following significant
caution : "People at home should be careful of trusting
reports, especially of Reuter's agents. The grossly dis-
torted home reports are publicly censured by the leading
Calcutta journals.   Amusement here this morning at
the cabled comments of the 'Daily Mail,' 'Times' and
'Standard' in their leading columns. They have been
misled by Reuter.—J. Keir Hardie."

In reply to a "Daily Mail" inquiry whether he had
really made this specific statement attributed to him, he
replied :—

"Calcutta, Thursday, October 3rd.

"The statements are fabrications. I said that the
prohibitions of meetings, etc., reminded me of Russia,
and the violation of Hindu women by Mohammedan
rowdies reminded me of Armenia, and that Colonial
Government was the ultimate goal.—Keir Hardie."

And yet, on the very same day on which he cabled

INDIA

his repudiation of the statement attributed to him,
Reuter's Calcutta correspondent sent a cable to the
British press in which he stated that "Mr. Keir Hardie,
M.P., admitted in an interview that the statements
attributed to him were not exaggerated." Thus lie
followed lie in a kind of cuttlefish endeavour to obscure
the truth, the real purpose of the detractors being to
discredit the very serious statements which Hardie
actually did make concerning the state of matters in
India.

Hardie's own exposure of these misrepresentations
was quickly followed by that of the Indian press, which
unanimously testified to the correctness of his bearing.
"None of the papers here, either English or native,"
said a Central News message, "has taken much exception
to his conduct, which is thought to have been, on the
whole, quite proper and discreet, as becoming the
honoured guest of the Maharajah of Mymensingh, one
of the signatories of the loyal Manifesto, and of several
prominent officials."

Most satisfactory was the attitude of his colleagues at
home in the face of all the obloquy and abuse. The
"Labour Leader," speaking for the I.L.P., declared
that "the Party would stand solidly with him in con-
veying to the Indian people the strongest expression of
the sympathy and support of British Socialists in their
struggle against social and political oppression."

Robert Blatchford, in the "Clarion," appealed to the
British press for fair play. Mr. Cunninghame Graham's
utterance was characteristic and at the same time representative of general Socialist opinion in the country.
Declaring that he honoured and respected Keir Hardie
for all he had endeavoured to do in Calcutta and British
India, he said, "There were many millions of population in the country, the discreetest millions of the dis-

251

creetest population the world had ever known, but there were few Keir Hardies—there were few men who, like Keir Hardie, had risen from the depths of poverty to such a position as he now occupied." Our position in India was but for a time, and he held that the utterances of Keir Hardie would do much to prepare the minds of the native Indians, and cause them to think of the benefits of free institutions. Instead of deporting Keir Hardie from India, he thought "they ought to send an ironclad to bring him home as the first man who had broken through prejudice, and given the right hand of fellowship to their down-trodden brethren."

These words undoubtedly reflected the views of the Socialist movement, and also of many people outside of it.

The attacks on Hardie, on this as on so many previous occasions, had exactly the opposite effect from what was intended, and he emerged from the tempest holding a higher place than ever in the estimation of the thoughtful sections of the community, while he had the satisfaction of knowing that public attention had been focussed on the question of the government of India as it had never been since the days of the Mutiny. Complacent and self-satisfied British citizens who had only heard vaguely of the partition of Bengal, and had no idea at all of what it implied, began to realise that all was not well in our manner of governing what the newspapers called the "Indian Empire."

Happily, it is not necessary to overload this memoir with a detailed account of Hardie's progress through India. That is to be found in his book "India : Impressions and Suggestions," first published in 1909; a second edition, issued in 1917 by the Home Rule for India League with a valuable foreword by Philip Snowden, is now available.

INDIA

He spent two months in India, and visited Bengal, Northern India, and two of the native States—Baroda and Mysore. He mingled with all classes—Anglo-Indian officials, native princes, rulers and magistrates, peasants and factory workers, Mohammedans and Hindus; with all on terms of equality—that being probably his greatest offence in the eyes of certain sections of the Anglo-Indians who regard the maintenance of the "colour line" as a necessary bulwark of British supremacy. Hardie, naturally, could not recognise any social or race barriers, and held steadfastly to his intention, publicly declared before leaving Britain, that he "would know no colour, race or creed." As a matter of fact, he knew them all, but made no distinction between any of them, and thereby won the esteem and confidence of all classes in India, and was enabled to see the inner life of the people as no previous visitor had been allowed to see it. In this respect, as in many others during the course of his life, he was a pioneer. The breach which he made in the wall of prejudice has never been quite closed, and through it there has passed much goodwill from the common people of Britain to the common people of India.

By this time Hardie was beginning to be somewhat homesick and longing to be in the thick of the political fray at Westminster. The visit to Ceylon was interesting but uneventful, and at Colombo he debated with himself whether it would not be better after all to leave out Australia and South Africa, and "make a bee-line for the Lugar, *via* the Red Sea." "The fact is," he wrote, "the trip is too long, and I see the new session opening and me still on the water, and I like not that." His health had evidently considerably improved, and with restored strength came renewed confidence in himself, and he was yearning to be free to face his critics.

J. KEIR HARDIE

His experiences in the Australian colonies were, in the nature of things, in strong contrast with his experiences in India. He was amongst a free people, in the one part of the world where genuine experiment was being made in the principles and practice of self-government, and he was naturally intent on studying—as far as his short tour would allow—the various phases and aspects of that experiment. But he made no claim that the notes which he sent home should be regarded as anything more than the personal impressions of a keenly interested wayfarer. He was well received everywhere, in West and South Australia, in Victoria, and New Zealand, and New South Wales, and regretted very much that he had to leave out Queensland and Tasmania. He had to speak at numerous public receptions organised in his honour. One or two attempts to raise prejudice against him, based upon the press reports of his Indian tour, melted away immediately on personal contact with him. He visited the gold fields at Koolgardie and Bendigo, the lead and copper mines at Broken Hill, and, of course, the coal mines at Newcastle—at all these places talking, as was his wont, as a miner to his fellow craftsmen. He renewed his friendship with Andrew Fisher, his early associate in the formation of the Ayrshire Miners' Union, then and now one of Australia's leading statesmen, and still true to his democratic upbringing. He met scores of old friends wherever he went, Scottish and Welsh friends especially claiming kinship and clanship. He spent many social hours with them cracking about old times in the old country and singing the old songs, and generally giving free scope to those social instincts which were always strong within him. At Adelaide he even went so far as to allow himself to be impressed into playing in a cricket match—Press and Parliament—and he records with a kind of boyish glee : "I carried off my bat for eight runs, one hit counting for four." Probably bowlers and fielders were kind to him. He enjoyed himself thoroughly, and from the health point of view the Australian visit was undoubtedly the most beneficial part of the world tour. Yet it came near making an end of his career. While on a short motor trip out from Wellington, New Zealand, the car in which he was travelling went over an embankment, throwing him some fifteen or sixteen feet down towards a stream at the bottom. He was only saved from a complete descent by contact with trees and shrubbery. No bones were broken, but he was badly shaken and had to rest for several days. Describing the occurrence in a letter home, he said : "The accident has quite upset my New Zealand tour so far as the South Island is concerned, but bad as this is, it might easily have been worse. Doubtless there are those who would account for it by quoting the old saw, 'Deil's bairns hae their deddie's luck.' If there be such, I am not the one to gainsay them."

From his summing up of his Australian experiences one passage may be quoted, especially as it seems to show some modification of his attitude towards the Citizen Army idea, a modification, however, which is overborne by his main argument. Referring to the fixed policy of a "White Australia," in defence of which he recognised that the Australasian "would fight as for no other ideal," and to the proposals arising out of that for an Australian navy and compulsory military service, he wrote : "Now, I who hate militarism and everything it stands for, readily admit that the conditions of the Australian continent are different from those of Great Britain. Further, if the choice is between an armed nation and a professional army, my preference is for the former. But in this, as in all else, everything depends upon who is to control the army. With Labour controlling the Parliament and owning the press, the danger of playing with arms would be reduced to a minimum. If, on the other hand, the professional sol-dier and the Imperialist politician are to run the show, the danger is too great to be taken on. Were I in Australian politics at this moment, I would resist to the end every proposal for giving militarism the least foot-hold in the Commonwealth. The Japanese bogey, when it is not a fraud, is the concoction of a frenzied brain, destitute of all knowledge of European politics. Great Britain is the last country on the map of the world with which the Japanese will care to embroil themselves. The experiment of keeping Australia white is a great one, the success of which time alone can decide."

From Australia to South Africa was like passing from a friendly into a hostile country. He had to run the gauntlet of an opposition carefully and vindictively organised by the gold and diamond mining interests whose influence largely dominated the public life and controlled the press of the South African colonies. Hardie was their declared enemy and the avowed friend of the Boers and of the natives. He had championed the Boer Republic all through the war. He had opposed bitterly, and not ineffectively, the introduction of Chinese labour. He had advocated the claims of the natives for fair treatment, and his impassioned protests against the Natal massacres were on record in the pages of "Hansard" and in the columns of the "Labour Leader"; and, greatest sin of all, he was the living symbol of organised Labour, now beginning to assert itself in South Africa as elsewhere. The opposition manifested itself in calculated and unbridled rowdyism, unchecked by the authorities, except at Johannesburg, where murder was feared. At Ladysmith, the windows of the hotel in which he stayed were smashed by the paid rowdies, "no one, not even the hotel-keeper, trying to restrain them." At Johannesburg a gang had been organised, and a detachment was sent to Pretoria, where the crowd, after the meeting, was the most turbulent of any, and smashed the carriage in which he drove back to the hotel with stones and other missiles. At Durban, there were similar disturbances. Yet at all these places he managed to address public meetings organised by the local Trades Councils and the Socialists, bodyguards capable of protecting him, at considerable risk to themselves, from actual violence to his person being provided from amongst his friends.

Through it all he moved unperturbed, and did not allow the rough treatment he had received to colour his impressions. Thus, for example, at Johannesburg, he describes a two thousand feet mine which he visited as being well ventilated and the timbering the finest he had seen anywhere. He noted that the compounds, especially the newer parts, were clean and comfortable, and that the Chinamen were living under much better sanitary conditions than they enjoyed at home. At the same time he points out that "there are empty houses, and unemployed workmen, and much woe and want in the Rand," and that, "nevertheless, the mines pay £7,000,000 a year in dividends."

He deplored the prevalence of the opinion, as much amongst working people as amongst other classes, that "South Africa should be made a white man's country and the nigger kept in his proper place," and he pointed out that the white man, by refusing to work and by getting the Kaffir to work for him under his supervision, was tacitly admitting that South Africa was not, and never could be, a white man's country. The native

question he regarded as South Africa's greatest problem, but made no attempt to dogmatise as to its
solution. He was impressed by the shrewdness and
intelligence of the South African native, who, he pre-
dicted, "would put up a fight against the farmer who
wants his land, and the miner who wants his labour at
starvation wage." Hardie urged that the Labour movement at home and in South Africa should combine to
save the South African natives from being reduced to
the position of "a landless proletariat at the mercy of
their exploiters for all time."

His somewhat pessimistic conclusions regarding the
South African outlook were, if anything, reinforced by a
day spent in the company of Olive Schreiner, with whom
he had been on terms of friendship since before the war,
and whose mind was filled with dark forebodings for
the future of her country. He was not sorry to shake
the South African dust from his feet and turn his face
homewards.

The tour, which for many reasons attracted as much
public interest as if he had been a royal personage, had
at least fulfilled its primary purpose. When he arrived
in Plymouth in the last week of March, he appeared to
be in splendid health. "I have never seen him looking
so well, though his grey hair has whitened a little," said
Glasier, who was amongst the welcoming party. "He
presented a most picturesque figure, as he stood, erect
as ever, sunburnt and aglow, in his tweed suit, his gray
Tam-o'-Shanter, and with his Indian shawl slung round
his shoulder, he struck one as a curious blend between
a Scottish shepherd and an Indian rajah. He avows
that he has stuck to his Scotch porridge for breakfast
six days a week with a 'tea breakfast' on Sundays."

Among the first news he received on landing was that
the Socialist students of Glasgow University had

nominated him for the Lord Rectorship, thus making him involuntarily the central figure in quite a new sphere of Socialist propaganda. The election, which created widespread interest, took place in the following October, after an unusually exciting fight. Hardie himself, in accordance with traditional etiquette in such contests, took no part. The nomination speech was made by H. M. Hyndman, and other speakers who addressed the students on behalf of Hardie's candidature were Cunninghame Graham, Herbert Burrows, Mrs. Cobden Sanderson, Victor Grayson and the Rev. Stitt Wilson, of America, while messages in support were sent by Dr. Alfred Russel Wallace, George Bernard Shaw, H. G. Wells, the Rev. R. J. Campbell, and others well known in the world of literature and politics. The leading spirit in this unique campaign was Thomas Johnston, a former student at the University, founder and editor of "Forward," and now well known as the author of the authoritative "History of the Working Classes of Scotland." The voting figures were as follows :—

Lord Curzon	947
Lloyd George	935
Keir Hardie	122

Twenty-two of Hardie's votes were from women students.
The narrow defeat of Lloyd George caused much chagrin amongst Liberals.

CHAPTER ELEVEN

ALMOST immediately on his arrival, Hardie found himself deeply immersed in work, and seemed bent on squandering somewhat freely the energy he had gained during his travels.

The period, indeed, is so crowded with events in which he was involved that it is well-nigh impossible to present a sequential account of his sayings and doings. There was the usual round of welcoming demonstrations which were calculated not only to show the esteem in which he was held by the Labour movement, but also to act as a stimulus to that movement. The meeting in the Albert Hall, London, was remarkable for size and enthusiasm, and the recipient of so much adulation might have been pardoned if he had succumbed, if only temporarily, to the disease known as "swelled head" —a failing not unknown amongst popular politicians. Hardie was not without his share of self-esteem, but he never allowed it to magnify into a grotesque proportion his place in the movement. These demonstrations he accepted as his due, but he valued them chiefly as Labour's answer to the misrepresentations and abuse that had been so lavishly showered upon him. If his own people believed in him, he cared not who was against him.

He had also to make a tour of his constituency, where his reception was such as to assure him that the attacks made upon him had not weakened, but had rather strengthened, the fidelity of his supporters. South Wales had now become a kind of second home to him, where he was as much at his ease, and had friendships as intimate, as in Ayrshire or Glasgow.

Following quickly upon these platform appearances came the I.L.P. Conference at Huddersfield, at which there were some signs of division over the Party's connection with the Labour Party. The trouble centred round Victor Grayson, who had been elected for the Colne Valley division in the previous year, under conditions which did not strictly conform to Labour Party rules, and which had prevented his official endorsement either by the N.A.C. or by the Labour Party Executive. The former body, however, made itself responsible for paying him his share of the Parliamentary Maintenance Fund, from which the I.L.P. helped its Parliamentary representatives. The Conference sustained the N.A.C. attitude by a large majority. Thereafter, a resolution—to which Grayson agreed—was passed, declaring that "during the remainder of Parliament his relations to the Labour Party should be the same as that of all the other I.L.P. members, except in the case of his being placed upon the Parliamentary Fund." This dispute, throughout which Hardie played the part of peacemaker, seems in perspective somewhat trivial, but at the time it looked to be very serious, and there were not wanting those who hoped to see it result either in the break up of the I.L.P. or in its severance from the Labour Party.

This Conference, however, was chiefly remarkable for its pronouncements on foreign affairs, and especially upon the agreement with the Russian Government, which it declared was equivalent to "giving an informal sanction to the course of infamous tyranny which has suppressed every semblance of representation and has condemned great numbers of our Russian comrades to imprisonment, torture and death." A resolution was also passed protesting against the "shameless exploitation of the Congo by the Government of King Leopold, and calling upon the British Government to take such action as may compel a more humane treatment of the natives of the Congo." This was followed by a resolution, moved by Hardie and seconded by Joseph Burgess, demanding "that the people of India should be given more effective control over their own affairs." In the course of his speech, Hardie cited the native States of Baroda, Mysore and Travancore as proof of the fitness of the Indian people for self-government. In one or other of these States, he affirmed, he had found parish councils established, he had found the caste system disappearing, and he had found compulsory free education, and in one of them there was a popularly elected Annual Parliament meeting and discussing national affairs. "The whole of the administration, from the humblest office right up to the chief, was filled by natives and the administration of the affairs of those States was a model to the rest of India." In face of the momentous issues raised by these resolutions, the Grayson incident dwindled into insignificance, and the somewhat rancorous feelings which it had evoked melted away in the general recognition of the great purposes for which the I.L.P. existed.

Three keenly contested by-elections occurring almost simultaneously, at Dewsbury, Dundee and Montrose Burghs, in all of which the Labour candidates were defeated, afforded opportunity for big scale propaganda in which, as a matter of course, Hardie played a prominent part, evidently quite forgetful of the fact that only a year before he had been almost at death's door.

At the same time, Parliamentary affairs developed in

such a way as to throw him once more very prominently into the limelight. Sir Henry Campbell-Bannerman had retired from the Premiership and was succeeded by Mr. Asquith, a decided change for the worse from the democratic standpoint, and almost of sinister import having regard to the new Premier's imperialistic tendencies and the international alliances which were in process of being formed. Notwithstanding the repeated inquiries of MacDonald and other Labour Members for information concerning the agreements which had been come to with the Czar's Government, no satisfactory or informative statement had been vouchsafed, and there were strong reasons for the suspicion that these agreements were of such a character as to involve this country in grave and unavoidable responsibility in the event of an outbreak of war in Europe. When, therefore, the announcement was made that King Edward was to pay an official visit to the Czar at Reval, these suspicions seemed to find confirmation, and it became the duty of all friends of international peace to protest. The fact that it was a Liberal Government which was pursuing a policy quite in line with the designs of the Tory Party threw the onus of opposition upon Labour, and against the combined forces of the two imperialist parties, Labour was in a hopeless minority and could do little more than make its protest in such a way as to arrest the attention of the nations.

Labour was opposed to the ostentatious recognition of the Czar's Government, not only because of the dangerous international commitments which it implied, but also because of the flagrantly despotic character of that Government which at that very time was engaged in suppressing with calculated savagery every semblance of constitutional rule. On every I.L.P. platform throughout the country the King's visit to the Czar was strongly condemned, Hardie, of course, being in the very forefront of the attack. Under the title, "Consorting with Murderers," he contributed a powerful article to the "Labour Leader," detailing the crimes of Czardom during the previous three years since the formation of the first Duma, which he contended had only been conceded for the purpose of giving confidence to European financiers so as to induce them to advance money to the Czar's Government, a contention which had found confirmation in the fact that immediately on the successful flotation of a loan of £90,000,000 the newly-formed Duma had been forcibly disbanded, and one hundred and sixty-nine of its members arrested and imprisoned on the flimsiest charge, while seventy-four members of the second Duma had shared the same fate. The article gave the official figures of persons butchered by the Black Hundred under Czarist auspices as 19,000 in two years, and the number of political prisoners executed during the same time as 3,205; and it stated that, during two months of the current year, 1,587 persons had been condemned to death or penal servitude for no other reason than for being Radicals or Socialists. "The Czar and his Government have been singled out for honour by a Liberal Government. What is the explanation?" The article went on to show that Russian finances were again in a bankrupt condition. The Budget for the year showed a deficit of £20,000,000. The Russian debt was £665,000,000, and there were projects for a new navy and a new military railway at a cost of £70,000,000. A new loan was necessary. "Financial reasons, therefore," continued the article, "probably explain why King Edward has been advised by his responsible advisers to pay this official visit to a monarch reeking with the blood of his slaughtered subjects. The Stock Exchange hook needed to be baited. Two years ago the bait was a popularly elected Duma; this time it is a Royal crown. Truly kings have their uses."

Language of this kind was not calculated to raise its author in the esteem either of royalty or of the financiers, nor was the persistence which the Labour Party showed in bringing the question into the House of Commons likely to be viewed with favour by the two other parties, who were at one on the question of Russian policy.

On June 3rd, Hardie came into conflict with the Speaker over the rejection of a question which he had put down as to the persecution of political prisoners in Russia—particulars of which he detailed—asking whether the British Government meant to make any protest or to continue relations with the Czar's Government. The question was disallowed as reflecting upon "a friendly Power"! Notwithstanding its rejection, he managed to gain full publicity for it, which was all he would probably have got even if he had been allowed to put it. With all his directness, he was an astute parliamentarian.

The following day, in committee on the Foreign Office vote, Mr. James O'Grady, speaking for the Labour Party, in an exceedingly effective speech, moved that the salary of the Secretary of State be reduced, in order that he might raise the question of the King's visit to Russia. In the subsequent debate, Hardie again incurred the censure of the chairman, who objected to the use of the word "atrocities" as applied to a friendly Power, and on Hardie replying that he knew no other word in the English language to express his meaning, a scene ensued, which provided the press with many columns of sensational "copy." The chairman insisted on the word "atrocities," which had only been used once, being withdrawn. Hardie declined to withdraw it, and continued on his feet, debating the chairman's ruling, and incidentally impeaching the Russian Government. Other members intervened, mostly in support of Hardie's position, until at last the chairman threatened to name Hardie, with a view to his suspension. His continued refusal brought the Prime Minister to his feet with a dexterous definition of Parliamentary law, and a direct appeal to Hardie to accept the chairman's ruling. After a very evident mental conflict, he reluctantly agreed to withdraw the term of offence, in order, as he said, "to secure a division." This was certainly a mistake in tactics, and was one of the very few errors of judgment made by him during the whole of his Parliamentary career. It was at least a refutation of the charge often made against him of being a seeker after notoriety. Suspension would have been his best card if notoriety had been his object, but it would also have been the most effective way of bringing home the nature of the controversy to the public mind, and for that reason it would have been better if he had held his ground.

The most unfortunate feature of this debate was the manner of its ending, Arthur Henderson moving the closure just as Victor Grayson rose to continue the debate. It was afterwards explained that an arrangement had been come to between the leaders of the three parties that the debate should close at a certain hour and be followed by a division, which Grayson's intervention would have prevented, but the fact that it was the Labour Party leader who intervened gave some colour to the accusation made in some quarters, that Grayson was being ostracised, and it certainly helped to roughen the already existing friction.

On this occasion it is noteworthy that more than one-half of the Liberal Party abstained from voting, while the Tories voted solidly with the Liberal Government, thus confirming Hardie's oft-repeated declaration that on questions of foreign policy, the Asquith-Grey-Haldane administration was in reality a Tory Imperialist Government.

There was a remarkable sequel to this debate, an account of which may be left to one of the persons directly involved, all the more as it provides us with another of those contemporary pen-portraits of Hardie which have genuine biographical value. The witness is Arthur Ponsonby, who had recently entered the House as the successor to Sir Henry Campbell-Bannerman in the representation of Stirling Burghs. Says Mr. Ponsonby: ''I first met Keir Hardie at a luncheon party in the House of Commons before I myself was in the House. Amongst others, another highly placed, successful, and prominent Labour leader was present. I remember contrasting the two, and I was immensely struck by Keir Hardie's reticence and his occasional incisive remarks, which were very different from his colleague's voluble assurance. I decided inwardly that K.H. was the genuine article. My upbringing and the fact that I was a Liberal connected more or less at the time with officialism, I thought might give him a prejudice against me, but, on the contrary, he regarded me approvingly and I felt sympathy in his extraordinarily kindly smile. But I had only a nodding acquaintance with him till 1908, when we were thrown together in very peculiar circumstances. I had only been a fortnight in the House when a debate came on in which the Government defended the advice they had given King Edward to visit the Czar at Reval. This explanation appeared to me entirely inadequate. The people of Russia were long oppressed and persecuted in an abominable way, and I thought it morally and practically wrong that this compliment should be paid to the oppressor by a country which should always be on the side of the oppressed. Without any hesitation I voted with a small minority of Labour men and Radicals against the Government. Keir Hardie was among the number. Shortly afterwards, King Edward gave a garden party to which all Members of the House of Commons were invited. But four exceptions were made. One member whose financial reputation was not the best, Grayson, who had made one or two ineffective demonstrations in the House, Keir Hardie and myself. I did not pay much attention at first, thinking there was probably some error. But when I discovered it had been done very deliberately, and at the King's orders, the incident assumed its honest proportions. It was no longer a private affair but an insult to my constituents and an attempt by the sovereign to influence votes of Members by social pressure. Keir Hardie also had been inclined to let the matter pass as an entirely unimportant incident. But when I put it to him that it was not a personal matter, but an official aspersion on our constituencies, he agreed, and he deliberated with his colleagues as to what course should be taken. The press took up the matter with embarrassing eagerness and the whole incident became embroidered out of all proportion. I need not follow the course of events so far as I personally was concerned, but Keir Hardie decided eventually to let the matter drop after explaining the position publicly in an interesting speech at Stockport in which he showed how throughout his career he had seen clearly that an attack on monarchy and the advocacy of republican principles was of very little consequence as compared with the attack on the economic system.

KING'S GARDEN PARTY

"We had many a talk, and need I say a laugh, over a cup of tea while the 'crisis' lasted, and we sympathised with one another in our efforts to avoid the pressmen. As regards the constitutional aspect of the incident, it is interesting to recall that high officials in no way in sympathy with our views had no doubt that the royal disapproval ought never to have been expressed in this way. In the 'Dictionary of National Biography' the incident is referred to thus : 'Unwisely the King took notice of the parliamentary criticism of his action, and cancelled the invitation to a royal garden party of three Members of Parliament. It was the only occasion during the reign on which the King invited any public suspicion of misinterpreting his constitutional position.'

"Subsequently, whenever I made a speech against the competition in armaments, or the policy of the balance of power, or on any subject on which I could only expect the support of a small minority, I invariably got a word of encouragement and approval from Hardie.

"There was always something in his uncompromising directness and complete indifference to the approval of the majority which attracted me. He was often blunderingly tactless and rough, and though he was strictly obedient to the forms of the House, he never indulged in the little complimentary politenesses which some Members find make life smoother. All this seemed to me part of the armour he wore deliberately against the insinuating influences of unaccustomed surroundings, and of the atmosphere of authority to which men brought up in a very different sphere of life not infrequently succumb. He seemed determined to preserve the integrity of his opinions—dangerously extreme as they were thought in those days, and to the end he succeeded. His geniality, his kindliness, and his appreciation of the gentler arts of life, came as a surprise to those who only knew him publicly."

Hardie's own references to the matter were characteristic. He had no use for Kings' garden parties. He had never attended any of them, and would probably never have known that on this occasion the invitation had not been sent had it not been that Ponsonby and Grayson were also implicated. "But," said he, "I am not going to allow either my position as a member of the Labour Party, or my Socialism, or my views concerning King Edward's visit to Russia, to control my principles as a Member of the House of Commons. I don't receive these invitations because I am Keir Hardie, but because I am a Member of the House of Commons, and if I am fit to represent the working classes of Merthyr, I am fit to attend the garden party at Windsor." His views concerning the monarchy had been defined on several previous occasions and it was hardly necessary for him to reiterate his opinion that it was a wholly superfluous institution, only tolerable as long as it did not actively interfere in the administration of the nation's affairs or in directing its foreign policy. That it was being so used in Russian (and, as we now know, in other) affairs, there could not be any doubt, and it showed its pettiness by this paltry ostracism. The Labour Party at once took up the matter. If a king could take cognisance of one Parliamentary act, then the constitutional theory of Parliamentary independence was gone. That week it therefore passed the following resolution and sent it to those concerned :—

"That the action of Mr. Hardie regarding the King's visit to the Czar, which incurred the displeasure of His Majesty and led to Mr. Hardie's name being removed from the list of Members of Parliament recently invited to Windsor, having been taken by instructions of the

KING'S GARDEN PARTY

Party, the Party desires to associate itself with Mr. Hardie, who, in its opinion, exercised his constitutional right on the occasion of the Foreign Office debate, and it therefore requests that, until his name is restored to such official lists, the names of all its members shall be removed from them.''

As a result, assurances were officially given that a mistake had been made, and the matter was allowed to drop.

Following close upon the Government's open declaration of friendliness to the Czar's regime, came a raging, tearing anti-German press campaign, and it was possible to discern in the propinquity of the two manifestations something more than accidental coincidence. Its tendency was undoubtedly to stimulate animosity between the people of Britain and Germany and render it difficult for peace lovers in both countries to make headway against their respective militarist elements. The British press campaign, naturally, had its reflection in the German press, which found in our Dreadnought programmes, our alliance with Japan, our Persian policy, and our highly demonstrative *entente* with France and Russia, the evidence of a policy designed completely to encompass and isolate Germany.

The obvious duty of Socialists in both countries was to give effect to the Marxian call, "Wage-workers of all countries unite," and the most serious feature of the British war scare was that the scaremongers included two leading Socialists, Blatchford of the "Clarion," and H. M. Hyndman of the Social Democratic Federation. Blatchford visualised an immediate German invasion of Britain and told hair-raising stories of embarkation rehearsals on the other side of the North Sea. Hyndman inveighed against all things German, and advocated, as he had always done, the formation of a citizen army, not primarily to resist capitalism, but to resist, if not to attack, Germany. Even Lord Fisher, who was getting his Dreadnoughts built, was constrained to characterise the scare as silly. "The truth is," said he, referring to the embarkation story, "that one solitary regiment was embarked for manœuvres. That is the truth. I have no doubt that equally silly stories are current in Germany." Unfortunately, in this country the "silly stories" had the endorsement of two prominent Socialists, one of whom was believed in Germany to be representative of British working-class opinion. During the course of this scare there were sneering references from Blatchford to the Labour Party as the "Baa-Lamb School who believe that we ought not to defend ourselves if attacked," as the "Ostrich School who, because they want peace, refuse to see any danger of war"; as the "Gilpin School, who had a frugal mind and wanted peace at the lowest possible price." There were also references to Hardie which approached the verge of insult. Thus the capitalist-militarist game was played and an international Socialist movement, which alone could then have averted war, was weakened.

Hardie retorted with a strong article, the very comprehensiveness of which renders it difficult to summarise. After showing that Germany had nothing to gain from war with Britain and that there were interests in both countries seeking profit out of the increasing expenditure on armaments, he deprecated the fomenting of antagonisms by avowed Socialists. He accused Hyndman of having ransacked the columns of the gutter press for inuendoes and insults levelled against the representatives of the German Empire, and of dishing them up with all the assurance with which he was accustomed to predict the date of the Social Revolution. "Blatchford and Hyndman," he said, "seem to have set themselves the task of producing that very feeling of inevitableness than which nothing could more strengthen the hands of the warmongers on both shores of the German Ocean, now known, I believe, as the North Sea. Is that work worthy of the traditions of Socialism? I assure our German Socialist and Trade Union comrades that Blatchford and Hyndman speak for themselves alone, and that their attitude on this question would be repudiated with practical unanimity by the Trade Union movement could it be put to the vote. The Labour Party stands for peace. We are prepared to co-operate with our German friends in thwarting the malignant designs of the small group of interested scaremongers, who in both countries would like to see war break out."

There was an immediate response to this closing appeal. Bernstein wrote emphasising the danger of stabilising the feeling of "inevitableness" as to war, and did not minimise the fact that it had already taken deep root amongst sections of the German people. He declared it to be "the duty of Socialists to lift their voice against the mad race in armaments which makes civilised humanity, to its shame, the slave of conditions which it ought to master." Bebel wrote prophetically: "A war between England and Germany would lead to a European—that is to a world—conflagration such as has never before taken place. The German Social Democratic Party will do its utmost to prevent such, but should it happen in spite of all their efforts, those who light this fire would also have to bear the consequences that await them. The vast majority of Germans are not thinking of war with England, and indeed do not do so for very sober, selfish reasons. We have nothing to gain, but much to lose."

This war scare temporarily died down, but its evil

effects remained. The rival governments went on unrestrainedly building navies and increasing armies against each other, and from this year, 1908, onward, it became more and more difficult to contend against the fatalistic expectations of war which had been created, alike by the jingoism of the press and by the European alliances entered into by Great Britain on the one hand and Germany on the other. We drifted into war. Few saw the tendency, and fewer strove to stop it. When it came, the scaremongers who made it hurried round and said with the air of prophets: "We told you so."

Meantime, Hardie was once more on the high seas, bound for Canada, having been invited by the leaders of the Dominion Trade Union movement to attend the Congress in Nova Scotia, on September 21st. On this occasion he was accompanied by Mrs. Hardie and Agnes, their daughter. He had also for ship companion Mr. Fels of America, the millionaire disciple of Henry George, with whom he had long been on friendly terms, and would fain have persuaded to accept the complete Socialist conception of an ideal society. There is nothing of much note to record concerning this Transatlantic trip. He took part in the Congress as an honoured guest, and endeavoured to convince the Canadians of the value of Labour representation as a means of reconciling elements which in Canada at that time were irreconcilable. He augmented his stock of knowledge regarding the industrial conditions of the Dominion, and crossed over into the United States, where he gathered impressions of the Presidential election then taking place, the Socialist candidate being Eugene Debs, who, for a wonder, was not in prison. But, on the whole, it was more of a pleasure trip than was usual with him, the companionship of his wife and daughter tending to save him from the propaganda traps lying in wait for him everywhere. He arrived back in Glasgow on October 11th, and, after a few days spent at Cumnock, was in London in time to take part in the welcome to Kautsky and Ledebour of Germany who had come on the invitation of the British section of the International Bureau. At the public meeting which took place in the St. James's Hall, both German delegates deprecated energetically the idea of war between the two nations. Kautsky especially, in language which to-day reads at once futile and prophetic, declared that capitalists themselves would be opposed to war. "Capitalism feared war to-day because it knew that after war there would be revolution. It was the certainty of revolution that would deter the exploiting capitalists of Europe from entering upon a struggle which would be death to capitalism itself." One can only say, alas! alas! We now know that though the war was followed by revolution, the fear of revolution had no deterrent effect upon capitalism.

Hardie's contribution to the speech-making was an impassioned appeal to organised labour to place no faith in armies, "whether citizen or by whatever name they might be called"—an exhortation which immediately roused the ire of the chairman, Mr. Hyndman, who, as we know, was a strong supporter of the citizen army idea. The fact that there were these divisions among British Socialists themselves, detracted largely from the value of this meeting as an influence for international peace.

Whilst this darkening shadow of impending international war was slowly gathering and filling the minds of serious men with ominous forebodings, there was serious enough trouble in the industrial world at home. A period of trade depression had again come round—

had indeed hardly been absent for several years—and month by month the records of unemployment went on increasing, accompanied by even stronger manifestations of discontent than on previous occasions. There had been disturbances in most of the big towns. At Glasgow a great crowd of workless men, led by members of the I.L.P., themselves unemployed, had stormed the City Council Chambers demanding work, and from thence had marched threateningly into the West End. At Manchester there had been similar scenes and violent conflicts with the police, resulting in arrests, and in several persons being sentenced to long terms of imprisonment. All through the summer, the Parliamentary Labour Party had been pressing the Government to give the financial aid which alone could make the Unemployment Act really serviceable, and to make the Distress Committee powers compulsory instead of permissive, and it had at last secured the promise of a statement from the Government as to its intentions.

On the day following that on which this promise was made, Mr. Victor Grayson created a scene in the House by moving the adjournment, his expressed desire being "that it should consider a matter of urgent importance—the question of unemployment." and on being told by the Speaker that, under the rules of the House, he could not move the adjournment at that juncture, he declared that he refused to be bound by the rules. After a somewhat lengthy altercation with the Speaker and many interjections from the members, he withdrew from the House, but not before he had stigmatised the Labour Members as "traitors to their class, who refuse to stand by their class." The following day, while the House was in Committee on the Licensing Bill, a similar scene ensued, which ended in Grayson being suspended.

INTERNAL STRIFE

Hardie's view of the matter had best be given in his own words : "Grayson came to the House of Commons on Thursday, but spoke to no one of his intentions, consulted no one and did not even intimate that he meant to make a scene. That may be his idea of comradeship; it is not mine. Nor is it what the I.L.P. will tolerate from one of its members. If the Labour Party, or if the I.L.P. members, had been invited to take part in a protest and had refused, then Grayson's action might have been justifiable, but acting as he did, no other result could be expected than that which happened. If a protest is to be made, it must be done unitedly, and in a manner to command respect."

Hardie, as we know, had no reverential regard for the rules of the House—though he had known how to make use of them for his own purposes, but he had very great regard for the prestige of the Labour Party in the House and in the country. He, of all men, could not be accused of indifference to the claims of the unemployed. What legislation on their behalf did exist was mainly the outcome of his efforts at a time when he stood alone. But now that there was a Labour Party in the House, he held that upon that Party rested the responsibility of forcing the hands of the Government, and that isolated action by one individual could only have a disruptive effect upon the Socialist movement without being helpful to the unemployed.

There was, moreover, some reason to believe that the Grayson histrionics were deliberately intended to produce the disruption deprecated by Hardie, and an incident which occurred outside the House, almost immediately after, seemed to verify that belief. Grayson and Hyndman refused to appear on the same platform as Hardie at a public meeting under the auspices of the Clarion Van Committee, a body existing for the

J. KEIR HARDIE

purpose of promoting the Clarion Van propaganda
carried on in connection with Blatchford's paper.
Hardie, Hyndman and Grayson had been invited by the
Committee to speak at demonstrations in the Holborn
and Finsbury Town Halls. Hardie had agreed to do
so and was much surprised to receive a letter from the
secretary on the day previous to the meetings, requesting him to "refrain from attending the meetings," the
reason given being that Hyndman and Grayson were
unable to join with him as speakers.

That this extraordinary and insulting attitude towards
the greatest of all working-class agitators was the outcome of something more than mere personal pettiness
was evidenced by the fact that the "Clarion" was at
this time devoting its columns to the promulgation of a
new Socialist Party, with the Clarion Scouts and the
Clarion Fellowship as the nucleus, and dissentient
I.L.P. members as potential recruits; whilst Hyndman
justified his action by reference to Hardie's anti-war
scare article, and to his attack on a citizen army at the
reception to the German delegation. The best comment
upon this disgraceful episode was supplied by an un-
solicited letter to the "Labour Leader" from M. Beer,
London correspondent of "Vörwarts," whose recently
published "History of British Socialism" is recognised
as the standard authority on the subject. Beer had
dissented strongly from Hardie's views at the time of
the class-war discussion, and his support of Hardie
now was therefore all the more valuable. The letter
has both biographical and historical interest, and is
therefore reproduced here intact. As an exposition of
the practical philosophy of the British Labour Party
movement from the point of view of a Marxian disciple it is worth considering at the present time. The
letter was as follows :—

INTERNAL STRIFE

"To the Editor of the 'Labour Leader.'

"Comrade,—Kindly permit me to express, first of all, my sincere and respectful sympathy for Keir Hardie with regard to the deplorable Holborn Town Hall incident. As a close observer of the British Labour movement, I regard the work of Keir Hardie to be of much more permanent value than that of Hyndman, Shaw, Blatchford, Wells, let alone Grayson. Of all British Socialists none, in my judgment, has grasped the essence of modern Socialism—aye, of Marxism—better than Hardie. Moreover, none has done in practice better work than Hardie. His silent, clear-headed and consistent efforts in the first years of the L.R.C. on behalf of the unity and independence of organised Labour, would alone be sufficient to raise him to the front rank of Socialist statesmanship. For what is the essence of modern Socialism as Marx taught it?—The political independence of Labour. And what is the foremost duty of a Socialist in the class struggle?—To divorce Labour from the parties of the possessing class. All that Keir Hardie has done, more by virtue of a practically unerring proletarian instinct than by theorising and speculating about revolution and so-called constructive Socialism. Socialism is not made, but it is growing out of the needs and struggles of organised Labour. The most simple Labour organisation, fighting for high wages, shorter hours and better Labour laws, does more for Socialism than all the Utopian books of Wells, all the Swiftean wit of Shaw, all the revolutionary speeches of Hyndman, and all the sentimental harangues of Grayson. I have been saying that for years in the 'Vorwärts,' in the 'Neue Zeit,' and sometimes in 'Justice.' And now let me make a confession. Soon after the election of Grayson, my editor asked me whether I did not think it advisable to interview

J. KEIR HARDIE

Grayson for the 'Vorwärts.' I replied it would be better to wait; the British Socialists, with their wonted hero-worship, were already spoiling him; there would be a meeting at the Caxton Hall (in September, 1907), when Grayson was to speak. I should then have an opportunity of arriving at some judgment about him. The meeting took place, MacDonald being the chairman, Curran and Grayson the chief speakers. After that meeting, of which I gave a report in the 'Vorwärts,' I wrote about Grayson. 'He is very self-conscious; his Socialism consists of commiseration with the poor; in his speech he didn't mention the Labour movement at all. Now, modern Socialism has very little to do with poor men stories but a great deal with organised Labour. Grayson has still much to learn about Socialism and he may learn it if he remains in close touch with the Labour Party.' ('Vorwärts,' September, 1907.) In approving wholeheartedly of the policy of Hardie, I also approve of the general policy of J. R. MacDonald. At the publication of his 'Socialism and Society' he had no severer critic than myself, because I suspected him of attempting to weaken the independence of the Labour Party. I still consider him what the Germans call a 'Revisionist,' but at the same time I cannot help perceiving that his general policy is at present thoroughly in conformity with the mental condition of the British Labour movement. Any other policy might at the present juncture spell disruption. We can't force movements of oppressed classes. We must allow them to develop and to ripen. 'Ripeness is all.'—Fraternally yours,

"M. Beer,

"London, November 22nd, 1908."

It should be said that this letter was followed by one from H. G. Wells protesting against being "lumped

INTERNAL STRIFE

with Hyndman, Shaw, Blatchford and Grayson, as
being opposed to the work of Hardie," and viewing "with
infinite disgust the deplorable attacks upon the I.L.P.
leaders." These attacks upon Hardie had the usual
effect of strengthening the loyalty of the I.L.P. rank
and file who, through their branch secretaries, literally
bombarded him with assurances of esteem and
confidence.

Amid it all, he went on with his work, and in the same
issue of the "Leader" in which Beer's appreciation
appeared, he had an appeal to the local education
authorities to give effect to the Provision of Meals for
Children Act and reminded them that they possessed
powers to supply each scholar in every public school
with two or three substantial meals each day. "I have
frequently," he said, "had occasion to point out that if
in this and other respects the existing law were put into
operation the hardships and suffering due to unemployment would be mitigated."

There never was a more practical idealist than J. Keir
Hardie. By blocking a North British Railway Bill, he
compelled that company to withdraw its dismissal of a
number of its employees who had been elected as Town
Councillors, and in December he introduced an "Emergency Unemployment Bill" to enable Distress Committees to use the penny rate levy for the payment of wages,
and to provide for special Committees where no Distress Committee was in existence. His object was to
make the present Act workable during the winter,
pending the promised Government measure. He also
protested strongly against the mutilation by the House
of Lords of the Miners' Eight Hours' Day Bill, but as
the Miners' Federation had agreed to accept the amendments rather than lose the Bill altogether, he had to waive
his objections. Every hour of his waking time seemed

to be filled with work. "I envy the editor of the 'Clarion,'" he wrote, "the quiet day at home in which to write his article on the political situation. Some of us are nomads and vagrants all the time, and have to write as odd moments offer, in the midst of many other and divers duties."

In proof of this, he appended his week's diary of work, which included attendance and speech-making in the House of Commons, six hours' sitting on the "Coal Mines Eight Hours' Bill Committee," a "Right to Work Executive" meeting, a "Labour Party" meeting, a conference with French workmen delegates, an I.L.P. Parliamentary Committee meeting, a week-end public meeting at Halifax, besides correspondence entailing over a hundred replies to personal letters. Hardie did not really envy Blatchford his life of leisured journalism, but he resented strongly the habitual assumption of pontifical authority on working-class questions by one who had no practical connection with the working class, who did not participate in any of the drudgery inseparable from the work of labour organisation, who was not in a position to understand working-class psychology, and who held himself safely aloof from all official responsibility. Hardie was amongst the workers every day. He knew every phase of working-class life, not only that of the toiling underground collier, but of the skilled artisan, the sweated labourer, the under-paid woman. His life purpose was to make the working class united and powerful, and conscious of its power; and he believed he knew better than Hyndman and Blatchford the methods whereby that purpose could be achieved. It had been no easy task to call the Labour Party into being, and he was certainly not going to allow it to be destroyed by the subversive and divisive tactics which were now being used. New parties might be formed bearing all manner of names, but the Labour Party would remain and be moulded towards Socialism by the I.L.P. as long as the breath of life remained in the founder of both organisations.

The climax came at the 1909 Conference of the I.L.P. held at Edinburgh. At this Conference, a proposal that the I.L.P. should sever itself from the Labour Party found only eight supporters against three hundred and seventy-eight in favour of ''maintaining unimpaired the alliance of Labour and Socialism as affording the best means for the expression of Socialism to-day.'' A further resolution declaring that "no salary be paid to Members of Parliament unless such Members sign the Labour Party constitution" was adopted by 352 votes to 64. Thus was reaffirmed with emphasis the fundamental principles of the Labour Party alliance. It was otherwise when the same principle reappeared in a form involving the discussion of Grayson's conduct outside the House of Commons.

A paragraph in the N.A.C. report explained the reasons why that body had ceased to arrange meetings for Grayson. They were that he had failed to fulfil engagements already made, and that his refusal to appear with Hardie on the Holborn Town Hall platform made it useless to fix up meetings for him through the Head Office. On the motion of Grayson himself, this paragraph was "referred back"—that is to say, deleted from the Report—by 217 to 194 votes. This could only be interpreted as an approval of Grayson's action, and of the motives which had actuated it. Hardie, Glasier, Snowden and MacDonald so interpreted it, and resigned from the N.A.C. to which they had just been re-elected by large majorities, Hardie, as usual, being at the top of the poll—a paradoxical

J. KEIR HARDIE

state of matters which evinced considerable mental confusion on the part of the delegates. The resignations were announced by MacDonald, who was chairman, in a firm speech in which he declared that he and his three colleagues declined to associate themselves with the growth of what seemed to them an impossiblist movement within the Party, with its spirit of irresponsibility, its modes of expression, and its methods of bringing Socialism; and he affirmed that it was not the mere reference back of the paragraph which made them take that action, but the source and antecedents of that event. The Conference, thus brought to face the implications of its censuring decision, quickly realised its mistake, and with only ten dissentients, passed the following resolution, which was, of course, equivalent to a rescinding of the Grayson motion : "That this Conference hears with regret the statement made on behalf of the outgoing National Administrative Council, and desires to express its emphatic endorsement of their past policy, and its emphatic confidence, personal and political, in Messrs. MacDonald, Keir Hardie, Bruce Glasier, and Snowden, and most earnestly requests them to withdraw their resignation." This the four members declined to do; Hardie, who spoke with strong feeling, declaring that they had been regarded as limpets clinging to office, and that members present and a section of the Socialist press had put forward that statement. The trouble with Grayson was that success had come to him too easily, and he was surrounded by malign influences that would ruin his career—a prediction that was unfortunately amply fufilled. Grayson, Hyndman and Blatchford had refused to appear on the same platform with him, and it had gone abroad that he had lost the confidence of the movement. Self-respect demanded that a stand

should be made. He valued the opinion expressed by
the Conference. He would like it sent down to the
branches, especially to those where there was that small,
snarling, semi-disruptive element. They must fight
that down, and if need be fight it out. With his colleagues he was going to test the question whether the
I.L.P. was to stand for the consolidation of the working-
class movement, or whether, departing from the lines
of sanity, they should follow some chimera called
Socialism and Unity spoken of by men who did not
understand Socialism and were alien to its very
spirit.

Thus, in the sixteenth year of the I.L.P., its founder
ceased to be a member of its executive, and with him
the three men most representative to the public mind of
the spirit and policy of the Party. Of the four, Glasier
was the only one who was not a Member of Parliament,
but he was editor of the "Labour Leader," which
expressed the policy of the Party. During his four-and-
a-half years of editorship, the circulation had increased
from 13,000 to 40,000, but, nevertheless, his editorial
conduct had been severely and unfairly criticised
during this Conference from the same sources which
had promoted the disruptive tactics, and in addition to
resigning from the N.A.C. he announced his intention
of ceasing to be editor as soon as another could be found
to take his place.

Superficially, it seemed as if the designs of the
enemies of the I.L.P. had been accomplished, and that
the Party had been rent in twain. Those who thought
so knew little of the I.L.P. or of the men who had
resigned from office in order to meet disaffection in the
branches. The influence of the four retiring men had
increased rather than diminished. The work of the
I.L.P. lay, where it has always been, in the country, and

the branches continued to do the work with an energy
that this internal strife only stimulated.

Eight months later came the General Election, with
the I.L.P. and Labour Party candidates in the field
working together, and the membership unitedly behind
them, fighting for Socialism and for working-class
political power. The efforts to disintegrate the Labour
movement had failed.

In the months prior to the General Election there
occurred opportunities of a kind to test the moral
courage of the Parliamentary Labour Party and demonstrate the need for the existence of such a Party. The
most outstanding of these was the visit of the Czar to
this country and his official reception by the Government
at Cowes. The significance of this would have passed
almost unnoticed but for the protest of the Labour
Party, so much at one were the Liberals and Tories on
the question of foreign policy. On July 22nd, on the
Civil Service vote, Arthur Henderson, as leader of the
Labour Party, delivered a strong speech denunciatory
of the Government's action as being in effect a condone-
ment of the crimes of the Czar and his Government
against the common people of Russia. His recital of
those crimes drew from Sir Edward Grey the memorable
and immoral declaration that "it is not our business
even to know what passes in the internal affairs of
other countries where we have no treaty rights," an
avowal which Hardie, who followed, had no difficulty
in proving to be without either historical or political
vindication, by recalling the action of Mr. Gladstone
with regard to the internal affairs of Naples and the
tyranny of King Bomba, and also the more recent
interventions in the matter of the Congo and of Armenia.
This was one of the finest utterances Hardie ever made
in the House of Commons. In his closing words he

appealed for a clear vote of the House on this subject of the Czar, as apart from the general discussion which had included other topics. "It was because he belonged to a Party whose whole sympathies were with the people of Russia in the great fight which they were making, and because he knew that every section of the advanced movement in Russia, from the extreme Socialist to the mildest Liberal, regarded the visit of the Czar to this country as, to some extent, throwing back their cause by giving him the official recognition of a great democratic State, that he, and those with him, opposed the visit."

This protest, which was re-echoed from every Labour platform in the country, had its effect. Not only did it wash the hands of British organised labour from the blood-guiltiness involved in the Russian alliance and left the Party free to oppose the development of the policy which that alliance implied, but, as a result, the Czar remained on board his yacht at Cowes and did not set foot on English soil. It is true to say that at the forging of every link which bound Britain to Imperialist Russia in a common policy, the Labour Party made an effort to prevent the chain from being completed; and it is also true to say that this was mainly due to the influence of the I.L.P. within the Labour Party, seeking thereby to perform its duty as a part of the International Socialist movement.

And not only with regard to Russia did the Labour Party maintain this attitude of sympathy with the oppressed, but with regard to every land whose affairs came in any way under the cognisance of the British Parliament. It championed the claims of the South African natives during the passage of the Draft Constitution of the South African Union; it protested by speech and vote against the suppression of civil liberty and the right of free speech in India; it supported the Irish Nationalists in their claims for Home Rule and joined hands with the Egyptian people in their demands for the establishment of their long withheld national independence. On foreign and colonial policy the Labour Party was, in fact, at this time, the only Parliamentary Opposition, and the only source from which emanated any virile criticism.

In all this work Hardie was bearing a very large share, not only in Parliament, but in the country and in the world. Thus, for example, we find him with George N. Barnes, representing the Labour Party at the Annual Conference of the Young Egyptian Party at Geneva, and hailed there as a valued friend and counsellor. One passage of his speech on that occasion should be preserved, if for no other reason than that it is in direct contrast to the conception of him prevalent in some quarters as an irresponsible firebrand and mischief maker. "Beware," he said, "of secret organisation and of all thoughts of an armed rising for the overthrow of British authority. Every patriotic movement which indulges in secret forms of organisation places itself in the power of the Government. Such organisations are sure to be honeycombed by spies and traitors. The experience of Ireland in former times, and of Russia at present, is all the proof needed on this score. Work openly and in the light of day for the creation of public opinion in Egypt and Great Britain, and have no fear of the result."

With this wide outlook upon the progress of democracy throughout the world, it is not surprising that abstract contentions about Socialist dogma sometimes seemed to him irrelevant and trivial, and the intrigues within the Labour and Socialist movement, petty and vexatious.

WOMEN

Nor must it be forgotten that all this time the Women's Suffrage movement was becoming more violently militant in its tactics, breaking up meetings of friends and foes alike, and acting generally on the principle that every other cause must stand still until the women's claims had been conceded. The women themselves were consistent and courageous in carrying through this policy, and nearly all the time there were numbers of them suffering imprisonment. To Hardie and Snowden they looked chiefly to champion their cause in Parliament and exploit their martyrdoms for propaganda purposes, and it is to be feared that they did not reflect that while harassing the Government they were also harassing their best friends and putting a serious strain upon physiques already overwrought. Nor was this all. Miss Mary Macarthur, of the Federation of Women Workers, has told us how, in the midst of her work of organising the underpaid and sorely sweated women of East London, Hardie was the one Labour Member upon whom she could always rely to come down and speak words of sympathy and encouragement to those victims of commercialism.

He responded to every call, and never counted the cost to himself, and when occasionally he ran off for a brief spell of rest it was an extremely wearied, though undaunted man, whom his friends among the Welsh hills welcomed to their firesides.

CHAPTER TWELVE

IN the two general elections of 1910, the man in the
limelight was Mr. Lloyd George who has managed
to retain that position fairly continuously ever since,
though he has long ago made friends of his whilom
enemies, and has thrust aside the semi-revolutionary
ladder by which he rose to fame and power. The agitations over the land taxation budget and House of Lords'
reforms seem now very remote, and in view of recent
jugglings with national finance extremely futile. But
at the time I have now reached, it was an exceedingly
noisy agitation and apparently sincere. Mr. George,
with his lurid hen-roost oratory, and the peers, with
their die-in-the-last-ditch constitutionalism, had, between them, created a decidely class-war atmosphere,
and there were timid people who actually believed that
the nation was on the eve of great events foreshadowing,
in the words of Lord Rosebery, the "end of all things."

The Labour Party in Parliament had naturally
supported the land taxation proposals and also those for
a super-tax on incomes, but only as initial concessions to
the Socialist claim that all unearned increment should
belong to the nation. Philip Snowden, now the recognised exponent of Socialist finance, made this unmistakably clear in a series of brilliant speeches at various
stages of the Finance Bill. On the question of the
House of Lords, the Labour Party stood for the

abolition of that institution, but, as a matter of practical politics supported any proposal having for its object the immediate limitation of the power of the second Chamber. The Labour and the Liberal Parties were thus, though in principle far apart as the poles, in apparent accord on electoral policy—a state of matters not to the advantage of Labour. The strategical weakness of the Liberals lay in the fact that they had not, and could not have, any policy on unemployment to counter the attractive and strongly boomed Tariff Reform proposals of the Unionists.

In the election which took place in January, 1910, the Liberals lost one hundred seats and the Labour Party lost five. All the leading Labour men, however, held their seats, Hardie keeping his by a greatly increased majority, though on this occasion he had a second Liberal opponent, in the person of Pritchard Morgan, whom he had defeated in 1900, and who now, as if determined on revenge, conducted the usual campaign of scurrilous abuse and misrepresentation. One very special lie circulated assiduously and insidiously, though not in print, represented Hardie as being a man of wealth, who owned an estate in Scotland and had sold the "Labour Leader" to the I.L.P. for £20,000. Up to the last there were credulous people who believed these stupid stories and pestered him for subscriptions to various kinds of ostensibly charitable objects. He, as a matter of fact, had refused to subscribe to local institutions such as football clubs and bowling clubs, for the sufficient reason that over and above his objections on principle, he had hardly enough income to meet the frugal requirements of his own household. The election campaign on this occasion was more prolonged and even more strenuous than the two previous ones, but need not be described here. The result seemed to carry with it the assurance that his position in Merthyr was absolutely impregnable. He had polled 13,841 votes as compared with 10,187 in 1906, and his majority had increased from 2,411 to 9,105.

An extract from his election address may be given as showing with what skill he raised the contest above merely temporary or local controversies. "There are issues that go deeper than any of those raised by the traditional parties in this contest. Mr. Balfour has said that he wants this election fought on the issues of Socialism and Tariff Reform. I accept Mr. Balfour's challenge, and put my Socialism against his Tariff Reform. He wants to use the State for the benefit of the rich. I want to use it for the benefit of all. Socialism is the one system whereby man may escape from the dreary labyrinth of poverty, vice and beggarliness in life in which the race is now aimlessly wandering."

He himself attributed his electoral success to the fact that Socialism had been made the supreme issue, and the following February, in his closing words as chairman of the Labour Party Conference, he affirmed adherence to that principle to be a necessary condition of success for the entire Labour Party. "Whether we like it or not, in every contest we wage, our opponents will see to it that Socialism is kept well to the front. Our candidates and workers will therefore do well to equip themselves for that line of attack. Socialism has no terrors for honest people. The caricatures and vile misrepresentation of Socialism fail entirely when the case for Socialism is put lucidly before the people. We do not want to see any vain beating of the air as is too often done in the name of Socialism, but it is imperative that every man who is put forward as a candidate under Labour auspices should be able to defend and expound Socialism when it is attacked by the enemies of Labour."

FOREIGN AFFAIRS

It must be confessed that there have been, and still are, many Labour candidates whose qualifications do not conform to the standard set up by the founder of the Labour Party.

In passing, it should be noted that this year the British Miners' Federation became affiliated to the Labour Party, and thus another decisive step was taken in the political consolidation of the working class.

All through the year the great constitutional controversy continued, and the people became so deeply engrossed shouting for or against Lloyd George that they forgot all about Sir Edward Grey, a much more fateful statesman if they had only known it.

The rival partisans debated hotly as to whether the House of Lords should be ended or mended, as to how many new peers it would be necessary to create to render that House impotent, or as to how many times a reformed Second Chamber should be allowed to throw out a Bill before it became law; and while this political comedy of "much ado about next to nothing" was proceeding, the diplomats and the Imperialists were not idle.

Lord Roberts continued his propaganda for compulsory military service, the introduction of which the War Office partially anticipated by encouraging railway companies and large employers of labour to make service in the Territorial forces a condition of employment. Mr. Haldane's "nation in arms" was materialising in spite of protests from Hardie and his colleagues. The Admiralty was getting its Dreadnoughts built. Germany was adding to its fleet. France was raising the peace-time strength of its army, and, more fateful than all, British and French financiers were investing their millions in Russia, and staking out concessions of industrially exploitable territory in that unhappy Czar-ridden country. In the midst of the evolution of a policy

U . 293

in which he took special interest and played a prominent part, King Edward died. His successor was enthroned. Liberals and Tories called a temporary truce. They mingled their tears for the dead monarch, combined their cheers for the living one, and then went on with the farce, "The Peers *versus* the People."

One tragic interlude there was, turning public attention for a few brief hours to the realities of industrial life. This was the Whitehaven disaster. Following close upon the death of King Edward came the death of one hundred and thirty working miners under appalling and, as many people believed, preventable circumstances; repeated recommendations by special scientific investigators for the minimising of risks of explosions in mines having been ignored alike by the Home Office and by the mineowners chiefly because of the expense. The feeling raised amongst the mining community by the Whitehaven disaster was, if anything, intensified by what many of them regarded as the too hasty closing up of the mine before all possible efforts at rescue had been exhausted. Hardie, ever sensitive where the lives of miners were concerned, gave public expression to his opinion that when the mine was bricked up the men were probably still alive; an opinion which Mr. Churchill, the Home Secretary, described as "cruel and disgraceful." Hardie, of course, was not the man to rest under such an aspersion. He repeated his statement in Parliament, and in an interview replied directly to Churchill's accusation, and raised the whole question of safety in mines. "Mr. Winston Churchill's comment," he said, "is characterised by righteousness which could only proceed from a total ignorance of what I said and of the facts of the case. In the course of the speech to which Mr. Churchill refers I gave it as my opinion, based upon my practical experience as a miner, that at the time it was decided to wall up the mine the miners were in all probability still alive. I adhere to that opinion. I further stated that had the spirit of the Mines' Regulation Act been carried out in connection with the working of the mine, the disaster would not have occurred. The fire which imprisoned the miners took place in what was known as the bottle-neck, and apparently this was the only means of egress from the workings beyond. The bottle-neck workings branch off in five main levels, and it would have been an easy matter to have had a safety road laid from this to the pit shaft, so that in the event of the main haulage road between the shaft and the bottle-neck getting blocked up, the other would have been available for the men to escape by. I suggested that these were matters which would require to be investigated, and it is this suggestion which the Home Secretary characterises as cruel and disgraceful. ˉWorking miners of the country will have a different opinion. I hope Mr. Churchill is not more concerned about shielding the mineowner than he is about finding out the truth." Whether Hardie was right as to the men being alive when the order to close up the mines was given, cannot now be proved, but his opinion had the support of men deeply interested in the matter, the rescue party having to be forcibly restrained from removing the brickwork and going on with their efforts to save life, even though told they would be throwing their own lives away.

This catastrophe occurred now eleven years ago. The mining community know best what improvements, if any, have taken place since then, and they also are best able to judge whether the kind of protests made by Keir Hardie were necessary or not. He never forgot that he was a miner, and a representative of miners.

In the endeavour to preserve some continuity in this

J. KEIR HARDIE

story of Hardie's life, the writer has up to the present found it difficult to bring into view one aspect of his nature which is, nevertheless, essential to form a complete estimate of the man. His love for and understanding of children was only equalled by the love of children for him. It was a case of "like draws to like." Young folk were drawn to him as he to them, instinctively. He has spoken of himself as the man who never was a child, and that was true so far as his own literal experience was concerned. Yet it might be even truer to say that he was all his life a child. Perhaps, even, it was his childlike directness and straightforwardness that rendered him immune from all kinds of sophistry and double-dealing and made him a perpetual puzzle to men of the world playing the game of politics. Be that as it may, it was certainly true that even in the midst of the most serious work he could lift himself out of the hurly-burly and become as a little child. In the many households which he entered during his goings to and fro, the presence of children always put him at his ease and made him feel at home. There are many grown-up men and women in the Socialist movement who cherish as one of the unforgettable things of their bairntime the occasion when Keir Hardie took them upon his knee, or hoisted them on to his shoulders and made chums of them. He could tell them stories, wonderful stories—stories sometimes of the wise pit ponies that were his own chums in the days of his boyhood, or of the ongoings of "Roy," the wise collie waiting to welcome him home far away in Cumnock, or of the Red Indians he had met in America, or, as often happened, a fairy tale made up "out of his own head"—that very head amongst whose grizzled locks the hands of the delighted youngsters were at that moment playing.

This love and understanding of children did not in

CHILDREN

any way interfere with or hinder his work for Socialism. It became part and parcel of it. In the 1910 volume of the "Young Socialist"—this very year when he and his colleagues were beset by so much political perplexity—there is a short story entitled "Jim" written by him. A story of a forlorn London slum laddie and of two equally forlorn London slum dogs—the only dogs in fiction I think that ever entered Heaven. It is a simply told tale blended of fantasy and realism, of humour and pathos, and of tender deep compassion. The literary world, of course, never heard of this child story by Keir Hardie, nor of others of the same kind which he wrote from time to time. They were not written to gain money, or reputation. They were written for the children of the Socialist movement. In the early years of the "Labour Leader" he, under the *nom de plume* of "Daddy Time," conducted a children's column and from week to week held homely converse with the bairns. Around this weekly talk there grew a kind of young folk's fellowship, which called itself "The Crusaders," and out of this again there came the Socialist Sunday School movement, the mere sound and rumour of which has made the hairs of so many pious but ignorant people stand on end. Good men and women gave their time and love to the building of it. Miss Lizzie Glasier, the sister of Bruce Glasier, Archibald McArthur (known as "Uncle Archie"), Clarice McNab, now Mrs. B. H. Shaw, Alfred Russell, Robert Donaldson, Fred Coates, Alex. Gossip, John Burns (of Glasgow), and a host of others, but all deriving their inspiration from Hardie, who, to them, was literally the "Great Exemplar." Thousands of young folks have passed through the schools and into the fighting and teaching ranks of the general Socialist advance. And so, in the words of William Morris, "the cause goes marching on," and with it the name and the memory of Keir Hardie.

September brought the International Socialist Congress once more, this time at Copenhagen. This Congress is memorable chiefly for the proposal by the I.L.P., with the approval of the British section, that the General Strike should be considered as a means of preventing war. This proposal took the form of an amendment to the resolution brought forward by the Commission on Anti-Militarism. Hardie had endeavoured to get his proposal incorporated in the resolutions, and, failing in that, now moved it as an amendment. In view of all that has happened since, and of what is happening still in the efforts to reconstitute a satisfactory Socialist International, it will be wise to reproduce these resolutions here, with the "General Strike" amendment.

"The Congress, reiterating the oft-repeated duty of Socialist representatives in the Parliaments to combat militarism with all the means at their command and to refuse the means of armaments, requires from its representatives :—

"(a) The constant reiteration of the demand that international arbitration be made compulsory in all international disputes;

"(b) Persistent and repeated proposals in the direction of ultimate disarmament, and, above all, as a first step, the conclusion of a general treaty limiting naval armaments and abrogating the right of privateering;

"(c) The demand for the abolition of secret diplomacy and the publication of all existing and future agreements between the Governments;

"(d) The guarantee of the independence of all nations and their protection from military attacks and violent suppression.

"The International Socialist Bureau will support all

MILITARISM

Socialist organisations in this fight against militarism by furnishing them with the necessary data and information, and will, when the occasion arises, endeavour to bring about united action. In case of warlike complications this Congress re-affirms the resolution of the Stuttgart Congress, which reads :—

" 'In case of war being imminent, the working classes and their Parliamentary representatives in the countries concerned shall be bound, with the assistance of the International Socialist Bureau, to do all they can to prevent the breaking out of the war, using for this purpose the means which appear to them to be most efficacious, and which must naturally vary according to the acuteness of the struggle of classes and to the general political conditions.

" 'In case war should break out notwithstanding, they shall be bound to intervene, that it may be brought to a speedy end, and to employ all their forces for utilising the economical and political crisis created by the war, in order to rouse the masses of the people and to hasten the downfall of the predominance of the capitalist class.

" 'For the proper execution of these measures the Congress directs the Bureau, in the event of a war menace, to take immediate steps to bring about an immediate agreement among the Labour parties of the countries affected for united action to prevent the threatened war.' "

It is easy now to make comment upon the inherent ineffectiveness of these proposals. They were, however, the outcome of years of deliberation by men of various nationalities who were sincerely desirous of two things, the abolition of war and the establishment of Socialism, and the real secret of their inutility may, perhaps, be found in the fatalism expressed in the preamble, which declared that "war will only cease with the disappearance of capitalist production." A belief in the inevitability of war is not a good foundation upon which to build measures of prevention. These proposals relied upon Parliamentary action to prevent war, and presupposed a much greater possession of political power on the part of Labour than has ever existed; and they certainly did not contemplate a world conflagration involving nations that had no parliamentary institutions whatever.

The I.L.P. amendment proposed extra-parliamentary action; direct action in fact, on an international scale. It was as follows: "This Congress recommends the affiliated Parties and Labour organisations to consider the advisability and feasability of the general strike, especially in industries that supply war material, as one of the methods of preventing war, and that action be taken on the subject at the next Congress."

The next Congress would be in 1913, and we can now see that if in the intervening years, the preparatory steps for enforcing this proposal had been taken, there would yet have been time for putting its efficacy to the test in August, 1914. In moving this amendment, the British section believed they were making a thoroughly practical proposal for the preservation of international peace. Somewhere there may be in existence a verbatim report of Hardie's speech. A very brief summary, mainly taken from the descriptive account of the Congress by Bruce Glasier in the "Labour Leader," will suffice here. Hardie began by stating that he desired that the position of the Socialist and Labour movement in Britain should be understood by their foreign comrades. It had been much misrepresented. The British Labour Party took a very definite stand against war. They were not only anti-war but anti-military, which was not quite the same thing. A standing army was an indication that the State was founded on force. Militarism and freedom could not exist side by side. It was a source of great pleasure to him to find that the Socialists of Denmark and Norway were not only against large expenditure in armaments, but were opposed to armaments altogether and had moved for their complete abolition. There was, he declared, a big place in history for the nation which has the courage and faith to disarm itself. No country, not even despotic Russia, would dare to attack an unarmed nation. Dealing with the argument used in the capitalist press for a large navy, he said that the refusal of the Hague Conference, in obedience to the British Government, to abolish the capture of merchandise at sea, did much to excuse, though it might not justify, that argument. He dissociated the British movement from the articles by Blatchford and Hyndman in the capitalist press, and in "Justice" and the "Clarion." He believed that the S.D.P. delegates would endorse his statement that on this question these men spoke only for themselves, and that every section of the Socialist movement in Britain disapproved of their utterances and their conduct in taking sides with the capitalist press. Ledebour, without knowing the difference between the German and the British Budget, had attacked the British Labour Party for voting for taxation, and Hardie replied. To vote for the rejection of the entire Budget, would be to vote against the provision of money for Old Age Pensions, against the payment of wages for the servants of the State, and against every social undertaking of the State. The I.L.P. in Britain were arranging for a great campaign against war. Jaurès and Vandervelde were coming to speak, and he hoped that Ledebour himself or some other German comrade would come also. Turning to his own amendment, he offered to Ledebour (the mover of the official resolution) to withdraw the addition, provided he would agree to the Bureau circulating a paragraph embodying the amendment. The French, American and South German delegates on the Commission agreed to support that, but Ledebour, on behalf of the Germans, declined. It was true that a general strike against war could only come by the international agreement of the workers. But did they not know that the miners at their recent International Conference had actually agreed that this very question should be referred to their Executive in order that it might be considered at their next Conference. The miners alone could prevent war by withholding supplies. We must give the workers a great lead. He did not expect that the workers were at present ready to strike against war. But they never would be ready to do so unless we helped to educate them by pointing out to them their duty.

The value, for us, of this utterance, even abbreviated, lies in the fact that it is illuminative. It throws light on the mental attitudes on both sides in the discussion, and we are forced to the conclusion that all these men were actuated by the highest motives and were sincerely striving to find a solution for the problems confronting humanity. The Germans would not mislead the Congress by voting for a resolution which they thought impracticable. Their Marxian theories of economic determinism made it easy for the Imperialist and Militarist forces to pursue their policy. They were like the rabbit paralysed by the serpent, but they honourably told the Congress that if a war came they did not believe that a general strike could be made to stop it. The "Time Forces" were against the International leaders. Capitalism and Imperialism were developing faster than International Socialism and proletarian power.

CHRISTIANITY

On this question it was not found necessary to divide the Congress. The resolution was carried on the understanding that the amendment should be considered by the International Socialist Bureau, the German section agreeing to this.

This was not Hardie's only visit to the Continent during this year. In May, he had been to Lille, in France, as chief speaker in a propaganda crusade organised by the National Council of the Pleasant Sunday Afternoon and the Brotherhood movements of Great Britain. To some scoffers the idea of British Nonconformists teaching continental workers how to spend pleasant Sunday afternoons was not without its humour; but that aspect did not appeal to Hardie. To him it was another opportunity for preaching Socialism and international goodwill, and he made full use of it. His name and fame brought together a great assemblage of working folk, and besides speaking in the great hall of L'Union de Lille, he had to address an overflow meeting of some six thousand in the Square, delivering an oration which, by its religious fervour and idealism, made him more than ever a man of mystery to the scientific Socialists who found in the materialist conception of history the only key to the explanation of every problem. What kind of a Socialist could he be who said, "Behind nature there is a Power, unseen but felt. Beyond death there is a Something, else were life on earth a mere wastage," and who declared, "I myself have found in the Christianity of Christ the inspiration which first of all drove me into the movement and has carried me on in it." Yet this man was an advocate of the general strike. They could not understand him. Nor could the commercialised professors of Christianity. To both he was an enigma.

There was nothing enigmatical, however, about his action a few weeks later, when, in the House of Commons, he was attacking the Home Secretary and the War Minister for having sent police and military into Wales during a miners' strike. This dispute had originated in the Rhondda Valley, where 11,000 miners had come out on strike, demanding an equalisation of wages with other collieries—demanding, in fact, a minimum wage. There had been some disturbance at Tonypandy, due, as Hardie alleged, to the importation of police from outside the district. In addition to the imported police, military had been sent into the district, and also to Aberaman, which was in Hardie's constituency, where he maintained there had not been even a semblance of riot or disturbance. In the strike district the police had interfered to prevent picketing, which he contended was still lawful, and, in fact, he charged Mr. Haldane and Mr. Churchill with using the forces at their disposal to protect blacklegs and help the masters against the men. In proof of his assertion that the rioting was due to outside influence, he pointed out that at Pen-y-craig, where there were no imported police, there had been no rioting, though there had been picketing and demonstrations of the kind common to a labour dispute. There was not even a window broken in this district. In raising this matter in the House, Hardie was, of course, supported by the Parliamentary Labour Party, and also by his Liberal colleague in the representation of Merthyr, Mr. Edgar Jones. A debate ensued, followed by a division, the only effect of which was to emphasise the fact that, in a quarrel between labour and capital, Liberals and Tories were united on the side of capital. From Hardie's point of view this was worth while. Every time this was demonstrated, the need for Labour representation was also demonstrated. This might not be the class war according to the Marxists, nor brotherly love according to the churches; but it was one of the roads to Socialism according to Hardie. He might, with some truth, have claimed that he was a better Marxist and a better Christian than either of them.

About this time he produced a scheme for the starting of a Socialist daily newspaper, the need for which had long been recognised, and had so far proceeded with his plans as to justify him in the hope that the first number would appear on May 1st of the following year. Another General Election, however, intervened, absorbing all the energy and spare cash of the Party, and later there emerged from the Labour Party a more ambitious, though not, in the opinion of the present writer, a more useful, scheme. The "Daily Citizen" was the outcome.

Night after night in Parliament he continued questioning and compelling discussion on the state of matters in South Wales, always producing fresh evidence in proof of the barbarous methods of the police authorities, and demanding an impartial inquiry into the whole circumstances of the dispute, until in the first week in December there came the General Election, and the transference of his activities to the actual scene of industrial strife. The strike was still proceeding. There was much distress in the Rhondda and in parts of the Merthyr constituency, and, in view of the action of the Government in the dispute, the Liberals did not dare to put up a candidate against him. There was a Unionist candidate, but without even a hope of success, and for Hardie the result was never in doubt. He polled 11,507 votes, and his majority was 6,230. It was the end. He did not know, nor could he nor anyone know, that he had fought his last election contest, and that that night he had heard for the last time the crowds hail him victor. His death was to cause the next Merthyr fight. And by that time Merthyr had changed; the whole world had changed.

J. KEIR HARDIE

The calamity which he dreaded, and which he fought so hard to avert, had come to pass. It was at least in keeping with his life that his last political campaign amongst the Merthyr miners should have had for its first and immediate issue the well-being of his class and craft.

In the outcome of this election the Labour Party more than regained its position. It went back to Parliament forty-two in number. Of these, eight were I.L.P. nominees, the most outstanding amongst the newcomers being George Lansbury and Tom Richardson; the latter's return as an I.L.P. nominee being a significant sign of the advance towards Socialism on the part of the North of England miners.

The Liberal and Tory Parties had exactly two hundred and seventy-two members each. The Liberal Government was therefore dependent for its continuance in office upon the Irish Party and the Labour Party. In these circumstances, had it not been that Liberal and Tory were alike Imperialist, there might have been no war in 1914.

It is strange to reflect that during the whole of this General Election the subject of war was never mentioned. Foreign policy was never mentioned. Armaments were never mentioned. Yet a Government was elected that took this country into the most terrible war the world has ever seen. As a decoy-duck Lloyd George was a success. He attracted the fire that should have been directed against Grey and Haldane and the British war-lords. Only the Socialists were alive to the impending danger. During November, the I.L.P. had carried through a strenuous anti-militarist campaign, holding big meetings in all the large centres of population, and in December, right in the middle of the election, and without any pre-arranged connection therewith, there

J. KEIR HARDIE, 1910

INTERNATIONALISM

took place in the Albert Hall, London, the great International Socialist Demonstration organised by the I.L.P. with the view of strengthening the solidarity of Labour in all countries against war. At this meeting Hardie was in the chair. France was represented by Jaurès; Germany by Molkenbuhr; Belgium by Vandervelde; Great Britain by MacDonald and Anderson; America by Walter T. Mills. The talk was all of peace and goodwill, and of the power of organised labour to preserve Europe from the scourge of war. Jaurès, the greatest of Socialist orators, spoke like one inspired— Jaurès, marked out as one of the war's earliest victims; yet happier was he than Hardie, for he was to fall quickly and suddenly and to be spared from beholding the full international collapse and the betrayals that followed it.

At least, they were there, the Socialists of France, Germany, Belgium, Britain, the nations that were, even then, being drawn into the whirlpool of blood; they were there, these Socialists, doing what could be done to prevent the catastrophe. But the people never heard them. The people were singing the "Land Song." They were listening to Lloyd George and "waiting and seeing," or rather, waiting and not seeing, what Mr. Asquith was going to give them; and the second General Election of 1910 ended like the first, in the achievement of nothing, except the blindfolding of the British people and the election of a House of Commons with neither political principle nor foresight.

Hardly had the election cries subsided, when there came the news in the last week of the year of another great mining disaster, this time in Lancashire at the Hulton collieries, known as the Pretoria Pit disaster. Hardie's last task for the year was to write an article for the "Labour Leader," similar to so many he had written in the course of his life, protesting against the callous indifference of the Government and all in authority to the continued needless sacrifice of the lives of the miners. Only those in close daily intercourse with him knew how these recurring calamities filled him with wrath almost to blasphemy. There was the usual coroner's inquest, inculpating nobody. There was the usual inquiry, followed by recommendations six months later, but valueless without Home Office compulsory powers. We do not require to remind ourselves that Parliament was dominated by the vested interests.

During all this time the Rhondda strike continued and the distress amongst the miners and their dependents increased. 1911, it will be remembered, was a year of industrial upheaval almost unprecedented in its universality. In nearly every industry the workers were at one time or other in revolt, but the outstanding disputes were those which produced the great railway strike, and prolonged this heartbreaking struggle in the Rhondda. In both of these, Hardie, by sheer force of circumstances, could not help becoming a prominent figure. His protest against the intervention of the police and the military in the Welsh dispute has already been recorded. It was the same cause, more tragically emphasised, which compelled the Labour Party to raise the matter of the railway strike in Parliament. The full story of the dispute need not be retold. The fundamental cause of the quarrel was the refusal of the railway companies to recognise the Railwaymen's Union, a refusal in which the companies had the encouragemnt of the Government. Even before the outbreak of hostilities, and while negotiations were proceeding out of which a peaceful settlement was possible, the Home Office, with the concurrence of the War Office, two departments of

INDUSTRIAL STRIFE

which Mr. Churchill and Mr. Haldane were the chiefs, had guaranteed to the companies the use of the forces of the Crown, and did actually implement their promise to such an extent that at one time it was estimated that every available soldier on home service was held ready for action. The result was what might have been expected. The railway directors stiffened their backs. The strike took place. Non-union blacklegs were given military protection. Men were shot down, one fatally at Liverpool, two fatally at Llanelly in Wales. In both cases the victims were wholly unconnected with the dispute.

The fact of the Government's preliminary guarantee to the companies was well established in the course of the parliamentary discussions, and the manner of their interpretation of their powers by the military was clearly illustrated by the evidence at the Llanelly inquest given by Major Stewart, who repudiated the suggestion that blank cartridges were fired, and declared that he had instructions from the War Office, empowering him to fire without orders from the magistrates : a state of matters which meant in effect, that a condition of martial law had been established without the sanction of Parliament, but with the sanction of a Liberal Government, or, in any event, of a Liberal War Minister.

The strike was settled ultimately by the full recognition of the Union and the appointment of a Royal Commission to inquire into the railwaymen's grievances. In the course of the discussion on the settlement, Mr. Lloyd George made a violent attack on Hardie for having stated that the Government had, while granting the aid of the military, made no attempt to bring pressure upon the directors to meet the men. Hardie had made this statement, referring to a declaration of the Prime Minister previous to the strike, but Mr. George, with

v   309

his customary slim dishonesty, sought to make it appear
as if Hardie's remark applied to a subsequent stage,
when the Government had belatedly endeavoured to
bring the parties together. Hardie, of course, held to
his original statement, the truthfulness of which was
testified to by the following resolution passed by the
Railwaymen's Joint Executive : "This Joint Executive
body repudiates the unwarrantable attack by the Chancellor of the Exchequer upon Mr. Keir Hardie for using
arguments which each of the forty representatives
present at the Board of Trade feels were quite justifiable after the language and attitude of the Prime
Minister. We further extend the best thanks of the Joint
Executive, representing all railway workers, to Mr. Keir
Hardie and the Labour Party for their splendid service
in helping, both to bring the men out, and get them back
again when the truce was called."

Another Labour dispute in which Hardie was very
directly interested, and in which he rendered invaluable
service to the workers concerned, was that which occurred
at the Dowlais Ironworks in his own constituency. This
dispute had features in common both with that of the
Rhondda miners and the railwaymen. It was a demand
to have the rates of pay equalised with those paid by
other firms in the same industry, and it was also a demand
for recognition of Trade Unionism. On both points the
men won after a protracted struggle, but not before
Hardie in Parliament had brought such pressure to bear
upon the Government for the enforcement of the Fair
Wages' Clause in Government contracts that the firm,
Guest, Keen and Nettlefold, Ltd., were compelled to
concede the demands rather than lose their contracts
with the Government of India and with other Departments. This was the kind of object lesson in the value
of Labour representation which even the most non-

political worker could appreciate, and the part played by Hardie enhanced his already very great popularity with his working-class constituents. Incidentally also it illustrated Hardie's remarkable capacity for assimilating knowledge in connection with other forms of industry than that in which he was himself expert. He showed himself able to discuss details and technicalities in connection with the steel and iron trade as familiarly as if he had been bred to the forge instead of the coalface. This adaptability applies to every other branch of industry in connection with which he had a case to uphold or defend. He was very thorough, and always made sure of his facts.

It will be perceived that during the whole of this session his time was spent alternating between the House of Commons and South Wales, and, as we shall see, in the former place there were other things than industrial strikes demanding attention. Meantime it should be noted that he was writing assiduously, and, in addition to occasional articles in the "Labour Leader" and other papers, was supplying two or three columns weekly to the "Merthyr Pioneer," a weekly paper which the local I.L.P. brought into existence in March of this year. In this journal he found once again the medium for the expression not merely of his opinions, but of his personality which had been the chief characteristic of the "Labour Leader" in its early days. Almost till the day of his death he made use of the "Pioneer" in this way.

With all this industrial strife and turmoil, and with an Insurance Bill and a House of Lords' Veto Bill to talk about, it is not surprising that the general body of the people had neither eyes nor ears for foreign affairs, and were not aware that the nation had been brought almost to the brink of war, though there were whispers that the possibility of the troops being required for service abroad had hastened the railway strike settlement.

The crisis over Morocco arising out of the rival interests of French and German financiers in that country, in which the influence of the British Government was manifested on the side of France, took place in June, but it was the end of November before, on the Foreign Office vote, a parliamentary statement could be extracted from Sir Edward Grey on a question which had so nearly involved the country in war. In the debate which followed, Ramsay MacDonald pointed out that it was the Socialist Party in the German Reichstag whose influence had prevailed upon the German Government to refrain from an immediate retort to Lloyd George's provocative Mansion House speech, and had thereby in all probability preserved the peace of Europe. MacDonald rejoiced that he belonged to a Party which was in this country the equivalent of the German Social Democratic Party in its efforts to avert international war.

Hardie, in the same debate, spoke with grave sarcasm of the self-confessed puerility of high State officials. "He did not know how the rest of the House felt, but when the Foreign Secretary was telling them how on one occasion the German Ambassador called upon him, and Sir Edward Grey asked for some explanation about the presence of the German warships at Agadir, the German Ambassador replied, 'I shall not tell anything about Agadir until you have explained Lloyd George's speech,' and the Foreign Secretary replied, 'I shall not explain Lloyd George's speech until you have told us about the presence of the warship at Agadir'—he could not help feeling that two statesmen of international repute were behaving like school children. Yet those were the men whom the two countries concerned were a:ked to trust implicitly with the control of foreign affairs."

In this same speech he went to the root of the matter. "Let them take the whole of the agreements concluded during the last five or six years between this country and other countries, about Egypt, about Morocco, and about Persia, and they would see what we were concerned with was not the promotion of the liberties of the peoples of those countries, was not the protection of the honour of the people of this country, but the protection of profits and dividends."

The situation, both in Morocco and Egypt, as it appeared to the I.L.P. leaders, and to other thoughtful, peace-loving people was fraught with peril, not only to this country, but to the whole of Europe.

We may well regret that this debate was not allowed . in June instead of in November. That it was not, shows that the Foreign Office had definitely made up its mind to conceal events from Parliament and hoodwink it should a crisis arise.

These casual extracts from the many utterances of MacDonald and Hardie, however, are placed here to show that for the ultimate catastrophe, they, and those for whom they spoke, were free from responsibility. That in the midst of all their other work, in Parliament and in the country, they should have been so vigilantly watchful in a sphere of politics to which the people in general were indifferent, was due, of course, to that belief in the international unity of interests which is inherent in the very spirit of the Socialist movement. They also knew far more than most Members of Parliament, and were better able to see what was coming and how to avert it.

MacDonald, at this very time, was himself passing through the Vale of Sorrow, the death of Mrs. Mac-

J. KEIR HARDIE

Donald in the previous September having bereft him of a companionship which could never be replaced, and which had been invaluable to the Socialist movement.

These last years of Keir Hardie's life—for we are now nearing the end—are very difficult to describe in such a way as to make vivid the environment, political, social and intellectual, which encompassed him. These years are so near to us in time and so unripened as to their harvest, that it seems like writing about current events, and yet they are separated from us by an intervening history so immeasurable in its effects, that they appear to belong to almost another epoch than ours. To recover the social and political atmosphere, to reconstruct the conditions, to appreciate the motives by which people were actuated in those days seem well nigh impossible. Yet that is what we must do if we are to have any conception of what those closing years were to Keir Hardie. We must see the world as it appeared to him in those days. How many of us, for example, can recollect or revisualise what was happening in 1912, much less recall what we were thinking about at that time.

In 1912, it will be remembered, occurred the great national miners' strike, which resulted in legalising, for the first time, the principle of a minimum wage for miners. 1912 was the year of the bitterly fought London dock strike, in which the workers were defeated, humiliated and actually starved into submission, with Mr. Tillett, the dockers' leader, praying theatrically on Tower Hill that God might strike Lord Devonport dead; the same Lord Devonport with whom, and with whose class, Mr. Tillett was in enthusiastic accord only two years later. 1912 was the year in which Tom Mann, Fred Crowley and Guy Bowman were imprisoned for advising soldiers not to shoot their fellow-workers on

THE BRINK OF WAR

strike, little thinking how near was the time when workers would be shooting workers on a scale unimaginable to those courageous protesters against working-class fratricide. 1912 was the year when there were hundreds of women in prison, hunger-striking and enduring the tortures of forcible feeding and unable, of course, to foresee how soon political right, withheld from them when claimed on grounds of justice, would be thrown to them as a bribe, or as a reward for war service—the very kind of service for which they were said to be unfit. 1912 was the year of the Irish Home Rule Act which never became operative. It was also the year in which Cabinet Ministers encouraged, and to some extent organised, rebellion in the North of Ireland, and when Mr. Bonar Law declared, blind to the possibility that South of Ireland rebels would hearken to those brave words and act upon them, "I can imagine no length of resistance to which Ulster will go which I shall not be ready to support." It was thus the memorable year when the leaders of the Unionist Party declared, and carried their Party with them in making their declaration, that a class which finds itself outvoted in Parliament may resort to arms and revolution to undo what was done through the ballot box. This was the year of the Unemployment Insurance Bill giving legislative recognition to the State's liability for the condition of the people. 1912 was the year in which the I.L.P. and the Fabians joined forces in a great "War against Poverty" campaign demanding the establishment of a minimum standard of life, and submitting proposals for the achievement of that purpose.

We have only to mention these movements and events to understand what would be the attitude of Keir Hardie towards each and all of them. His principles were fixed, his record was open. By his past conduct you

315

could always tell what his present or future conduct would be in any given set of circumstances. In much that was happening in the industrial world he could see the outcome of his own past labours. The national strike of miners: what was it but the outward and visible sign of that unity in the coal industry which he had advocated as far back as 1886 when he became the first Secretary of the Scottish Miners' Federation? The Insurance Bill: what was it but one of the fruits of his long years of agitation in and out of Parliament on behalf of the unemployed? It was not what he wanted. It was not the "right to work." He described it as a slipshod measure and sarcastically commented that its beneficiaries would still have plenty of opportunity for the cultivation of habits of thrift; but makeshift though it was, it was better than nothing. In essence, its second part was an admission of the workless man's right to live, and it would not have been there but for Keir Hardie.

For British Socialists the time was one of high hopes, alternating with almost paralysing fears. The hopes lay in the evidences of the growing solidarity of organised labour; the fears had their source in the ever-present danger of an outbreak of war in Europe which would overwhelm all plans for human betterment. In Hardie's mind, on the whole, the hopes overbalanced the fears. In the case of the Morocco crisis, war had been arrested. It might be so again and again until the sheer stupidity of having recourse to such a method of settling disputes would become universally recognised and the means of preventing it by international action would be strengthened. He was naturally an optimist and fain to persuade himself that the power of international Socialism and the common sense of humanity would be stronger than the Imperialist and capitalist forces making for war. It was well for him at this time to be able to cherish, even doubtfully, such a faith. Otherwise he would have had little zest in life during these remaining years. Unlike some other Socialists, he could find no compensating comfort in the theory that a European war, with all its evils, would at least precipitate revolution. For him, the possible fruits of a revolution were not worth the terrible price that would have to be paid for them. He had always believed, and still believed, that Socialism could be ushered in without violent and bloody revolution. That was why he was in Parliament. That was why he favoured the general strike. That was why he strove to destroy the militarist idea in association with the Socialist movement and opposed resolutely all "citizen army" proposals. For him, a war-engendered revolution was no gateway to any promised land. Though he knew well what kind of war the Great War would be, if it came, he refused to admit that it was inevitable, and in this frame of mind he went on with his work.

This year, much to the satisfaction of Hardie and his South Wales supporters, the I.L.P. Annual Conference was held at Merthyr, the object being to mark the general movement's appreciation of the stalwarts who, in the darkest hour of the Independent Labour Party had sent its leader to Parliament and had steadfastly stood by him ever since. The chief subject of debate at the Conference was Parliamentary policy, involving the vexed question which had troubled the movement ever since the formation of the Parliamentary Labour Party, as to whether that Party, and especially the I.L.P. members of it, should vote on every question on its merits, or should be guided by the general political exigencies which the Party had to face from time to time. The latter policy was endorsed by the Conference, Hardie

J. KEIR HARDIE

speaking in support of it; but as a matter of fact, on this occasion the Conference itself was a secondary function, compared with the public manifestations of Socialist feeling in the constituency and personal attachment to Hardie. The local comrades were proud of their Member, and he was proud of them. Francis, Davies, Morris, Barr, Stonelake, and all the others who had done the spade-work and the fighting, took pride— as they were well entitled to do—in their past achievements, and were full of confidence for the future. He would have taken great risks who would have suggested that anything could ever happen to dim the popularity of their hero in Merthyr Tydvil. To their credit and honour these men all stood firm when the hour of trial came. They came through the fire like fine gold. At that moment such a trial seemed so far off as to be impossible. Yet it was near at hand.

During the parliamentary session he took his full share of the work, and with George Lansbury was specially active in protesting against the vindictive treatment of the suffragist women in prison, whilst as usual he was also very much in evidence on the propaganda platform, and in various ways showed himself to be full of life and vigour. In the early autumn, preparatory to going to America for an eight weeks' tour in support of Eugene Debs's candidature for the Presidency, he spent a short holiday in Arran with his wife and daughter.

A rhyming note which he sent from there in reply to some birthday congratulation in verse reveals him as being in good health and spirits.

"Dear Comrade, if you flatter so,
You'll make an old man vaunty:
I'm six and fifty years, 'tis true,
And much have had to daunt me.

318

AMERICA

"But what of that? My life's been blest,
With health and faith abiding;
I've never sought the rich man's smile,
I've never shirked a hiding.

"I've tried to do my duty to
My conscience and my neighbour,
Regardless of the gain or loss
Involved in the endeavour.

"A happy home, a loving wife,
An I.L.P. fu' healthy;
I wadna' swap my lot in life
Wi' any o' the wealthy."

"—Keir. Arran, Aug. 15th, 1912."

Mere holiday jingle, of course, and meant only for
Tom Mackley of Woolwich, who had sent the birthday
epistle, but indicating that the agitator "off the chain"
was enjoying himself.

The American tour, like Debs's candidature itself,
was simply Socialist propaganda. He addressed forty-
four meetings, including four in Canada. He was well
received everywhere, and well reported by the American
press. The enthusiasm which he aroused in such places
as Chicago, Pittsburg and Indianapolis must be taken
as a tribute to his personality, for he was no platform
"spell-binder" such as American audiences are said to
be fond of. He had never aspired to the reputation of
being an orator. At Chicago he reminded his audience
of this. "Those who know me best are aware that I am
never much of an orator. If I have any reputation at
all it is not that of a talker, but it is rather this : that
during the thirty odd years that I have been out in the
open for the class to which I belong, whether in Parliament or out of Parliament, I have stood by that class
through good report and ill."

A good deal depends on what is meant by oratory.

319

J. KEIR HARDIE

Hardie could not play upon the emotions of an audience by means of voice modulations and inflections and dramatic gestures, but he could, nevertheless, sometimes set the heart of his hearers beating in perfect tune with that of his own. He was guided by no rules of elocution except that which enjoins clear enunciation. His sentences nearly always ended on a rising note, which in an insincere speaker would have sounded like querulousness, but from his had the effect of intense earnestness. When closing a speech on a note of passionate appeal the last word of the last sentence would ring out like the sound of a trumpet, and call his auditors involuntarily to their feet; they knew not why except that they had to get up and cheer. For lucidity in definition and explanation of principles in oral speech he was unrivalled. He was never obscure. You always knew what he meant. Take, for example, the following reference to the State in this same Chicago speech : "The syndicalist starts from the assumption that the State is a capitalist institution. The State, however, is nothing of the sort. At the present time every State in the world, and every kingdom in the world, is capitalist. Why is that so? Because the workers elect the capitalist class to govern the State. The State itself is neither capitalist nor anti-capitalist. The State is simply a good old donkey that goes the way its driver wants it to go. When the capitalists rule, of course, the State serves the capitalists. When the workers get sense enough to stop sending capitalists, and send Socialists drawn from their own ranks, to represent them, then the State becomes your servant and not the servant of the capitalists."

He sent home, as was his custom, a series of articles descriptive of industrial and social conditions in America, very valuable at the time, but not so interesting for us now as the accounts of his meetings with old friends from the home country. At every stage of his journeyings they seemed to have gathered round him. His tour took him through many of the coal-mining districts, and we hear of social evenings with comrades of his youth now, like himself, growing grey, but fain to shake hands and be merry with him for auld lang syne. We hear of "Hardie singing 'Bonnie Mary o' Argyle' and 'Robin Tamson's Smiddy,'" and of "big Bob Macbeth in 'The Battle of Stirling Brig,'" and of "Barney Reilly dancing an Irish jig with as clean and light a step as he did thirty years ago in the 'Quarter.'"

This was Keir Hardie as the party politicians and press interviewers never knew him, but as he was known in hundreds of I.L.P. households throughout Great Britain and also to the delegates at I.L.P. conferences in the social hours when the day's work was done and the controversies forgotten. On such occasion, to look upon Keir Hardie and Bruce Glasier letting themselves go in a foursome reel was, as the Scotch phrase has it, "a sicht for sair een." This, his last American trip, seems to have given him very great pleasure, a fact the knowledge of which has a measure of consolation for some of us who know what time and fate had in store for him.

Hardly had he arrived home when the Party was called upon to face the troubles for international Socialism created by the war in the Balkans. A special international Congress had been summoned to meet at Basle. The separate Balkan States had united against Turkey, and there was very great danger that the war would not be confined to the Near East and that the much dreaded European conflagration would break out. So imminent was this possibility that the International Socialist Bureau had already cancelled the arrangements for the 1913 Congress due to take place in Vienna. The contiguity of Austria to the theatre of war, and the ambitions of its rulers and diplomats and its interests in the balance of power in the Balkans, made it seem certain that, if the struggle were prolonged, Austria would speedily be involved and would drag the others in also. Europe was again on the edge of the precipice. So, when the Congress had to be postponed till 1914, it was decided to call immediately an emergency Congress in Switzerland. We know what happened in 1914, and why it came about that this at Basle was the very last Congress before the break-up of the International. It should be noted that the British members of the International Socialist Bureau were strongly opposed to the postponement of the 1913 Congress and were alone in this opposition. Who can tell but that if it had met, it might have been able to radiate sufficient moral force to prevent the calamity of the following year? To be wise after the event is, of course, easy, and these post-war conjectures may seem futile; yet it is natural for us to regret what seems a lost opportunity for a last great effort for the prevention of the world-war.

At the Basle Congress, twenty-three countries were represented by five hundred and fifty-five delegates, Great Britain sending thirteen. By the time the Congress met, the Balkan States had effectually defeated Turkey and an armistice had been declared with the Balkan League holding the mastery of the situation. This had not lessened the danger of war in Central Europe. Not only was there the likelihood that in the settlement the Great Powers would intervene and come into collision with each other, but there was also the danger, which realised itself only too speedily, that the victorious Balkan States would turn and rend each other. The actors on the Balkan stage were too much puppets controlled by the rival Powers who plotted, bribed and egged on from behind the scenes.

The Basle Congress was a magnificently impressive International Socialist demonstration against war; but that was all it could be. It drafted and issued a manifesto to the Socialists of all the countries represented, defining what measures they might take for the preservation of peace. This manifesto, the last issued by any authoritative International Congress, might well be republished. It sets forth in vivid detail the conditions and international relationships out of which the Great War eventuated, conditions and relationships which, if re-established, whatever the grouping of the different interests may be, must produce the same evil results.

There was deep seriousness at this Congress, and, at the great peace demonstration in the Cathedral, high and noble utterances by Bebel, Jaurès, Adler, Hardie and other international representative men. It was an historic Congress, in a sense of which none who participated could have any knowledge. None of them could know that this was the last. Nor could Bebel and Hardie know that this was their final meeting. But so it was, Bebel, now in his seventy-third year, had only a few more months of life, and happily did not see his beloved German Social Democratic Party first voting war credits and then torn to pieces. Hardie looked almost as venerable as Bebel, but had greater vigour. Basle wound up an old generation, ended an old chapter, was the close of many hopes.

The Rev. James Wallace of Glasgow, who was one of the British delegates, has preserved for us a very pleasant glimpse of Hardie in the streets of Basle. "After the excitement of the public meeting," says Mr. Wallace, "I accompanied the tribune of the people on a tour to see the 'uncos' of Basle, and, as in Bunyan's

J. KEIR HARDIE

'Pilgrim's Progress' Hopeful had to fall back on Christian to translate the writing on a pillar 'for he was learned,' so I proved of service to Keir Hardie in the case of French or German sentences and specially by enabling him with some ease to make a purchase of a keepsake for Mrs. Hardie in a small jeweller's shop. Blessing on the honest Swiss saleswoman whose shop seemed so fragrant with honesty that we both felt completely at home, and the desire for gain or profit was simply nowhere with her compared with the full play of human kindliness and good feeling. Whether she recollects the two Scotsmen or no, I cannot tell, but to the two Scotsmen her shop with its fragrant honesty was a green spot in our memory. As we passed along the pavements we admired the noble street architecture of the old city, but Keir Hardie was also much interested in all the different kinds of dogs, large or small, that crossed our paths. The most contemptible 'tykes' attracted the great man's notice. During the whole course of our peregrinations working men broke into smiles at the sight of Keir Hardie, and kept him very busy pulling off his cap in reply to their salutations, while an Egyptian, with a profile exactly reproducing the features of his ancestors on the monuments of Luxor four thousand years ago, approached us with all eagerness to complain of the high-handed acts of British officials in the land of the Pharaohs. Keir Hardie listened to him very sympathetically and offered to air his complaint in Parliament; but so far as I could judge there was a want of definiteness about his statements, as if they were rather the expression of a general restiveness of his country under the regime of Britain, and might even be fomented by German intrigue. Very naturally our footsteps gravitated towards the Art Gallery of Basle. 'There's Jaurès,' said Keir Hardie, and went forward to shake the great Frenchman's hand. A man more unlike the typical Frenchman as depicted in our comic papers it would be impossible to find. Indeed, take a shrewd farmer from the Ayr or Lanark market, and there you have a Jaurès. It was the last meeting of these two great men on earth. What sphere have they now for the exercise of their beautiful energies? 'We are such stuff as dreams are made of.'" Mr. Wallace was wrong. Hardie and Jaurès were to meet again before the end.

And so the year 1912 drew towards its close, with the war-clouds hanging dark and threatening over the nations, and the minds of all Socialists full of foreboding. "The moment is critical," wrote Hardie, "and European war will almost certainly lead to European revolution, the end of which no man can foresee"; yet was he still an optimist. "It was a great gathering," he summed up, speaking of the Basle Congress, "and full of significance for the future of our race. For those gathered there represented not so many nationalities, but the disinherited of all lands. These have now no country : they are the mob, the proletariat, the oppressed. These are the ties that bind them. The International is uniting them in their fight against bondage." He was great of heart, and he needed to be.

CHAPTER THIRTEEN

SOUTH AFRICA AND IRELAND—COMING OF AGE
CONFERENCE—THE WORLD CONFLICT

IT is not easy to describe Keir Hardie's activities during the succeeding eighteen months of turmoil. So many different events, political, industrial and international, were happening concurrently, in all of which he was interested and implicated. Perhaps the simplest way will be to take the more outstanding of these events in their chronological order.

At the I.L.P. Annual Conference held at Manchester, in March, he accepted once more the position of Chairman of the Party, the chief reason for his election being that he, as founder of the I.L.P., might preside at the "Coming of Age" Conference and celebrations to take place the following year at Bradford. His remarks in accepting the honour were brief and characteristic. "Twenty years ago I was elected to the Chairmanship. I then said I accepted the office reluctantly. I say the same thing to-day. Nature never intended me to be a leader. I find myself happier among the rank and file. But one thing let us determine. During the next twelve months we are all going to be young men in a hurry."

In Parliament a fortnight later, Hardie found himself almost in the position which he had occupied at the beginning of his parliamentary career. He stood alone, or nearly so. The occasion was the introduction of what was known as the Government's "Cat and Mouse" Bill, the object of which was to enable the Home Secretary to release suffragist hunger strikers when they were at the point of death, and, when they had recovered in health, to reimprison them without trial. Hardie moved the rejection of the Bill and got only seven other members to follow him into the lobby. There was magnanimity as well as courage in his lonely championship of the militants.

Only a few days before, these same women had not only shouted him down, but had actually assaulted him. Hardly by a word did he blame them. Nor did he look for gratitude from them. He opposed the Bill because it was the right thing to do, and he opposed it with so much vigour and persuasiveness that in the final division before it became law, his seven supporters had increased to fifty, a proof that he had stirred some of the parliamentary guardians of liberty to a perception of the danger of vesting such arbitrary power in the hands of a Secretary of a Government department. So far as the militant suffragists were concerned, he appreciated their fighting spirit, though he deplored their lack of judgment in the conduct of their campaign. The leaders, Mrs. Pankhurst and Mrs. Pethick Lawrence, both of whom had suffered imprisonment, were, or had been, his personal friends. Mrs. Pankhurst had declared war on the Labour Party because it had declined to adopt the policy of voting against every Government measure until the women's demands had been conceded, and, of course, Hardie, as a member of the Labour Party, had been included in that declaration of war, and treated, or rather maltreated, as if he were a foe to the suffrage movement instead of its strongest advocate.

Recent developments had added exasperation to the sense of injustice in the minds of the women. The Government had introduced a Reform Bill which made no provision for votes for women, but had tacitly agreed that if amendments embodying such a provision were carried, they would be included in the Bill. There was a practical certainty that such amendments, proposed by the Labour Party, would be carried; but the hopes thus raised had been frustrated by the Speaker's ruling that such amendments would constitute an entirely new Bill, which would require to be introduced anew, and the Government had thereupon abandoned the measure altogether. The militant section, violent in their methods before, were more violent now, and seemed more wrathful even against the Labour Party than against the Government, notwithstanding that the I.L.P. Conference had pledged itself to oppose every franchise measure which did not include women. That very Conference the militant women had tried to wreck, and mobbed and hustled Hardie and Snowden. He did not blame the women. He blamed the Government which denied them the rights of citizenship, much in the same way as he had held that unemployed workmen could not be expected to conform to a system of laws which did not guarantee to them the right to work. In tactics the militant suffragists were wrong : in principle they were right. It should be said that the tactics of violence had never been endorsed by the National Union of Women's Suffrage Societies under which the majority of the women were organised and which had supported the Labour Party throughout in its methods.

Early in the month of April, Sir Edward Grey disclosed that a European war had again nearly broken out over a quarrel between Montenegro and Albania—a part of the aftermath of the previous year's fighting in the Balkans. Only the most meagre information was vouchsafed and no opportunity was provided for public discussion. "I suppose," commented Hardie, in his gravely satirical way—"I suppose we shall be allowed to say a word or two before war begins." Put in the past tense, these words are an accurate description of what actually took place sixteen months later. Parliament was allowed "to say a few words" before the Great War began. Responsible Socialist leaders had certainly at this time other matters than the franchise question to engross their attention.

In June, he travelled further across Europe than he had yet been, to Budapest, to attend the Annual Congress of the International Women's Suffrage Alliance, not as a delegate, but as a guest. This fact emphasises how widely he was recognised as a friend of the cause, some of whose advocates in his own country were throwing stones at him. He found the Hungarian capital to be a beautiful city, but a city in which democracy could hardly draw breath. Trade Unions were tolerated as long as they were harmless to the employers, there was a franchise which excluded the workers from any share in legislation or administration, and military law was dominant over all. Reading his description, we can realise how helpless the Socialist elements would be to rally any anti-war force, and how the whole populace would be rushed automatically into war when the crisis came. Side by side with the autocratic power, he found a certain amount of wisdom in the municipal management which made life tolerable, and there is no indication of any premonition of the terrible ordeal which awaited this fair city on the Danube fated to be scourged by war, pestilence, and famine, and, later on, by the infamous White Terror. He visited Vienna, where he found much the same conditions, and conferred with Dr. Adler and other Socialist leaders, and in Brussels, on the way home, with Huysmans, the subject of talk between all these representative Socialists being, we may be sure, the ever darkening war-cloud and the possibility of dispelling it.

He does not seem to have derived much benefit in health from this Continental trip, as, almost immediately after his return, he had a temporary but rather alarming breakdown. On the last Friday in July, Mr. and Mrs. W. C. Anderson, on their way to an I.L.P. summer conference at Keswick, found their leader in a railway carriage at Euston in a state of acute exhaustion. He was due to speak at Whitehaven that evening, but finding his condition so serious, Mr. Anderson sent him home in a cab, and himself took his place at Whitehaven. Hardie turned up two days later at Keswick looking very pale and shaken, but assuring his friends that he was all right. As a matter of fact he had very frequent attacks of this kind, known only to the friends with whom he happened to be staying. Seldom did he allow them to prevent the fulfilment of his public engagements.

In Parliament the following week he was, with Mr. Outhwaite, demanding an inquiry into the industrial trouble which had broken out in South Africa, and incidentally providing the British public with the finest reliable information as to the nature and cause of that trouble. The Rand miners had at last realised that the conquest of South Africa had not been undertaken primarily in their interests, and when in order to better their working conditions they had begun to organise and to hold public meetings, they found that the very law which, when passed by the Boer Government, was declared to be one of the justifications for British aggression, was now used to prevent British labour in South Africa from organising itself. A public meeting in the Square at Johannesburg had been suppressed by armed force and twenty men killed and one hundred

BEBEL'S FUNERAL

and fifty wounded. The Governor-General, Lord Gladstone, had allowed himself to be made the tool of the mineowners, had given the sanction of his authority to the outrage, and had thereby brought dishonour on British rule in South Africa. Such, with many additional particulars of the evil conditions prevailing in the mines, was the impeachment put forward by Outhwaite and Hardie. The Government had practically no defence, and an inquiry was granted, the subsequent outcome of which is no part of this narrative. What is noteworthy is how instinctively labour in revolt, whether in South Africa or elsewhere, looked to Hardie for championship. He could always be relied upon. It almost seemed as if in this resolute, unswerving man the working-class struggle the world over had become personified.

In August, Hardie, with Socialist representatives from many lands, was called to Zurich to the funeral of Bebel, whose place in the German Socialist movement was very similar to that of Hardie himself in this country. Jaurès was absent through ill-health. The public mourning for Bebel, as described by Hardie, must have been deeply impressive, but more impressive to us are Hardie's simple words : "The end came sudden, which at seventy-three is meet and proper. In the evening he retired to rest, apparently in his usual health, and ere the morning he had entered upon the rest everlasting. What now remains is but the memory of the mighty life, and the calm, peaceful death."

In the first week of September he was in Dublin at the invitation of the Irish Transport Workers' Federation investigating the cause of the serious disturbances in that city, the memory of which has been dimmed by the subsequent more terrible happenings with which we are all too familiar. Indeed, the events of that

331

time—outrageous though they were—seem now like a mere dress rehearsal for what was to follow. The city was given over to "Castle" rule, administered by the R.I.C. which was almost equivalent to being placed under military law. As at Johannesburg, public meetings were forcibly suppressed and lives lost in the course of the suppression. The organiser of the Transport Workers' Union, Jim Larkin, was arrested on a charge of sedition, which, as Hardie pointed out, could, if upheld, be construed to apply to the whole of Trade Union activity. "There never was a meeting held in connection with a strike or a Labour dispute in which the same charge could not have held good." This was not the "Irish Question" as the politicians understand it. It was not England *versus* Ireland. It was Capital *versus* Labour, and was in reality an attempt on the part of the employers, directed by W. M. Murphy, an Irish capitalist, to destroy organised labour in Ireland before it became too strong. In six years' time, Larkin, a man of volcanic energy, had achieved something like a miracle. The Irish industrial workers were already nation-conscious. He had made them also class-conscious, and had brought into existence a force which, in the event of Home Rule being established, boded ill for capitalism in Ireland. Larkin was the leader, the inspirer, of the new movement; but there was another quieter, brainier, but equally determined man, James Connolly by name. These two were creating an organisation and a spirit which was at once Nationalist and Socialist, and a mutual instinct of self-preservation made Dublin Castle, the army in occupation, and Murphy, the capitalist Nationalist, join forces for the destruction of this new phenomenon.

Hardie knew well how dangerous it was for any British-born agitator to obtrude in Irish affairs, but nevertheless declared it to be the duty of British Trade Unionists to take part in the resistance to what he described as "a conspiracy to destroy the Trade Union movement." He protested against the Government taking sides with the employers, and pointed out that, at that very moment, Carson and F. E. Smith were fomenting rebellion in the North of Ireland with apparently the approval of Dublin Castle. From Dublin he passed to Belfast where he addressed a meeting under the auspices of the I.L.P. and sought to convince the Trade Unionists of the North that it was their duty to make common cause with their fellow Trade Unionists in the South and West.

The week following he was at Jena as the fraternal delegate from the British Labour Party to the German Socialist Congress, his real object being as ever, to assist, if only by the weight of a single word, in consolidating the International Socialist forces against war. In his greetings to the Congress he restated practically his whole Socialist and anti-militarist creed. "In these days of international commerce, finance, art, literature, and the increasing solidarity of the working-class movement of the world, the rulers and statesmen of Europe could, had they the will, abolish armies and navies in one generation. We could at least easily have the United States of Europe in that time, but they do not want to. Their rule is founded on the sword, and, were that to be abolished, the democracies of the world would soon abolish class rule. In the Socialist parties there is growing up a State within the State. The new State will not be based on force, but on economic equality and personal liberty."

He does not seem to have been much impressed with the proceedings at the German Congress, and was disappointed that the general strike idea had not yet been embodied in any practical proposal, while, in the friction between the Christian Unions and the Social Democratic Unions, he saw a fatal obstacle to unity at a time when unity was the one thing needful. He knew from experience not so far away as Germany the evil consequences of sectarian differences. Thus the weeks and months passed, every day full of strife and agitation, the year closing with a national I.L.P. campaign against Conscription, in which, as usual, Hardie took a leading part, and with another impressive international demonstration in London with Adler, Vandervelde, Jaurès, Hardie all delivering the same message, these four standing side by side almost for the last time. The year of the Great War was at hand.

And yet it seemed as if the danger had receded. These distinguished foreigners were in London to attend the meetings of the International Socialist Bureau, the chief business of which was to arrange for the postponed International Congress, which it was, after all, decided could be held in Vienna. In the minds of these men the danger of European war had, for the time being, vanished, else they would not have been arranging for Vienna in August, 1914. When August came, Vienna was the scene of a congress of another kind—a congress of armed men. The conscripts were then mustering and were being marched out into Hell.

While in London the Socialist Bureau lent its influence on behalf of the movement for Socialist unity in this country which seemed now at last on the point of being achieved. This, also, the war rendered impossible.

The springtime of 1914 was a time of great satisfaction for Keir Hardie. It brought him a sense of achievement. The Independent Labour Party had existed for twenty-one years. It was now a power in the land. It had created a political Labour Party expressive of working-

"COMING OF AGE"

class ideals, and its principles were accepted by the great Trade Union movement. In all this his own personal effort was manifest. His had been the guiding hand, not always visible, but always operating. The influence of the I.L.P. was apparent, not only in Parliament, but in every sphere and phase of local government. In Town Councils, County Councils, Parish Councils and School Boards, members of the Independent Labour Party were at work, and the effect of their presence was already beginning to humanise the administrative work of these bodies. Almost imperceptibly, a new collectivist spirit was permeating the public life of the country, and a consciousness of power was growing amongst the working class. In all this the Independent Labour Party had been the driving and the inspiring element. The very fact that it was the mark for special attack by the vested interests was the proof of this. Many times during those twenty-one years the capitalist press had exulted in the appearance of division, and had gloated over the coming disruption— which never came. It was now celebrating its "coming of age" as a political party, and the man who presided over it on the day of its birth was presiding over it now. Keir Hardie, like the Party, had survived through abuse, ridicule and misrepresentation. He was able, literally, to look upon his handiwork and find that it was good. To consolidate organised Labour and shape it into an invincible power for the realisation of Socialism. That was his purpose. Only a beginning had been made, but it was a good beginning. A path had been cleared along which others might follow.

It was in something of this spirit that the I.L.P. met at Bradford, the place of its birth. Congratulations came from every Labour organisation in Britain and from every Socialist Party in the world. From many of these also came delegates in person. Camelinat, who had been a member of the First International and Treasurer to the Government of the Paris Commune, beaming over with kindliness, gave his blessing to the I.L.P. pioneers for liberty. Huysmans, of the Second International, told how the great fraternity of Socialist effort was growing in all lands, and paid tribute to the Independent Labour Party's share in that work. Herman Muller, of Germany, spoke in the same hopeful strain. There was eloquent speech-making and brave and stirring music, including a Song of Liberty, specially composed for the occasion by Granville Bantock to words written by Mrs. Bantock. The early pioneers of the Party were much in evidence; Robert Smillie, Fred Jowett, M.P., Bruce Glasier, Mrs. Glasier, with many a rank-and-file delegate from the first-year branches of the Party, fighting their battles over again. The general feeling was one of confidence and optimism, and for the moment, at least, they had put out of their hearts and minds the fear of war. Even Hardie's presidential address made no reference to the European spectre. He looked to the past and to the future, and if for that future he had any fears, he kept them to himself. "The past twenty-one years," he said, "have been years of continuous progress, but we are only at the beginning. The emancipation of the worker has still to be achieved, and just as the I.L.P. in the past has given a good, straight lead, so shall the I.L.P. in the future, through good report and ill, pursue the even tenour of its way, until the sunshine of Socialism and human freedom breaks forth upon the land."

It was a rejoiceful time for the I.L.P. marred only slightly by attempted outbreaks of violence from the militant suffragists, and even they, could they have peered into the near future, would probably have held their hands.

"COMING OF AGE"

Hardie's closing words in vacating the chair constitute the most self-revealing public utterance he ever made, and as they have also a bearing on present—and probably future—developments within the I.L.P., it is well that they should be preserved. They are also biographical, in the truest sense of the word. "I think I have shown that I can be a pioneer, but I am not guided so much by a consideration of policy, or by thinking out a long sequence of events, as by intuition and inspiration. I know what I believe to be the right thing and I go and do it. If I had, twenty-one years ago, stopped to think about what the future would bring, I would not have dared to accept the responsibility of entering the House of Commons. During those first three years my wife kept my house going, kept my children decently and respectably clothed and fed on an income which did not even exceed twenty-five shillings a week. Comrades, you do well to honour her. Never, even in those days, did she offer one word of reproof. Many a bitter tear she shed, but one of the proud boasts of my life is to be able to say that if she has suffered much in health and in spirit, never has she reproached me for what I have done for the cause I love. I leave the chair, then, as I did at the end of the first Conference, to be a pioneer. I said the other day that those of us who are advanced in years may easily become cumberers of the ground. I am not going to die if I can help it, but there is a dead spirit which blocks the path of the young. I am not going to stand in their way. I shall die, as I have lived, a member of the I.L.P., but I want the Party to have freedom to grow, and I do not want young men and women to say, 'We might have done this or that if it had not been for old Keir.' I will accept no position which will give me standing over you. I will fight for what I think the right thing,

337

but I will trust your judgment. While I have anything
to give, it shall be given ungrudgingly to the child of
my life—the I.L.P."

This was Easter, 1914. The delegates returned to
their districts to report the proceedings to their branches
and to prepare for the usual summer propaganda work
and for the coming general election which was expected
before the end of the year. The possibility of war did
not enter into their calculations. Indeed, it is a remarkable fact that the great upheaval, so long feared and
dreaded and prophesied, came at the last unexpectedly,
almost like a thief in the night, and gave the democracies
of the various countries no time to organise any
resistance, much less to collaborate internationally on a
common policy. The people of this country were not
dreaming of any European War in which they would
possibly be involved. On the Saturday and Sunday—
twenty-four hours before Sir Edward Grey made his
fateful speech which brought the war spirit into the
heart of the country—there could be seen on the London
streets groups of men and women on their way to
Germany to convey to the German workers the fraternal
greetings of groups of British Adult Schools and of
British citizens innocent of what had gone on behind the
scenes.

So far as politics were concerned, people were
deeply interested in two subjects only. One was the
increasingly outrageous lawlessness of the militant
suffragists. The other was the threatened Ulster
rebellion in resistance to the Home Rule Act due to
be put in operation shortly. Shiploads of ammunition—
said to have been imported from Germany—had been
landed in Ireland for the arming of the Ulster Volunteers. Certain officers of high rank, responsible for the
control of the military forces in Ireland, had let it be

known that they could not be relied upon to act against the Ulster rebels, and to the threat of rebellion there was thus added the threat of mutiny, and though these officers had somewhat modified their mutinous declarations, the utterances of such politicians as Sir Edward Carson, F. E. Smith and Bonar Law were the reverse of reassuring. The situation was regarded as serious. The people of this country were more concerned about the Curragh of Kildare than about the Market Square of Sarajevo.

The Socialist movement, too, was, as has been indicated, for the time off guard. Philip Snowden, in rather poor health, went off with Mrs. Snowden on a world tour. If he had thought so great a crisis was imminent he would certainly have stayed at home. Even the assassination of the Austrian Grand Duke at Sarajevo did not awaken serious apprehension of a general European war, though such a possibility was not absent from the minds of the I.L.P. leaders. That possibility was indicated in an article by W. C. Anderson in the "Labour Leader" of July 30th, but even at that late date he felt justified in writing : "Despite all signs to the contrary, there will, I believe, be no war; nothing, at any rate, in the nature of extended warfare." And so was it with the international movement.

On July 29th, the International Socialist Bureau met at Brussels, hurriedly summoned to consider the state of matters created by Austria's declaration of war on Servia. "But," says Bruce Glasier who was present with Hardie and Dan Irving from Britain, "although the dread peril of a general eruption of war in Europe was the main subject of the deliberations, no one, not even the German representatives, seemed apprehensive of an actual rupture between the great Powers taking place until at least the full resources of diplomacy had been exhausted." So little was a general European war expected that it was decided to go on with the International Congress, only changing the place of meeting from Vienna to Paris because of the state of war in Austria, and fixing the date for August 9th instead of the 23rd, the original date. By August 9th, neither Paris nor any capital in Europe could give hospitality to an International Socialist Congress.

In the evening after this Bureau meeting in Brussels, a great anti-war meeting, attended by 7,000 people, was held in the Cirque. Vandervelde, of Belgium, presided. Haase, of Germany, Jaurès, of France, Hardie, of Britain, all spoke movingly. Jaurès, in this last speech he was ever to make, warmly thanked the German Social Democrats for their splendid demonstrations in favour of peace, and with impassioned eloquence invoked the workers to rescue once and for ever civilisation from the appalling disaster of war.

Forty-eight hours later Jaurès himself fell, not by the hand of a German, but of a fellow-countryman, inflamed, it was said, by war madness, though to this hour no serious attempt has been made to discover whether any other motive power directed the assassin's arm. It was here then, in Brussels, that Hardie and Jaurès met and parted for the last time. It was in Brussels that on this, the very eve of Armageddon, the citizens, men and women in their thousands, marched through the streets displaying their white cards with the strange device, "Guerre à la Guerre" (war against war). We know what happened to Brussels in the time that was near at hand.

Yet, still there was hope, amounting almost to a belief, that the crisis would pass. Assuredly in Great Britain that was the prevalent conviction, and it was only when it was realised that Russia was mobilising her troops, and massing them where, in time of peace, no Russian troops should be, and that German forces were threateningly near to the Belgian frontier, that the people of this country woke up to a real sense of peril, and it must be said that they did not wake up with any enthusiasm. The common people did not enter into war. They were dragged into it. That they could be dragged into it was due to the fact that they had been kept wholly ignorant of the doings of their diplomatists, and they had not believed the I.L.P. when it tried to inform them. The I.L.P. now, and up to the last possible moment, directed all its efforts towards keeping the nation out of the war.

With a spontaneity which was a striking proof of how surely rooted in principle was the organisation, every section of it moved in the same way. The National Council, the Divisional Councils, the Federations, the branches—even the smallest and most isolated of these— acted as by a common impulse; and on Sunday, August 2nd, in every city, town and village where there was a branch or group of the Independent Labour Party, a public protest against the nation being dragged into the war was made, and a demand that whatever might happen in Europe, this country should stand neutral and play the part of peacemaker. Hardie, if he had time to think of it—which he probably had not—had reason to be proud of his beloved I.L.P. that day.

He himself was in Trafalgar Square taking part in a demonstration organised by the British Section of the International Socialist Bureau, of which he was Chairman. The Bureau had already issued a Manifesto which is here reproduced for two reasons, first, because Hardie was one of the signatories, second, because it is important to preserve this documentary proof that organised labour in this country was unitedly opposed

J. KEIR HARDIE

to the war. Had it continued to be so after war was declared, history would to-day have had a different and better story to tell than it can now present to posterity. The Manifesto was as follows :—

"AN APPEAL TO THE BRITISH WORKING CLASS.

"(Manifesto by British Section of the International Socialist Bureau.)

"The long-threatened European war is now upon us. For more than a hundred years no such danger has confronted civilisation. It is for you to take full account of the desperate situation and to act promptly and vigorously in the interests of peace.

"You have never been consulted about the war. Whatever may be the rights and the wrongs of the sudden crushing attack made by the Militarist Empire of Austria upon Servia, it is certain that the workers of all countries likely to be drawn into the conflict must strain every nerve to prevent their Governments from committing them to war.

"Everywhere Socialists and the organised forces of Labour are taking this course. Everywhere vehement protests are made against the greed and intrigues of militarists and armament-mongers.

"We call upon you to do the same here in Great Britain upon an even more impressive scale. Hold vast demonstrations in London and in every industrial centre. Compel those of the governing class and their press, who are eager to commit you to co-operate with Russian despotism, to keep silence and respect the decision of the overwhelming majority of the people, who will have neither part not lot in such infamy. The success of Russia at the present day would be a curse to the world.

"There is no time to lose. Already, by secret agreements and understandings of which the democracies of the civilised world know only by rumour, steps are being taken which may fling us all into the fray. Workers, stand together therefore for peace. Combine and conquer the militarist enemy and the self-seeking Imperialists to-day once and for all.

"Men and women of Britain, you have now an unexampled opportunity of showing your power, rendering a magnificent service to humanity and to the world. Proclaim that for you the days of plunder and butchery have gone by. Send messages of peace and fraternity to your fellows who have less liberty than you.

"Down with class rule! Down with the rule of brute force! Down with war! Up with the peaceful rule of the people!

"Signed on behalf of the British Section of the International Socialist Bureau,

> "J. KEIR HARDIE (Chairman).
> "ARTHUR HENDERSON (Secretary)."

There is a strange ring about that appeal now. It still seemed as if organised Labour would hold together for the preservation of peace, or for its speedy restoration if war should come. But it was too late. The country was in the rapids and was being rushed to the doom of the waterfall. Within twenty-four hours both temper and outlook had changed. The heavy blares of the war trumpets were beginning to perform their magic.

The Trafalgar Square demonstration, which the "Manchester Guardian" described as "the biggest held for years," was representative of all sections, as is shown by the list of speakers, which included Mr. J. Stokes, Chairman of the London Trades Council; George Lansbury, now of the "Daily Herald"; Robert Williams, of the Transport Workers' Federation; Will Thorne, M.P., of the General Labourers' Union; Mary R. Macarthur, of the Federation of Women Workers; Margaret Bondfield, of the Shop Assistants' Union; Dr. Marion Phillips, of the Women's Labour League; Herbert Burrows, of the British Socialist Party; Keir Hardie, of the I.L.P.; Arthur Henderson, of the National Labour Party; Mrs. Despard and Mr. Cunninghame Graham. The latter gentleman's speech was said to have made the most profound impression, and to have been "the best he had ever delivered," which was saying a great deal. "Do not," he implored, "let us do this crime, or be parties to the misery of millions who have never done us harm."

In another part of the country Robert Smillie said that if it were yet possible to stop the war by a cessation of work all over Europe he would be glad to pledge the miners to such a course. On August 2nd, labour was against the war.

On the following night interest was transferred to the House of Commons, and Parliament was "allowed to say a few words" before the war, already decided upon, really started officially.

The few words, from the I.L.P. point of view, were spoken with unmistakable emphasis by MacDonald and Hardie. Never did speakers speak under difficulties like those men. The facts had not been disclosed; the crowded House was in a frenzy and wished to listen to no reason. "I think," said MacDonald, "Sir Edward Grey is wrong. I think the Government which he represents and for which he speaks is wrong. I think the verdict of history will be that they are wrong. There has been no crime committed by statesmen of this character without these statesmen appealing to their nation's honour. We fought the Crimean War because of our honour. We rushed to South Africa because of our honour. The right hon. gentleman is appealing to

us to-day because of our honour. So far as we are
concerned, whatever may happen, whatever may be said
about us, whatever attacks may be made upon us, we
will say that this country ought to have remained neutral,
because we believe in the deepest part of our hearts that
is right, and that that alone is consistent with the honour
of the country."

Hardie, some time later on in the debate, made a
speech of extraordinary dignity and earnestness.
Addressing himself in the first place to the consequences
rather than the causes of the war, he impressed everyone
with a sense of the extent of the distress that might be
expected. Unemployment would spread and, lacking
wages, the poor would be robbed by the manipulators of
the various food rings. He darkened the picture of
suffering as only one could who had seen it so frequently.
"How," he asked, "were the Government going to
relieve it?" He pointed out that earlier in the sitting a
Bill to help the bankers had been rushed through all its
stages by the Government. Where was the Bill to help
the workers? He passionately denied that the mass of
the workers of the country were for war. "Had they
been consulted, war would not have happened. Why
were not they consulted?"

Both MacDonald and Hardie knew only too well that
their speeches and protestations were now in vain. They
had made these protestations years before, when they
ought not to have been in vain. What they were doing
now was to clear themselves and their Party from
responsibility for the crime, and, if possible, hold the
Labour movement of this country true and faithful to the
spirit and pledge of International Socialism. It was a
tremendous ordeal for both, but especially for Hardie,
who was the older man, and physically unwell, and only
sustained against collapse by the intensity of the crisis,

which made him forgetful of bodily infirmity. These had been two weeks of terrible strain. The critical Conference at Brussels; the emotional experience of that great public gathering there; the murder of Jaurès, revealing, as by a flash from the fires of hell, the potential horrors opening out upon humanity; the I.L.P. Council deliberations; the Labour Party Executive meetings; the Socialist Bureau's meetings and decisions; the Trafalgar Square demonstration; and now, this last solemn hour in the House of Commons. The wonder is that he was able to pass through it, and that he did not break down then instead of a year later. There are occasions for some men when the spirit triumphs over time and circumstance and fate itself. But for such men the penalty in pain is very great.

Hardie had yet another ordeal to pass through, and he resolved to face it at once before going home to the quietness of Cumnock. He had to see his constituents. He knew well that the drums of war that were already beating would, in proportion, as they roused national pride and prejudice, drown reason, and that if he was to get a chance to explain his position it would have to be immediately. On August 6th, he spoke in Aberdare. What happened there had best be described by one who was present. "As soon as the hall began to fill it was obvious that a large hostile element was present. There was no disturbance when Hardie, Richardson and the Chairman, Councillor Stonelake, mounted on the platform. The Chairman spoke without interruption, but as soon as he called on Hardie the uproar commenced. A well organised body of men had taken up a strong position near the back of the hall, a huge dreary building, which was usually the local market. They were the members of the Conservative and the Liberal Clubs who had always hated Hardie. Their opportunity had come

THE WORLD CONFLICT

at last. 'God Save the King' and 'Rule Britannia' were sung lustily, and the clang of a bell could be heard amongst the general pandemonium. The crowd in the front attempted to quell the disturbance. It soon became evident that Keir Hardie was not going to be heard that night. Hardie continued to speak for about half an hour utterly undaunted by the noise, but his voice could not be heard further than the front seats. Once or twice a few scraps of phrases could be heard amidst the din. He was heard to refer to the German workers as good, kind natured people and the noise drowned the rest. At last he sat down. Richardson met with a similar reception and soon gave it up. A Union Jack was displayed, but it soon disappeared. Evan Parker had seen to that (an incident which was to tell against him in a D.O.R.A. prosecution months after). A small body of the comrades closed round Hardie. There was a rush near the door but the street was reached safely. The crowd surged down the side street, but in the main street it began to get less. But several hundred men followed us up the main street singing their jingo songs. Hardie was unperturbed; he walked straight on with his head erect, not deigning to look either to the right or the left. He was staying with Matt Lewis, the school teacher, secretary of the local Labour Party. As we turned up the road the crowd became gradually less and, as the house was reached the sight of Mrs. Lewis with the baby in her arms dared the rest. Several of the comrades kept watch for some time. Hardie sat down in the arm-chair by the fire and lit his pipe. He was silent for a time staring into the fire. Then he joined in the conversation, but did not talk so much as usual. I had to catch the nine o'clock train down the valley. He shook hands, and said, 'I understand what Christ suffered in Gethsemane as well as any man living.'"

J. KEIR HARDIE

A report of the meeting in the "Western Mail," which had for its headings

"Mr. Hardie Hooted.

"Hostile Reception in his own Constituency.

"Wild Scenes at Aberdare Meeting."

confirmed the foregoing account in every particular, but, in addition, credited him with having restrained his supporters from retaliating, thereby preventing outbursts of actual violence. From this report we learn also that "amid a hurricane of booing Mr. Hardie said that the whole Liberal press stood for British neutrality until they heard Sir Edward Grey's speech last Monday. The effect of that speech was that the Liberal Party found itself committed to war without having been consulted in any shape or form"; and that in his concluding words he declared that "he had won this seat as a pro-Boer, and he was going to oppose this war in the interests of civilisation and the class to which he belonged." The other meetings were abandoned and he returned to London, where, broken in spirit for the time, he unbosomed himself to a friend. The result was that another meeting in Merthyr was arranged and MacDonald, Glasier and Hardie had a triumphant reception.

Nor is it too much to believe that if he had lived till an election came round, he would have still held the seat for Labour. He spoke several times in the constituency during the ensuing twelve months without molestation, and continued his weekly criticism of the Government in the "Merthyr Pioneer." There was evidence that his strong personality was beginning to prevail again over the temporary war prejudice. He had, however, received

THE WORLD CONFLICT

a mortal blow, and that Aberdare meeting gave the fatal
wound to the man who had lived his life for his fellows.
He derived great comfort from the knowledge that his
Welsh I.L.P. comrades were staunch. Except "one who
was numbered with us," there were no deserters. Di
Davies, Lewellyn Francis, John Barr, Evan Parker,
Matt Lewis, Stonelake, Morris, the Hughes family, all
the stalwarts who had fought and won with him, were
now ready to fight and lose with him, and to stand by
him, even unto death if need be. He had reason once
again to be proud of his I.L.P. He did not hide from
them nor from himself the seriousness of the outlook.
"This war," he told the Merthyr comrades, "means
conscription," and there were tears in his eyes as he said
it. "My own boy may be taken, and I would rather see
him in his grave than compelled to fight against other
workers."

He went home to Cumnock to see the boy, and the
boy's mother and sister, and to rest himself for a little
while. It was more than time.

Similar experiences to those of Hardie befell
the other I.L.P. Members of Parliament. MacDonald
at Leicester, Jowett at Bradford, Richardson at
Whitehaven, Snowden—when he reached home—at
Blackburn, had all to pass through the same ordeal of
calumny and abuse, growing ever more bitter and
unscrupulous as the years of war lengthened out, and
constitutional methods of government were displaced by
militarism and bureaucracy. Hardie did not live to see
the evil thing at its very worst. For the others there
is at least this consolation : they have lived to see their
principles vindicated, and may yet live to see their
cause triumphant and their position honoured.

CHAPTER FOURTEEN

THE LAST YEAR

HARDIE'S rest-time at Cumnock did not last long. He was not in good health, and never was again; but while any capacity for work, mental or physical, remained, he could not lie idle, a mere onlooker at the new phases of the conflict in which he had spent his life, the conflict between war and peace, between Capitalism and Socialism. The forces of evil had triumphed and were in the ascendant. That was all the more reason for continuing to fight against them. He had fought with his back to the wall before. He would do so now, though it should prove to be the last fight of all.

On August 27th, he had an article in the "Labour Leader" which showed no falling off in vigour of expression or lucidity of statement. It was in answer to the specious plea put forward on behalf of those Socialists who had become aggressively pro-British and needed some plausible justification for their lapse from the principles of Internationalism. Their plea was that this country was not at war with the German people but with the Kaiser, and that the overthrow of Kaiserdom would be in the interests of Socialism in Germany. The victory of the Allies, in fact, would be a victory for Socialism. Logically, though the apologists shrank from committing themselves to the statement in so many words, the war, from the British point of view, was a Socialist one. Hardie reminded the people who argued in this fashion that one of the Allies was the government of the Czar, and he wanted to know how Socialism would gain by the substitution of Czardom for Kaiserdom. If he had lived, he might have been able to show that it was only when Czardom ceased to be of any value as an ally that Socialism was able to make headway in Russia. As it was, he was able to show that it was this very fear of the supremacy of Czardom that had made some German Socialists also forget their Internationalism. One passage from this article should be quoted as it gives the point of view which largely determined Hardie's attitude towards the war both before its outbreak and during its process in the remaining months in which he was to be a spectator. "Let anybody take a map of Europe and look at the position of Germany : on the one side Russia with her millions of trained soldiers and unlimited population to draw upon (its traditional policy for over a hundred years has been to reduce Prussia to impotence, so that the Slav may reign supreme), and on the other side France, smarting under her defeat and the loss of her two provinces, Alsace and Lorraine, in 1870. For a number of years past these two militarisms have had a close and cordial alliance. What was it that brought the Czardom of Russia into alliance with the free Republic of France? One object, and one alone, to crush Germany between them. German armaments and the German navy, were primarily intended to protect herself and her interests against these two open enemies. If this reasoning be correct, it follows that our being in the war is a matter of the free choice of our rulers who appear to prefer that Russia should become the domineering power of Europe. I do not write these words in order to say that we should now withdraw from the conflict. That is clearly an impossibility at present. But if we can get these facts instilled into the mind and brain of our own people, and of the working class generally, we shall be able to exert a much greater influence in bringing the war to a close much more speedily than the military element contemplates at present."

In this same article he pointed out that Lord Kitchener's new army scheme involved the raising and training of not merely one hundred thousand men, but of five hundred thousand, and that the final outcome thereof would be, and was intended to be, Conscription, a prediction which the Socialist patriots pooh-poohed as being the one thing from which their voluntary recruiting campaign was going to save the country! Hardie's prediction, much to his own sorrow, was just on the verge of fulfilment when death took him away from it all. He was at least spared from seeing this humiliation and enslavement of his class, for whose independence he had fought all the days of his life.

The article concluded: "Some British Socialists are unfortunately ranging themselves on the side of militarism, and we shall require to take the strongest possible action to make it clear to our comrades on the Continent that the hands of the I.L.P., at least, are clear, and that when the conflict is over, and we have once again to meet our German, French, Belgian and Russian comrades, no part of the responsibility for the crime that has been done in Europe can be laid at our door."

By this time it had become evident that the I.L.P. would be the only political party or section in this country refusing to accept any share of responsibility for the prosecution of the war. The Government started a great recruiting campaign and called upon all political and Labour organisations to assist. A majority of the Labour Party Executive accepted the invitation, as did

THE LAST YEAR

also the Parliamentary Labour Party, and both placed their organising machinery at the service of the War Office.

The I.L.P. representatives on the Labour Party Executive opposed this decision and reported to their own Head Office, while MacDonald had resigned from the position of Chairman of the Labour Party, actions which were endorsed by the National Council and by the entire I.L.P. movement. The reasons for this line of conduct must have been evident to all who had any knowledge of the origin and history of the Independent Labour Party. To have joined with the other parties would have been equivalent to ceasing to be an Independent Labour Party, and neither the leaders nor the rank and file were prepared to commit moral suicide in support of a war which they had for ten years back strenuously striven to obviate. The National Labour Party might, if it choose, merge itself with its bitterest opponents, but the I.L.P. could not do that. Even if Hardie and MacDonald had favoured such a policy--an unimaginable supposition—they could not have carried the Party with them. Most of the Divisional and Federation and Branch officials would have resigned, and there would have been an end of the I.L.P., a consummation which would doubtless have gladdened the hearts of the orthodox party politicians.

The National Council, in its recommendations to Branches, declared : "If advice has to be given to the workers, we hold it should come from our own platforms, preserving the character and traditions of our movement, and we refuse to take our stand by militarists and enemies of Labour with whose outlook and aims we are in sharpest conflict, and who will assuredly seize this opportunity to justify the policy leading up to the war. Now that the country has been drawn into a deadly and desperate war, which may involve, in the end, our existence as a nation, it is not a matter for speech making, least of all from those who will not themselves be called upon to face the horrors of the trenches."

We can well understand that the spectacle of the Labour Party (in the creation and fostering of which he had given so much of his life) transforming itself into a War Office annexe was a mortifying and painful spectacle to Hardie. Even more poignant were the emotions evoked by the consequent estrangement between men who had been his intimate friends and comrades, some of whom owed whatever endowment of political prestige and opportunity they possessed to their association with himself. A violent onslaught in the press by H. G. Wells affected him not at all, but parting company with George Barnes and some others hurt him deeply and permanently. He was stricken not only by the world, but from within his own household.

The steadfastness of the I.L.P. was the one sustaining fact proving that all was not lost, and giving to life still some zest and comfort. But even here there were individual defections that cut him to the heart. In the same week in which the already quoted article appeared, he, with James Maxton, Chairman of the Scottish I.L.P. Council, and the present writer, attended a district conference at Edinburgh to explain and discuss the Party's policy. From Glasgow he telegraphed to a trusted Edinburgh friend to meet him at the station. This friend was one of those who had kept an open door for Hardie, who had pressed always to be nearest to him on public occasions : a most devoted follower. At the station the friend was not. Instead, there was a messenger to say that he had another engagement. Hardie understood. Another personal tie was broken never to be renewed. There were others. It was all

THE LAST YEAR

part of the price. There were more war-wounds than
those of the battlefield, and just as deadly.

This conference at Edinburgh, and one the following
day at Glasgow, endorsed fully the policy outlined by
the National Council, which was indeed simply a
reflection of the will of the Party in general. At both
conferences Hardie spoke with vigour and clearness and
seemed to be the same man he had always been, save
for a slight tendency to irritability, most unusual with
him, and probably indicating some nervous derangement
due to his recent trying experiences.

That his mental powers were unimpaired was shown
in a strong and uncompromising reply to the critics of
the I.L.P. in the "Labour Leader" of September 10th.
Amongst these critics were included Mr. H. G. Wells,
of whom and his friends in the controversy Hardie said
they "must make up their own minds as to what they
must do. That is their own affair. But one thing they
must not do. They must not lie about those who differ
from them. When Mr. Wells writes that I am 'trying
to misrepresent the negotiations which took place before
the war,' he writes an untruth. Mr. Wells is shouting
with the multitude and it is unworthy of the man to
speak of either Mr. Ramsay MacDonald or myself as
having whined in our criticism of the policy of the
Foreign Secretary. But, after all, Mr. Wells has a
reputation, not only in newspaper articles, but in his
books, of taking a mean advantage of those whom he
does not like." The manner of Mr. Wells' retort proved
that Hardie had not lost his old faculty for making his
opponents very angry while he himself remained perfectly cool. In this article, on the question of recruiting,
he had a query for Trade Union leaders. "It was in the
year 1911 that the British army was last mobilised—and
two men were shot dead at Llanelly. Would any railway

355

man have touted for recruits for the army then? And is not the enemy of the worker the same now as then? The most prominent of the South African exiles has been to Germany and comes back with the declaration that 'the only attitude for the British Empire to adopt, I am convinced, is to fight with every available man until the Prussian military despotism is beaten. I am pleased to learn that South Africa is rising to the occasion.' Now, is was not 'Prussian military despotism' that sent troops to massacre striking miners in Johannesburg, or that sent into exile, where they still are, the writer of that passage and his colleagues."

What was wrong with Hardie and the I.L.P. was that their memories were too retentive. They could not forget that there was a capitalist system and a capitalist class, or that there was a British policy which openly labelled itself "Imperialism," nor could they forget history and its story of how all wars began—and how they ended.

During the month of September, similar conferences to those at Edinburgh and Glasgow were held all over the country, those at Ipswich, Leeds, Liverpool, Manchester and Eccles being addressed by Hardie who continued to show the same energy which had characterised his propaganda work all through life, so that there seemed some justification for the belief amongst those who were not in close touch with him that his leadership would be available for many years to come, and that the end of the war, which it was hoped would come soon by means of negotiation, would find him still in the van of the progressive movement.

In October, he was back in his own constituency where the reception given him (the meeting to which reference has already been made) was in striking contrast to the organised hooliganism at Aberdare in the first week of

the war. With him were MacDonald and Glasier, and
to an audience of three thousand in the skating rink at
Merthyr the trio of the I.L.P. champions explained and
defended the policy of the Party. They were well
received and loudly cheered, and the indications were
that Hardie had not lost his hold on the constituency, and
that any defection there may have been was more than
counterbalanced by new adherents won by his courage
and straightforwardness. He also held meetings of the
I.L.P. branches in the constituency, at Merthyr, Mountain Ash, Aberdare and Penrhiwceiber, receiving votes
of confidence in each place. This was at a time when
the war fever was mounting and the recruiting campaign
was in full swing. He was still continuing his weekly
articles in the "Merthyr Pioneer," which circulated all
through the constituency, and the people in the district
were thoroughly familiar with his views and opinions on
the war, his attitude towards recruiting and his general
outlook. The fact that there were no manifestations of
hostility during this visit might have been an indication
of the existence of a spirit of fair play in the Merthyr
community sadly lacking in most other districts, or it
might have been due to the personal respect which his
past services had won from them. Probably both
influences were at work.

In the "Labour Leader" of November 5th, Hardie
had a review of Brailsford's book, "The War of Steel
and Gold," written before the outbreak of war, but as
readers of the book know, substantiating both by fact
and argument the Socialist analysis of the causes which
produced the war. As was to be expected, Hardie gave
the book high praise. The opponents of the war,
standing against overwhelming odds, with the entire
British press against them and a Defence of the Realm
Act already looking for sedition in every pacifist

J. KEIR HARDIE

utterance, were naturally glad to avail themselves of
every intellectual contribution which might fortify them
in the defence of their convictions. At the outset of
the war the withdrawal from the Government of such
men as Lord Morley, Lord Loreburn, Mr. John Burns,
and Mr. C. P. Trevelyan was of itself a comforting
though silent witnessing on their behalf, while the
searching criticism of foreign policy by Bertrand
Russell, Gilbert Cannan, E. D. Morel, and Arthur
Ponsonby, M.P., none of whom could at that time be
described as Socialists in their outlook, was also of
great value. In the same category was Mr. Brailsford's
book, and it was eminently satisfactory to Hardie because
it emphasised the sinister influence of Russia, upon
which he had insisted so strongly in all his platform and
press declarations. He urged that it should be widely
circulated by all I.L.P. branches and propaganda
agencies.

George Bernard Shaw's pamphlet, "Common Sense
about the War," which first appeared as an article in
"The New Statesman," and was the cause of much
controversy and the subject of hostile criticism in "The
Citizen," a paper originally promoted as the organ of
the Labour movement, gave Hardie much satisfaction,
chiefly because it tore to shreds that British self-
righteousness which saw motes in the diplomatic German
eye, but never a beam in that of the British or the Allies.
He wrote the following letter to Shaw :—

"House of Commons,
"November 26th, 1914.

"Dear Bernard Shaw,
"As my disgust with the 'Citizen's' attitude over the
war is great, I have not even looked at it for some weeks.
Thus it comes that I knew nothing about its attack on

358

THE LAST YEAR

your 'New Statesman' article until someone told me of your letter in to-day's issue. I am sending for the issue containing the attack and shall see what can be done to raise the Socialist and Labour unions to make protest. The paper is making rapidly for the void. The circulation, after going up to 70,000 [a great under-estimate] a day, is now less than it was before the war broke out. A big effort is now about to be made to raise more funds to keep it going, but nothing can save it so long as the present bumptious and reactionary cad is in the chair.

"May I now say that which I failed to muster enough courage to say when first I felt the thrill of your article, that its inspiration is worth more to England than this war has yet cost her—in money I mean. When it gets circulated in popular form and is read, as it will be, by hundreds of thousands of our best people of all classes, it will produce an elevation of tone in the national life which will be felt for generations to come. In Scottish ploughman phrase, 'God bless ye, and send ye speed.'

"I prohibit any reply to this, or even acknowledgement. It is the expression of a heart which now throbs towards you with almost feelings of devotion.
"Sincerely,
"J. KEIR HARDIE.
"P.S.—Only a Celt could have done it."

Shaw's article did not produce "an elevation of tone in the national life." All the angelic hosts could not have done that. It only added to the volume of damning. The tone-producers were Northcliffe, Hulton, Bottomley, and such-like, and their combined output was the reverse of elevating.

The fervour of gratitude in the closing words of Hardie's letter gives some indication of how much he was feeling the need for sympathy and support. With

J. KEIR HARDIE

all his courageous facing of the situation on the platform and in the press, so far as it was available, the
conditions growing up around him were such as to make
life for a man of his temperament and principles, almost
unbearable. He could hardly move without coming
in contact with the things that were hateful to him.
The very colour scheme of the streets had now militarist
khaki for its dominant note. The noises in the streets
were militarist noises, even the cries of the newsboys
were "shouts of war." The marching and drilling of
men, the drum-beatings and bugle-calls, the open training of young boys in bomb-throwing and in bayonet
exercise with dummy figures to represent Germans, and
with accompanying obscene expletives to stimulate
hate and blood-lust, were rehearsals of the foul sport
deliberately calculated to brutalise the public mind.
The overbearing vulgar swagger of many of the officer
class, the steady supersession of civic authority by
military rule, the abdication of Parliament itself in favour
of the militarists, and, added to all, the news and ever
more news, of colossal bloody murder on the battlefield,
made the world into an inferno for him. He could not
get away from it. Wherever he turned it was there. In
the House of Commons, in the House of God; in the
streets, in the railway stations and the train compartments; amongst the hills and glens and valleys, on the
open highway—everywhere omniscient and omni-
present, ruthless in the lusty day of its power. The thing
he had fought, Militarism, was triumphant. Perhaps
worst of all, he saw in this the coarsening of the public
mind, the swamping of its intelligence, and, in spite of
fine words, the lowering of its ideals. If these things
read hard, they must stand here as they were Hardie's
thoughts, and time has already begun to deliver its
verdict upon them.

THE LAST YEAR

In the midst of all this, Shaw's "Common Sense about the War," even with its acceptance of the war as a fact which could not now be run away from, was to Hardie like a gleam of sunshine through the darkness—like a drop of water to a very thirsty man.

In the last week of November, he went to Blackburn, Philip Snowden's constituency, and spoke three times in the district. Snowden was at the time in New Zealand, but he had found means, by speech and interview, to let his constituents and the world in general know that he was at one with his I.L.P. colleagues at home in their policy on the war. It was necessary, in his absence, to have that policy made clear, and to give the fullest encouragement to his supporters. Hardie evidently succeeded in doing so, for the "Northern Daily Telegraph" declared that, "both at the Trades Hall and the I.L.P. Institute, Mr. Hardie was greeted in a most cordial manner, his reception possibly being warmer because of the way he has been attacked during recent weeks."

He had, however, for the time being at least, exceeded the limit of his powers and had once more to turn his face homeward suffering from what appeared to his friends to be a very dangerous nervous breakdown. During the greater part of December he rested at home, but did not show much sign of improvement. It was this illness which gave rise to a rumour that he had been attacked by paralysis, a rumour which travelled far, as we shall see. The trouble was quite serious enough, and it would have been good for him if he could have been prevailed upon to continue resting. It was perhaps part of the trouble that he could not do so. He was restless and unsettled, and could not stay quietly as a looker-on at events. He had to be faithful in his storm-tossed world.

J. KEIR HARDIE

On the first Saturday of the New Year, he was in Glasgow addressing the annual Scottish Divisional Conference of the I.L.P. Here an incident occurred of a kind not calculated to be helpful to a man suffering from nervous trouble. It was a conference of delegates to which the public had no right of admission, but it was found that four persons had obtained entrance to the ante-room of the hall without the necessary credentials and were known to be detectives. They were asked to withdraw, and did so. The Defence of the Realm Act was now in full operation, but the officers of the law had not yet fully realised the powers which it conferred upon them. Otherwise they might have insisted upon remaining, in which case there would probably have been serious trouble arising not out of any words spoken by Hardie, but out of the resentment of the delegates to the presence of spies. Hardie was not informed of the incident till after he had spoken, but it annoyed him and rankled in his mind. He was accustomed to open opposition and to press misrepresentation. But to be spied upon in his own country was a new experience, and too much akin to Russian and German methods. It troubled him greatly and preyed upon him.

His speech was simply in the nature of advice to the delegates to hold fast to the I.L.P. organisation during the troublous times through which they were passing. He counselled them to continue their propaganda for Socialism, and to seek representation on Citizen Committees and all other bodies through which it might be possible to safeguard the rights and interests of the common people without taking responsibility for the conduct of the war. He also advised them to associate with other agencies and movements working for the speedy restoration of peace.

THE LAST YEAR

On the following night—Sunday—he spoke in Hamilton, making his last public appearance in the district where, thirty-five years before, he had started out as an agitator. Theie were men there who had worked in the pits with him, and who still worked in the pits. They were proud of the record of the comrade of their youth, but some of them perturbed and doubtful of the wisdom of his attitude on the war. His speech was a vindication of that attitude as being in conformity with the whole of his past career. He showed that the Liberal Party had held the same attitude as himself towards the war, but had changed in a single day. His own principles, as they knew, had never been of that flexible quality, and he held that because the Foreign Office secret alliance with Russia had involved the country in an unnecessary war, that was no reason why he, or the Party to which he belonged, should approve of the war, but rather the reverse. He spoke argumentatively and clearly, but without passion. Mrs. Hardie was with him on the platform, and few in the audience could have guessed that she had wished to keep him away from the meeting and that her one concern was that it should come to an end quickly that she might get him away safely to the place where he ought to be, in bed, and within call of medical attendance.

After a week's rest he began to regain strength, so much so, that by the end of January his colleagues of the N.A.C. sent him congratulations on his recovery. The re-assembling of Parliament drew him up again to London as by a magnet, to live again lonely in the Nevill's Court lodgings and to attend to his Parliamentary work.

On February 25th, he spoke in opposition to the proposal to relax the educational by-laws to enable children under twelve to be employed in agricultural

J. KEIR HARDIE

work, the alleged reason being the shortage of men caused by the war. He contended that working-class children should not have their educational opportunities curtailed because of the war, and declared that the real object aimed at was to enable the farmers to obtain cheap labour. "The by-laws," he said, "issued to protect our children are being practically swept out of existence. I think it can be demonstrated that they are being swept aside, not because of any special necessity for child labour, but very largely as a means of perpetuating uneducated sweated labour in the agricultural districts." He had a partial alternative, in the suggesting of which there came out some personal reminiscences of an interesting kind. "There is one proposal upon which I do not know whether my colleagues would be unanimous, but which I think might be used to great account in solving this problem during the war period. I refer to the employment of women. I can remember in Scotland, my own mother, who was a farm servant, often at work after she was married, with her family growing up. I have seen her employed in the fields at kinds of work which I would not like to see women employed at now : but there is much work about a farm which is perfectly respectable and clean, and which calls for a certain amount of intelligence, such as milking, the handling of milk, the making of butter, and many other occupations which a woman can do with advantage to herself and to others. But the average woman brought up in the town has lost all instinct for, and all contact with, the life of the farm."

On this occasion, for the first time in his life, he claimed indulgence from his fellow Members of the House of Commons on the ground of ill-health, giving that as the reason for lack of energy in his treatment of the subject. It was fitting that his last recorded parliamentary utterance should have been on behalf of working-class children.

About this time it would be that he met by chance Lord Morley. His note on the incident in the "Merthyr Pioneer" has for us even a deeper pathos than it had then. Not Lord Morley, the octogenarian, was the first to pass from the scene, but Hardie the much younger man. "Passing along the Lobby the other day, I met a familiar figure, the outstanding figure of the trio who resigned from the Ministry rather than soil their consciences by the bloodshedding in which we are now engaged. He stopped and shook hands with me. 'You have been ill,' he said; 'what was the matter? Was it the war which so weighed upon your soul and spirit that it made your body sick?' I had to smile a vague assent to the question. 'The war,' he said, 'when will it end? If we lose, we shall pay an awful penalty; if we win, the penalty may be greater still.' He sighed as he walked away with the weight of eighty years bending his shoulders. I stood and watched the retiring figure, and thought to myself, there goes the last of England's great statemen. To-day, it is not statesmanship or principle which actuates those who hold office. They are as completely under the power of the capitalist as any ordinary member of the Stock Exchange."

And thus these two sincere men, diametrically opposed to each other in political and philosophical outlook, met now on common moral ground. To both, the war was a crime, and Britain's part in it wicked and foolish. And both were helpless to prevent it or to stop it.

On March 25th, he had an article in the "Labour Leader," the last he ever wrote for that paper, though, as we shall see, not his last press utterance. There was nothing valedictory about this article, nothing to indicate that he had come to the limit of his power or that he himself felt conscious that the end was near. The title of the article was "Patriotism Measured in Millions." Therein he traced the growth of the Imperialist idea in British foreign policy, synchronising with the growth of capital investments in the colonies and in foreign countries, and, in order to show to what this had led, he quoted Lloyd George's reply to a question, on March 13th. "The total British capital invested abroad amounts to four thousand million pounds (£4,000,000,000), and the income from interest on colonial and foreign investments is two hundred million pounds (£200,000,000) a year."

The following passage from this article is well worth producing now. "Very many millions will be needed to finance our allies, and *to induce some to join in the murderous mêlée* who now stand aloof. When the war is over these will require large sums for the renewal of their navies, and the creation of new, and the repair of war-destroyed, railways and the like. There will also be unlimited scope for new companies to open out the great mineral, oil and other industries of Russia, Persia, and the Balkans, which are yet in their infancy, and the British investor will be the only man left with money to float them. France and Germany will alike be bankrupt, and only *the United States will remain as a possible competitor with Lombard Street.*"

He did not foresee the Bolshevik intervention to spoil sport for the British financiers, but, had he lived, he would have had no difficulty in explaining the malignant attempts to prevent the Socialist regime from establishing itself in Russia.

Withal his realistic vision of the dread consequences of the war, he had not lost hope in humanity, nor faith in Socialism. "When the war is only a stinking memory of a bloodstained nightmare, and we are again face to

THE LAST YEAR

face with the real things of life, then surely there will be a great and mighty agitation for complete enfranchisement of democracy, man and woman alike, who will then be able to win control over both domestic and foreign policy, and break the rule of those to whom Imperialism and Militarism mean wealth and power, and to instal all the peoples of all lands in authority, and thus bring plenty, peace and concord to a long-suffering race."

This was his last "Labour Leader" article, but it might have been written in his prime, so vigorous was it, so clear in the marshalling of fact and argument, so dignified in diction. It was not to be wondered at that the movement was deceived into believing that the end of the war would find Keir Hardie still guiding and inspiring it, especially as during all this time he had, by an extraordinary exercise of will power, or else by sheer force of habit, been contributing almost without a break his weekly article to the "Merthyr Pioneer," and did so up till as late as April 17th.

Curiously enough, on the same date as this final "Labour Leader" article, March 25th, the "Merthyr Pioneer," reproduced from an American paper, the "Boston Evening Transcript," an obituary sketch of Keir Hardie's career, the rumour of the attack of paralysis having evidently been accepted as true. The sub-heading of the sketch, "Another of England's Picturesque Figures Passes from the Scene," though premature, was not inapt. Keir Hardie had not passed, but he was passing. He had made his last speech in Parliament; he had written his last article in the "Labour Leader"; and now he was going to attend his last I.L.P. Conference.

It was held at Norwich under conditions unprecedented in British history. Great Britain was governed as if it were a beleaguered country. There had been night-

367

time Zeppelin raids on the Norfolk coast, and when, on Easter eve, the I.L.P. delegates, many of whom had been travelling for twelve hours in crowded trains, reached Norwich, they entered a city of dreadful night, and had to be piloted through utter darkness to their hotels and lodgings. When Easter morn came, and with it the blessed sunshine, it revealed a city full of soldiers, with officers billeted in all the hotels, and with bugle-calls and drum-beats mocking the peaceful message of the chiming Eastertide bells. An attempt had been made to prevent the I.L.P. Conference being held, through the cancelling of the halls engaged for the Conference and the public meeting. In the interests of free speech the Primitive Methodist Church placed its Schoolroom at the disposal of the Conference; and it has to be recorded—and remembered—that two other religious organisations, the Scott Memorial Church and the Martineau Unitarian Church, had also offered the use of their meeting places.

At the Conference, Hardie, who was looking very ill, spoke only once, and just at the close, in support of a special resolution protesting strongly against severe sentences passed upon fifty-three members of the Russian Seamen's Union and on the five Socialist Members of the Duma, and asking the British Government to bring pressure to bear on the Russian Government with a view to their ultimate freedom. In his speech he declared that the fifty-three seamen were in prison for no offence except membership of a trade union. Their secretary was illegally arrested in Egypt, he was sent to Russia, and there sentenced to Siberia. "Some of us tried in the House of Commons to get Sir Edward Grey to intervene, or at least to have him tried in Egypt. Grey then said that this country could not interfere with the political affairs of another country.

THE LAST YEAR

One of the biggest risks we run is being allied to a nation whose past and present record is a disgrace to civilisation and progress. The alliance with Russia is not to help Belgium. It is to open up fresh fields for exploitation by capitalists. We register our protest against all the infamies of the bloody cruelty of Russia."

These were the last words of Keir Hardie at a Conference of the Independent Labour Party. Never again would the delegates hear the voice or grasp the hand of the man who for twenty-two years had been their leader, comrade and friend.

Yet he was not finished, nor his fighting quite done. His speech at the public meeting on the Saturday evening brought him once again into public conflict with authority. The circumstances are within memory, but Hardie's own words which ruffled Mr. Lloyd George to anger, will best recall the situation. "In time of war, one would have thought the rich classes would grovel on their knees before the working classes, who are doing so much to pile up their wealth. Instead, the men who are working eighty-four hours a week are being libelled, maligned and insulted; and, on the authority of their employers, the lying word, accepted without inquiry by Lloyd George, went round the world that the working class were a set of drunken hooligans. That is the reward they got. The truth is, that the shifts could be arranged so as to overtake all the work in hand. Mr. John Hill, the Secretary of the Boiler-makers, has shown that if the shipbuilders would reduce their contracts ten per cent., the Government could get all their work done, but the shipbuilders will not do that because ships were being sold at two and three times their value before the war."

Popularity was then, as always, essential to Mr. Lloyd George; loss of it, a thing to be dreaded. At that moment especially it was needful for him to stand well in the opinion of the working classes. He hastened to essay the task of clearing himself from the charge involved in Hardie's remarks. On Monday he sent a telegram to Hardie, quoting the offending passage, and concluding with a query for which the quotation afforded no basis whatever. "Would you kindly let me know where and when I am supposed to have uttered such words or anything that would justify so monstrous a deduction." Hardie's telegram in reply was as follows : "I pointed out that the employers, when before you, concerning output of armaments, etc., had put the whole blame on the drinking habits of the workers, and that you, by accepting this statement without challenge, had given world currency to the fiction that the workers were drunken wasters. I never said 'bullies' nor have I seen the report from which you quote.—Keir Hardie."

Mr. Lloyd George, notwithstanding this explanation, sent a denunciatory letter to the press accusing the I.L.P. leader of "reckless assertion," "wild accusation," "mischievous statement," "excited prejudice," but at the same time found it necessary to explain that he himself had referred only to a small section of the working classes, a qualifying excuse which would probably never have been given but for Hardie's public protest on behalf of the reputation of his class. Lloyd George's letter received the fullest prominence in the press. Hardie's letter in reply was relegated to the back columns, and in some cases sub-edited to distortion.

With this incident the public career of Keir Hardie came to a close. He ended, as he had begun, standing up for the working people. The British public heard no more of Keir Hardie until the closing days of September, when the newspapers announced his death. During the intervening months it was borne in upon his intimate friends

THE LAST YEAR

and colleagues that the days of their leader were numbered. Indeed, early in May it seemed as if the end had come. The illness from which he had been suffering intermittently since the previous August reached an acute stage, producing what looked like complete collapse. He was in London at the time, and after a week, at the end of which it had become evident that the necessary care and attention was not possible in the Nevill's Court lodgings, and that in his physical condition travelling home to Scotland was also out of the question, he was removed to Caterham Sanatorium, where he had alike the benefit of skilled medical and nursing attendance, and the devoted service of personal friends, chief amongst these being the ever faithful Frank Smith and Tom Richardson, M.P. Mr. Smith took charge of his correspondence and warned all inquirers, of whom there were hundreds, against addressing any letters to Hardie himself, such letters being more disturbing than helpful. At the end of the first month he was still unfit for railway travelling, and Mrs. Hardie came up from Cumnock and remained with him until he was able to face the homeward journey four weeks later. During all this time there had been alternating periods of oblivion, acute physical suffering, and apparently normal alertness. It was during one of the normal intervals that he, with the consent of the medical advisers, determined to make for Cumnock. He broke the journey at Newcastle and stayed for a few days with Mr. and Mrs. Richardson, arriving home in Cumnock at the end of July, Frank Smith and Tom Richardson being his travelling companions. A week or two of rest in the home circle seemed to bring him some renewal of strength, and he ventured to cross over to Arran where his son Duncan was having a brief holiday—the elder son, James, had been settled in America for some years

J. KEIR HARDIE

and was therefore unable to be with his father during these last weeks. From Arran, after a few days, he went on a visit to his brother George at Clarkston, Glasgow, where the utmost care and attention awaited him. Neither the breezes of Arran, nor the comforts of home, nor the solicitude of friends could now ward off the approach of that "White Herald" of whom he had once spoken as a welcome friend rather than a foe to be dreaded.

On Wednesday, September 22nd, a change for the worse took place, and on the advice of the doctors, who still seemed to think that some partial recovery was possible, removal to a home for special treatment was decided upon. On the Saturday a great weakness overcame him, and in the evening pneumonia set in. On Sunday at noon, September 26th, he passed peacefully away in the presence of his wife and daughter.

Thus, in his sixtieth year, in the second month of the second year of the Great War, which he had tried to avert and of which he was unquestionably one of the victims, died Keir Hardie. Next morning, when the newspapers announced his death, they carried heartfelt sorrow into many thousands of British homes, sorrow, not alone for the loss of a great agitator and Labour leader, but for that of a dear personal friend. Probably never was any public man so sincerely and deeply loved by so many people as was Keir Hardie.

On the following Wednesday, a great concourse of mourners of all classes, but mostly of the working class, joined the funeral procession which followed his remains through the streets of Glasgow to the Crematorium at Maryhill, where eight years before he had said farewell to his father and mother. Some were there who had accompanied him through the greater part of his public life, Robert Smillie, Bruce Glasier, Sandy Haddow, George Carson, William M. Haddow, Alex. Gilchrist,

THE LAST YEAR

James Neil, Cunninghame Graham, and others, recalling memories of the early days of struggle ere fame or even the promise of success had come as a stimulus to labour and self-sacrifice. His colleagues of the I.L.P. National Council were, of course, there, as many as could attend, Ramsay MacDonald, T. D. Benson, W. C. Anderson, Fred Jowett and the others, serious and sad at this last parting with the comrade of so many years of ceaseless endeavour for the betterment of the common people. Delegates came all the way from Merthyr Tydvil, members of the election committee who had fought side by side with him in those never-to-be-forgotten political battles and who now realised sorrowfully that never again would Keir Hardie lead them to victory.

At the funeral there were no delegates from foreign lands to lay wreaths upon the bier of the man who had striven so resolutely for international unity of purpose among Socialists, and who had refused to join in a struggle which he held to be fratricidal and unnatural. The war which had slain Jaurès of France, and Franck of Germany, had now claimed Keir Hardie of Great Britain, and had made it impossible for any of the men and women with whom he had fraternised in the common efforts for international Socialist achievement to manifest in person their respect for him and his work.

A simple burial service was conducted by the Rev. A. M. Forson, of London, whose associations with Hardie dated back to the early evangelising days. A few words from Bruce Glasier calling upon those present to honour the memory of their lost leader by preserving his ideals and continuing his work. A brief exhortation in a similar strain to the multitude outside from W. C. Anderson—both have since followed him into the unknown country of which Hardie used to speak as the "Beyond"—and the mourners dispersed.

z   373

J. KEIR HARDIE

Here ends the work of the present writer. He has tried to tell as fully as possible the story of Keir Hardie's life, and leaves it to others to estimate the value of his work and example. Time itself will probably prove to be the truest commentator, and it is the firm belief of the writer that the passing of the years will establish Keir Hardie as one of the permanently historic figures in that great age-long progressive movement which must find its complete realisation in the establishment of human equality on a basis of mutual service by all members of the human family. An essential part of that process is the struggle of the working class in all countries for the abolition of class. In directing that struggle Keir Hardie played an important part during an important period. In future years, whatever may be the prevailing form of society, men and women will have to turn their thoughts back to that period, and will find James Keir Hardie to have been one of its outstanding characters. Perhaps even this imperfect account of his life will help them to know the kind of man he was, and to visualise the environment amidst which he lived. That his worth and the nature of his rendered service is already beginning to be understood is apparent. The monument which the Ayrshire miners are erecting is only one of the signs of that recognition. The annual Keir Hardie celebrations held by the Independent Labour Party is another. These organisations themselves stand as a proof of his courage, foresight and resolute energy. But the time will come when miners' unions and political Labour Parties will be unnecessary, and even then there may linger some dim memory—traditional it may be—of an incorruptible man of the common people, who, in his own person, symbolised the idea of independence, and in his message proclaimed the practicability of Brotherhood.

CHRONOLOGY
AND
INDEX

CHRONOLOGY

1856.
J. Keir Hardie born (August 15th).

1866.
In the mine. Trapper.

1879.
Marries Miss Lillie Wilson (June 3rd).
Appointed Corresponding Secretary, Hamilton Miners (July 3rd).
Appointed Miners' Agent (August).

1880.
Miners' Strikes in Lanarkshire.

1881.
Ayrshire Miners' Strike (October).

1882.
Joins staff of "Ardrossan Herald" and "Cumnock News."

1884.
Franchise Act: Household and lodger franchise extended to the counties.

1886.
Ayrshire Miners' Union formed.
Appointed Organising Secretary.
Scottish Miners' Federation formed.
Appointed Secretary.

1887.
No. 1 of "The Miner" issued (January).
Ayrshire Miners declare for a Labour Party.
Adopted as miners' candidate for North Ayrshire.
Udston Colliery Disaster (May).
First attendance at Trades Union Congress, Swansea (September).
Speech at Irvine (October).

1888.
Mid-Lanarkshire By-election (April 27th). Result:—

J. W. Phillips (L) 3,847
W. R. Bousfield (C) ... 2,917
J. Keir Hardie (Lab) ... 617

Declines Sir George Trevelyan's offer of £300 a year from the Liberal Party.
Scottish Parliamentary Labour Party formed (August 25th).
Attends International Trades Union Congress, London (November).

1889.
Attends International Congress, Paris.
First No. of the "Labour Leader" (monthly) issued (February).

1892.
General Election. Elected for West Ham (South). Result:

J. Keir Hardie (I.L.P.) 5,268
Maj. G. E. Banes (C) 4,036

Refuses financial help from Mr. Andrew Carnegie.
First question in Parliament (August 18th).
Declines £300 a year offered by the Misses Kippen.

1893.
Presides at Conference at Bradford at which the Independent Labour Party is established (January 13th and 14th).
First speech in Parliament (February 7th).
Hull Dock Strike.

376

CHRONOLOGY

1894.

Elected Chairman of I.L.P., Manchester Conference (February 2nd and 3rd).
"Labour Leader" issued weekly from March 31st.
Visits Ireland.

1895.

General Election, Defeated for West Ham (South). Result ·
Maj. G. E. Banes (C) 4,750
J. Keir Hardie (I.L.P) 3,975
First visit to America.
Refuses offer of $100,000 to commit the I.L.P. to support of Bi-metallism.

1896.

Attends International Socialist Congress, London (July).
Boggart Hole Clough Free Speech Agitation.
Bradford East By-election (November 10th). Result :
Capt. Hon. R. H. F. Greville (C) 4,921
A. Billson (L) 4,526
J. Keir Hardie (I.L.P.) 1,953

1898.

South Wales Miners' Strike.

1899.

. War with the South African Republics.

1900.

Scottish Workers' Representation Committee established, Free Gardeners' Hall, Edinburgh (January 6th).
Labour Representation Committee established, Memorial Hall, London (February 27th).
Resigns Chairmanship of I.L.P. at Conference held at Glasgow (April 16th and 17th).
Contests Preston and Merthyr at General Election. Results :
Preston—
R. W. Hanbury (C) ... 8,944
W. E. M. Tomlinson (C) 8,067
J. Keir Hardie (I.L.P.) 4,834

Merthyr—

D. A. Thomas (L) ... 8,598
J. Keir Hardie (Lab) ... 5,745
W. Fritchard Morgan (L) 4,004

1901.

Moves Socialist resolution in House of Commons (April 23rd).
Taff Vale judgment.

1902.

Death of father and mother (April).
South African War ends (June).
Holiday on the Continent after illness.

1903.

Presides at Unemployed Conference at the Guildhall, London (February 23rd).
Undergoes operation for appendicitis.
Gives up editorship of the "Labour Leader" and transfers paper to the I.L.P. (December).

1904.

Visits Continent to recuperate after illness.
Attends International Socialist Congress at Amsterdam.

1906.

General Election. Re-elected for Merthyr. Result :
D. A. Thomas (L) 13,971
J. Keir Hardie (L.R.C.) ... 10,187
H. Radcliffe (L) 7,776
Visits Ireland.
Chairman of the Parliamentary Labour Party.
Fiftieth birthday celebration. Presentation at Memorial Hall, London.

1907.

Re-elected Chairman of the Parliamentary Labour Party.
Publishes "From Serfdom to Socialism."
Left Liverpool for tour round the world (July 12th).
International Socialist Congress, Stuttgart.

377

CHRONOLOGY

1908.

Return from world tour. Welcome Home meeting at the Albert Hall, London (April 5th).

Election for Lord Rectorship of Glasgow University (October). Result.

Lord Curzon 947
Lloyd George ... 935
Keir Hardie 122

Omitted from invitation to the King's Garden Party.

Attends Dominion Trades Union Congress in Nova Scotia (September).

1909.

Chairman Labour Party.

Publishes "India: Impressions and Suggestions."

Resigns from National Council I.L.P. (April).

Attends Egyptian Party Congress, Geneva.

Osborne Judgment.

1910.

General Election (January). Merthyr result:

E. R. Jones (L) 15,448
J. Keir Hardie (Lab) 13,841
A. C Fox Davies (C) 4,756
W. Pritchard Morgan (I.L) 3,639

Presides at Labour Party Conference, Newport (January).

Visits France—speaks at Lille.

Proposes establishment of Socialist Daily Paper.

Attends International Socialist Congress, Copenhagen (September).

General Election (December). Merthyr result:

E. R. Jones (L) 12,258
J. Keir Hardie (Lab) 11,507
J. H. Watts (C) 5,277

International Demonstration at the Albert Hall, London (December).

1911.

Re-elected to I.L.P. National Council.

Railway Strike.

1912.

Visits America and Canada.

Attends International Socialist Congress at Basle (November).

1913.

Re-elected Chairman I.L.P., Manchester Conference (March).

Attends International Women's Suffrage Alliance Congress at Budapest (June).

Attends funeral of Bebel at Zurich (August).

Visits Dublin at invitation of Irish Transport Workers' Federation (September).

Attends Congress German Social Democratic Party at Jena (September).

International Demonstration at the Kingsway Hall, London (December).

1914.

Presides at Coming-of-Age Conference of the I.L.P., Bradford (April).

Attends meeting International Socialist Bureau, Brussels (July 29th).

Assassination of Jaurès (July 31st).

Germany declares War on Russia (August 1st).

Trafalgar Square Peace Demonstration (August 2nd).

Speech in House of Commons (August 3rd).

War declared against Germany (August 4th).

Hostile meeting at Aberdare (August 6th).

Responsive meetings in Merthyr and other towns (October).

1915.

Last speech in Parliament (February 5th).

Passed peacefully away in presence of his wife and daughter (September 26th).

Funeral at Maryhill Crematorium (September 29th).

INDEX

INDEX

J. KEIR HARDIE

INDEX

J. KEIR HARDIE

INDEX

385

INDEX

Printed in the United Kingdom
by Lightning Source UK Ltd.
129639UK00001B/145/A